Character, Politics and Responsibility

Restarting the Heart of the American Republic

Mary,
Happy holidays! Glad to be
closer to you + the rest
of the family. Heres to
many holidays together

Honorable Brian Baird Ph.D.

4PiRSq ◆ *Seattle*

ISBN 978-0-578-06642-4

Cover design and photograph by Richard Fields

To William and Edith Baird, who taught me about integrity and lived it themselves. To my brother and sister and to my wife, who support me when integrity is demanded but not easy. Most importantly to my sons William and Walter, they are the reason for this book and why character and responsibility matter.

CONTENTS

INTRODUCTION

This book is about what Congress, the administration and, most importantly, the American people can do to get our country moving in the right direction again. Having served in Congress for twelve years I am convinced that we need comprehensive reforms in virtually every major aspect of government. Piecemeal, symbolic and half-hearted gestures will not work, and the changes that need to be made will require courage and integrity.

The title of this book says it all: we need sound Character, changed Politics, and personal Responsibility to restart the heart of the American republic. If there was ever a time to set aside partisanship and political opportunism, this is it. The stakes are too high, the challenges too great and the issues too complex for us to craft solutions unless we all work together and find common ground.

Much of what needs to be done will be extraordinarily difficult politically. In writing this book, which has been more than four years in the making, I set out to tackle some of the most significant and daunting problems and propose actions that I think are necessary, regardless of any political calculus or consequences. In the process, I will say things and recommend actions that I know will upset some of the most powerful interests in the country, including many people and groups that are and have been long time friends and supporters. Elective office is not meant to be a risk-free occupation and the job of serving this country is not meant to be easy or secure.

This book does not attempt to cover every issue or challenge we face. Neither would I pretend that every idea presented here is exclusively my own. Taking credit is not what this is about. It is about getting things done.

While specific topics and chapters are of necessity addressed individually, in practice the proposals are meant to be taken as an integrated whole. Efforts to stimulate the economy will be best achieved if combined with changes in tax law, energy policy, improved education, and control of health care costs. So, too, restoring fiscal responsibility depends on

8

reducing spending while growing the economy. This, in turn, depends on responsible entitlement reform, changes in Congressional procedures, and adjustments to defense policies.

In contrast to those who might argue that we can only address one or two changes at a time, I firmly believe that the more we combine and coordinate efforts across the board, the more successful the overall outcome will be.

As the father of twin five-year-old boys, I know that if we fail in our task, their future, and the future for all our children and grandchildren will not be as bright as it should be.

With those principles in mind, here, in brief, are some of the highlights of what follows:

Character – The book begins with the principle that no programs or policies can succeed if the people who create and carry them out lack character. For America to meet the challenges of today and the future, elected leaders and the people must put values into action and demonstrate real honesty, integrity, responsibility, courage, a sense of community, and humility. It may seem strange for a politician to talk about character before policy, but without character, even the best policy will be unsuccessful.

The Deficit and Debt – Our nation is facing crushing financial debts that will bury our children and destroy the country if not turned around. The second chapter describes the current and projected fiscal deficit and debt, then raises issues of personal debt, state indebtedness, the infrastructure deficit and more. To end the deficits and lower the debt we must grow the economy, increase revenues through taxes, and cut expenditures on all fronts – including social spending, defense and entitlements. There is no other way. This means Democrats and Republicans alike must be willing to compromise and modify some of their core political positions for the greater good of the country.

Taxes – Taxes should be simple, fair, easy to administer and comply with, and must generate sufficient revenue to pay for government expenditures. To achieve this, we should eliminate the income tax, throw away the tax code, do away with hidden "tax expenditures" and free people from the millions of human hours spent filing income taxes. In place of the income tax there should be a progressive national sales tax, reformed estate tax that protects family farms and businesses, a progressive time-indexed capital gains tax, and targeted tariffs – including higher gas taxes. By law, combined revenues from these sources must be sufficient in a given year to match spending.

"Entitlement" reform – We must maintain a safety net of social programs to support those truly in need, but we should do away entirely with the terminology and idea of "entitlements" and mandatory spending. The government has made too many promises that it simply cannot afford to keep and the sooner we own up to that the better.

While maintaining a safety net, we should recognize that the safety net is insurance, not a guaranteed benefit. We should also reiterate the fundamental importance of personal responsibility. Consistent with an insurance principle, we should needs-test all Social Security, health care and other social insurance benefits, we should key any future benefit increases to cost of living not wages, and we should include the full costs of the programs in all budget calculations, both in the short and long term.

The Economy – To get the economy on track and sustain growth for the future, we must have a trained and motivated workforce; sound infrastructure; a regulatory structure that is fair, predictable and efficiently administered; affordable and reliable energy; a level playing field with foreign competitors; and access to capital for investment and growth. Many chapters in this book are dedicated specifically to each of these requirements. This chapter focuses on the core structure of our economy and how to support and grow employment. Streamlining regulations, a national infrastructure and industrial strategy, and strong trade enforcement are some of the key topics addressed.

Education – The primary responsibility for education must be refocused on parents before all other education reforms. We must get our priorities straight, turn off the TV, put sports in their proper place, and make our kids study. There should be comprehensive reform of teacher and principal education, selection and pay.

Substantial across the board pay increases for teachers and principals should be established, but this should be accompanied by merit pay, the elimination of tenure, and the more expeditious removal of teachers and administrators who are not up to the task. To meet the needs of our mobile society, there should be a standard voluntary national curriculum, combined with greater technology aided individualized instruction, use of adaptive testing, and elimination of the No Child Left Behind AYP approach. There should be substantial reforms to special-needs and special talent education, changes in how education is funded at the local level, and dramatic cuts to the education bureaucracy at every level.

Energy – To lower spending on foreign oil and gas, stimulate the economy, end our dependence on petro-dictators, and lead the world in greenhouse and ocean acidification reduction, we should set and meet a goal of national reduction in energy consumption and carbon emissions by 20 percent in 20 weeks. To achieve further savings, we need massive investment in renewable energy infrastructure today, plus a Manhattan Project or Apollo-like commitment to renewable energy research and engineering.

As further incentive and funding for change there should be taxes and caps on carbon-based energy consumption and emissions of CO_2 and other global overheating and ocean acidifying gasses. This includes increases in taxes on gasoline and diesel fuels for passenger vehicles, with lesser increases for commercial, freight or agricultural uses. Proceeds from these taxes must be dedicated solely to transportation and energy efficiency or deficit reduction, not new spending on any other programs.

Health Care – Health care in our nation suffers from high costs, limited access, and outcomes that are below what they should be. Legislation recently passed Congress that is well-intentioned and will likely make things better than they currently are. This change notwithstanding, I believe the result is still unnecessarily complex and costly. There is a simpler, more affordable and more effective alternative.

As a starting point, we must assure anyone who has health insurance that they are perfectly free to keep what they have, while those in genuine financial need will still receive assistance. With those assurances, all current Federal and state government funded health programs for people of all ages should be eliminated and replaced with means-based assistance that covers basic prepaid medical, dental, vision and mental health with no insurance forms.

Catastrophic insurance would then cover high-cost occurrences plus long term care, with individuals choosing from for-profit or not-for-profit plans that are state, regional or national with a national insurance commissioner. Basic care and insurance coverage would be mandatory. Discrimination against pre-existing conditions or genetics would be banned for all plans, but incentives would promote positive health and prevention.

Comprehensive malpractice reforms would provide alternatives to litigation and reduce defensive medicine and abusive lawsuits. There should be an end to direct-to-consumer drug and medical device advertising but also effective incentives to pharmaceutical and medical device manufacturers to develop new treatments particularly for likely pandemic and drug resistant diseases or illnesses.

Foreign Policy and Defense – Our military personnel and capabilities are the best in the world, and we must keep it that way. But we must also ensure that our foreign policy and military engagements are consistent with our core values and truly in our national interest. We must free ourselves from dependence on petroleum and petro-dictators and not spill blood, ours or anyone else's, to feed this dependency.

In the present economic circumstances and dangerous global environment, we must strengthen our defense while reducing defense spending. To achieve this, we must encourage all Americans to serve their country, control the military/industrial complex, modify the defense acquisition process and priorities, and do more to strengthen statecraft and civilian support both to prevent wars and help rebuild after and during conflicts. Members of Congress and the Administration must not be influenced by any groups who advocate the political interests of other nations at the expense of our own independence, interests or values.

Immigration – The population of the U.S. is growing far too large and far too rapidly. In the interest of managing population growth, strengthening the economy and protecting domestic security, we must control immigration, both legal and illegal. At the same time we must directly confront and reject racism and prejudice wherever it occurs.

To achieve this, we must reduce or eliminate the demand and rewards for illegal immigration. This should involve establishing a single national biometric identification card, rigorously enforcing employment and tax laws, ending birthright citizenship, promotion of English language and a phase out of translation services and expenses.

To address the legitimate workforce needs of agriculture and certain other industries, and to deal with people who are already here illegally, there should be a three-tiered structure. Those who have committed criminal acts should be immediately deported or incarcerated. Individuals who have worked without paying taxes should be deported but eligible to return if a guest worker program is established. Those who have lived and worked here, paid taxes, and who have an employer who will vouch for both employment and tax payment, should be allowed to continue working under a new status. Legal immigration and citizenship procedures should focus on those most able to contribute to the economy. We must make it easier, not harder, for select individuals with highly valuable skills to stay and work here, and we must overhaul how legal visitors are treated at our consulates and embassies and when they arrive at our borders.

Politics – The single most important and beneficial reform for our nation would be a complete ban on candidates or elected officials raising or accepting campaign contributions or spending any personal funds on campaigns. Limited public financing should be the only funding directly available to candidates and for limited time periods. Strict and prompt transparency and contribution limits should be imposed to constrain expenditures by "independent" groups and additional matching funds should be provided to candidates targeted by those groups. There should be an end to political gerrymandering of Congressional and legislative districts; the Electoral College should be replaced by direct vote for the Presidency; and we should consider adopting instant runoff voting.

Congressional Reform – All legislation should be available to be read by members of Congress, the public and the media for a minimum of 72 hours before voting, and Congress should be in session for full five-day work week throughout the year with periodic recesses scheduled for district work and other business. The daily schedule in Congress should limit conflicts between committee hearings and votes and should prevent in so far as possible conflicts between floor votes and committee hearings or markups.

There should be strict bans on conflicts of interest for members of Congress and their staff and all appropriations or tax change requests should be made public. Biannual budgeting and appropriation should be implemented, authorizing and appropriating responsibilities and committees should be integrated, jurisdiction of certain committees should be redistributed, and spending and revenue bills and amounts should be directly linked to ensure budget balance.

Within the Senate, individual legislative holds should end, the number of votes needed for cloture should be lowered, there should be a limit to the numbers of times an individual Senator can filibuster, and there should be consideration of a germane rule comparable to the House. Replacement of Senate vacancies should be accomplished through a means other than partisan gubernatorial appointment. Finally, drawing upon the example of George Washington at the Constitutional Convention, it is worth considering selection of a non-partisan speaker of the House to ensure the people's business gets done for the sake of the people, not politics.

As ambitious as this list is, there is no time to waste. The challenges are great, but so are our country and our people. The time to act is now.

1.

CHARACTER

In the great rotunda of our Nation's Capitol there is a large painting of General George Washington handing a sheet of paper to a group of seated men. As a work of art, the painting itself is not very striking, but the act it portrays is astonishing.

Having led the army that defeated the British, then the most powerful nation in the world, Washington is turning over his commission as commanding general to the elected civilian government of the Continental Congress. In that remarkable gesture, Washington, a successful and revered military leader, gave power to a civilian government rather than claiming it for himself and his forces. By doing so, Washington demonstrated more courage, more faith, and more integrity than at any time in the war and perhaps more than any other victorious leader in human history.

A decade later, Washington presided at the Constitutional Convention. The Framers of that document knew full well that it was not perfect and that it would be received with criticism by many. They also knew that the Constitution wagered the fate of our nation on the willingness of the people to look honestly at their current situation, to accept the responsibility that goes with citizenship and self-government, to sacrifice for the greater good, and to have the courage to change. Those qualities are the essence of our republic and we must call upon them today to meet the nation's challenges once again.

From the beginning, the American people have always been willing and able to overcome any difficulty and achieve any goal. At their core, Americans want to do what is right for their country and for the world, and time after time our people and our nation have done just that. It is true that we make mistakes along the way -- sometimes large mistakes -- and the challenges at times may seem insurmountable, but if the people and their elected leaders hold firm to their deepest values and work together for the common good, we have always prevailed.

As we look at our nation and the world today, we face extraordinary challenges both domestically and internationally. The list is long – the economy, unemployment, Iraq, Afghanistan, terrorism, declining home values and the mortgage crisis, the collapse of major and local financial institutions, national security, health care, the budget deficit, record debt, an inefficient and incomprehensible tax code, rising energy costs, global warming and ocean acidification, population growth, immigration, failing infrastructure, job loss, education, global economic competition, and extremism at home and abroad. The list goes on.

Facing this list could easily be dispiriting and cause one to wonder if we can really meet all the challenges, if we really can take our nation and the world forward again. How could one be human and informed and not have concerns about what lies ahead?

As serious as the challenges are, I believe and I know the vast majority of Americans believe, we can and must meet them. Ultimately, constitutional democratic republics like ours are based on faith – faith in the fundamental wisdom, decency and abilities of the people, faith in our ability to turn crisis into opportunity, faith that the people really are willing and able to look truth, even unpleasant or difficult truth, in the eye and do the right thing when called upon.

It is time to call upon that faith in our people, in our great nation, and in the democratic process itself to move our country forward once again. It is time to remember that we are all in this together, time for our nation and each of us as citizens to reach a new level of honesty, a new level of courage, and a new level of responsibility. It also time to call upon our elected representatives and leaders, and on all our people, to demonstrate the deeper virtues, the greater courage that these times demand. The stakes are too high and time is too short for anything else.

For every one of the challenges before us today, there are also opportunities to solve them and make things even better by doing the right things, making the right choices. Unfortunately, this is not happening because our system is stuck in the status quo. On the one hand, our leaders and our voters are too afraid of the political fallout of truly bold ideas, too busy shouting and blaming others rather than taking personal responsibility, too attracted by easy promises rather than hard truths, too reluctant to make the fundamental changes we need to make to take our country forward again. At the same time, many of our citizens are so filled with anger and frustration that they are turning to demagogues with little experience and no real solutions, just anger.

As we look at the challenges not being confronted, the opportunities not being pursued, and as we contemplate the potential harm our nation will face if we do not act boldly and honestly, I am far more concerned about the consequences for our nation than I am about any political risks that I or others may face if we start telling the truth in a much deeper and more forthright way.

The greatest risk we face is not political. It is the risk of knowing that we saw the real dangers and opportunities facing our nation and our future, but we did not confront those risks honestly, and did not pursue the opportunities fully because we were too afraid of the political consequences or too angry to think clearly. I believe it is time for us all to say nuts to the political consequences; let us say and do what is honest and right.

The most important place to start any real process of change is not by the usual route of listing all the programs or legislation we endorse. We will get to those later. More important is something far more fundamental to success and far too seldom talked about in politics: Character.

Much has been said in political circles about values. Candidates talk about their values and pundits refer to so called "values voters." It is actually all too easy to say one has or votes their values, especially if those values are distilled to one or two litmus test issues.

Character, however, demands much more. Anyone can talk about their values, but character means dealing with the full complexity of life and putting values into actions. That is not so easy politically or personally.

We must begin with character because the key to success or failure of any venture lies not in programs but in the people. Unless you start with the right people with strong character, you cannot succeed even if you have the best plans and programs in the world. If people have the right character, motives, skills, and work ethic, anything is possible. If people lack these qualities, very little can be accomplished that is worthwhile.

Without character in our leaders, in our citizens and, indeed, within our culture itself, all the policies, campaign promises and government programs in the world cannot succeed.

When elected leaders do not tell the truth, when their actions are not consistent with their words and values, when they refuse to take responsibility for solving problems and instead pass that burden onto others, they are not showing real character. When they rely on inflammatory emotional appeals and pander with easy sound bites, when they focus more on party or personal power than common good, and when they show no willingness to run personal or political risks, it is no wonder the people lose faith in and respect for government.

On the other hand, if elected leaders truly respect the people who elected them, and have the courage and integrity to lead by the example through their honesty, responsibility, judgment and sense of community, the people will support them and rise to the occasion. From there, anything will be possible and we can restore the brilliance that has always been at the heart and soul of this great nation.

We must insist on choosing leaders with character, but we must also acknowledge that the success of our constitutional democratic republic depends first and foremost on the character of the nation and of the people themselves. We cannot turn to elected leaders or government programs to solve our problems for us unless we first look at ourselves. We have to be willing to be part of solutions and that may mean we have to make some changes.

Whatever they may claim as party affiliation, most voters care far more deeply about their country than about political parties. Most voters want to hear solutions rather than assign blame. They are willing to listen to unpleasant truths, confront daunting challenges, and to make even difficult changes, if they believe their leaders are honest and willing to lead by example.

What are the core qualities Americans look for in political leaders and in ourselves as citizens if a constitutional democratic republic like ours is to endure? There are many possible answers, but at the core must be Honesty, Integrity, Responsibility, Community, Courage, and Humility.

Honesty

Far too many political consultants would say that complete honesty is a recipe for political suicide. They may be right. However, if we do not start by telling the truth as political leaders, and if the citizens do not sincerely want to hear, see, understand and acknowledge even difficult or complex truths, how can we ever hope to solve problems and make real progress?

In spite of what pundits, consultants or pollsters might suggest, I am convinced the American people would welcome real honesty from their leaders. The people are not stupid; they are not ignorant and they love their country.

They see what has happened to our nation and to our government and they don't like the sight. They are sick and tired of political spin and are justifiably suspicious of the motives of the media and politicians alike. They are angry about the corruption and dysfunction in government, and they want people in office to stop the pettiness, the negativity, and do what is right before it's too late.

They ask, what does honesty mean in the context of setting policy and politics? What does it require of us as citizens and as elected representatives?

Honesty means more than just speaking the truth. It means being willing to listen to different sides, and evaluate varying perspectives fairly and openly.

Honesty means telling the people what the facts are, not what we think they want to hear or what we think will get them to vote for us.

Honesty means not asking what do I already believe or want to be true; rather, it means asking what is actually true, what is false and what is unknown based on the best available evidence from all sides.

Honesty means looking objectively at the situation from many different perspectives and recognizing that some opposing ideas are worth considering and some of our own should be rejected. If we are honest, we do not just accept the status quo, we evaluate both the current approach and alternatives with equal rigor. Honesty means making decisions through reason, not blind obedience, wishful thinking, fear, anger, intimidation or raw power.

Integrity

As important as honesty is in principle, it means little if it is not backed by deeds -- by real and consequential action. That is where integrity comes in. To live and act with integrity we must strive to make our actions consistent with our values and our knowledge to the greatest extent possible.

To claim that we hold certain values, but then act contrary to those values, demonstrates that we only hold those values when they are convenient or easy, not when they require real choices, action or consequences.

To acknowledge that we face a problem and that our own behavior contributes to that problem, but then fail to change our behavior, reflects a lack of integrity. To deny that our behavior may be part of the problem and instead blame others also lacks integrity. To recognize the merits of an alternative approach or agree with certain facts, but then seek to disguise the facts or give no credence to that alternative, shows that we do not truly value honesty.

When we look at the history of our nation and find times when the leaders and the people have acted with true integrity, those have been the proudest moments and the times of true greatness for America. Now is the time to find that integrity once again.

Responsibility

Let us state something very bluntly: government is neither the cause of nor the solution to our problems. Government does not owe anyone anything except protection of basic rights and opportunities.

Those who look to a government leader or program to "fix" all our social problems are mistaken. At the same time, those who blame and tear down government are equally mistaken. It is just as much a dodge of personally responsibility to depend on government for all solutions as it is to blame the government for all problems.

Government is all of us, no better and no worse. Before we look to government for solutions or blame, we must first look to ourselves and ask how we personally contribute to the situation and could help to solve problems.

We, the people, are the key to government. That means we, the people, are the key both to the problems and the solutions and we must accept personal responsibility for both.

When John Kennedy called on our nation to "Ask not what your country can do for you, ask what you can do for your country," he was talking about accepting responsibility and a commitment to the greater community.

Our nation's most challenging problems can best be solved only by individual citizens taking personal responsibility for our own actions, looking clearly and honestly at how those actions square with our values, and taking responsibility for how our actions affect our future and that of others.

Consider any of the issues people care most about – the economy, education, health care, energy, safe communities, the environment, national security. For each of these the most important part of the solution depends upon individuals accepting personal responsibility for what they do and how what they do affects everyone else and the nation as a whole.

If elected representatives promise solutions that don't have personal responsibility as the foundation, they are not being straight with voters. This has to stop. No one else is going to solve our problems for us and everyone must be part of the solution.

Community

As we work together to find solutions, we must keep sight of the fact that we are all part of a larger community. It is an ancient but eternal truth that we must strive to do unto others as we would have them do unto us. We must also strive not to do to others what we would not want done to ourselves.

One of the greatest strengths of our nation is the extraordinary commitment of citizens to helping others through community involvement and service. Whether through religious institutions or voluntary organizations like Rotary, Kiwanis, Lions or countless others, Americans are more involved in charitable giving and civic involvement than any other nation on earth. This participation and generosity should be celebrated and respected both at home and internationally.

Unfortunately, while our nation leads the world in examples of civic organizations and private philanthropy, it is also true that we seem to be losing a sense of community and responsibility. Evidence of this can be found at all levels of our society.

On one hand, too many people believe that government or someone else owes them something regardless of their own actions or choices. People who refuse to work for a living, who do not spend or save responsibly, who feign or exaggerate disabilities, who knowingly produce faulty or dangerous products, people who file lawsuits without justification, who destroy their lives and families through substance abuse, all seem to have lost both the sense of personal responsibility and the awareness that they are part of a larger community to which they must contribute, not detract from.

At the same time, at the very highest levels of wealth and income, it is far too common for the most advantaged people in the nation to feel they are entitled to vast amounts of money with little or no sense of justice and no regard for how their actions affect other individuals or the nation as a whole.

Serving in Congress, one is besieged by people and interest groups who are constantly asking for more for themselves with little concern about how their requests impact others or the overall well being of the nation. On many occasions, when I have asked such individuals or groups how they would deal with the fact that the new spending, benefits or tax cuts they advocate would either pass more debt on to our children or lead to cuts elsewhere, the response has literally been, "That is your problem, not ours," or, worse, "we don't care."

This attitude of selfishness and self interest above all else, and the willingness of elected representatives and candidates to pander to it, is a large part of why we are where we are today as a nation. Unless that changes, it will be impossible to solve our problems in the future.

Courage

It is easy to write or speak about honesty, integrity, responsibility, judgment and community, but putting those values into actual practice -- living them, defending them, embodying them -- takes courage.

Not everyone believes in honesty, many people find it easier to say one thing and do another. It is easier to avoid responsibility and let someone else take the blame or pay the price. Working for the good of the larger community may mean our selfish interests are in conflict with the overall good. That is why courage is an essential part of character for the people and for their political leaders.

Courage is also required of the people and political leaders because it takes courage to put one's faith and trust in the people and in the power of their good judgment and character. There is risk in trusting a government of, by and for the people. There is risk in truly listening to and fairly considering the ideas of others. There is risk in putting forward ideas of your own or taking actions that might not be popular. Politics, elective office and responsible citizenship are not meant to be risk-free pursuits.

The second paragraph of the Declaration of Independence begins with the words,

> *We hold these truths to be self evident. That all men are created equal, that they are endowed by their Creator with certain unalienable Rights, that among these are Life, Liberty, and the Pursuit of Happiness - That to secure these Rights, Governments are instituted among Men, deriving their just Powers from the Consent of the Governed.*

It took tremendous courage to state such a bold proposition, such an outrageous premise so directly and so blatantly in contrast to millennia of rule by kings, priests and warlords. As evidence of that courage, the Declaration concludes by committing everything that mattered to the great cause –

> *And for the support of this Declaration, with a firm Reliance on the Protection of divine Providence, we mutually pledge to each other our Lives, our Fortunes and our sacred Honor.*

The people who signed the Declaration knew the stakes, knew the risks, and knew the odds. They signed nevertheless because they had courage and vision and were willing to wager everything for a better life and a better nation. And the better life they sought was not simply for themselves but for everyone and for their posterity.

Humility

Finally, no matter what an individual or nation achieves, when compared to the immensity of space and the course of history, things must be kept in perspective. We would do well to keep a sense of humility ever present about ourselves as individuals, about our political parties and agendas and about our nation.

Respecting the achievements and strengths of others, understanding our own limitations as well as our own strengths, and being open to new ideas and new ways is a sign of true strength. Practicing and demonstrating genuine humility would go a long way toward reducing the divisiveness and partisanship that have paralyzed and distorted our government of late. It would also help reduce some of the anger in the public and would restore the rest of the world's appreciation for our nation and its people and leaders.

There are many reasons to argue for humility, but here is one of the best I know. The Hubble Space Telescope has captured an image known as Deep Field that is stunning in its beauty and its implications. Focusing for ten days and gathering light from an apparently dark area of space that to our eyes would fill a part of the sky about the size of the head of a pin held at arm's length, Hubble's cameras revealed an image of more than 10,000 never-before-seen galaxies. Each one of those galaxies consists of billions of stars and planets, and the light from those most distant galaxies left before our own solar system even existed.

As people and as a nation, we must never overestimate how much we know, nor underestimate our ability to learn. Our nation has been and should be great, but there are other great nations on this planet. We have much to learn and admire in others. The greatest leaders and the greatest nations earn respect through genuine and noble actions, giving respect to others for their qualities and achievements as well.

The Challenges

As I was working on this book, two experiences highlighted both the challenges and the unlimited potential of our nation and its people.

The first experience was a trip to visit our soldiers serving in Iraq and Afghanistan. There I met with men and women from around our nation and from our allied nations who are serving with extraordinary courage, professionalism and compassion on the front lines of an extraordinarily difficult and dangerous conflict. I also met with U.S. government and military leaders and with civilian personnel, all of whom are trying desperately and against tough odds to make those nations stable, safe and civil.

The second experience happened just a few weeks later as my wife and I traveled to see a friend launch into space as part of the crew of the Space Shuttle. As the sun set in the west, the rockets roared to life and in a matter of just minutes the most complex device ever created by humans lifted the crew and their cargo into the heavens to build and resupply the International Space Station.

There can be no question that these are incredibly challenging and dangerous times and many of our fellow citizens in Iraq, Afghanistan and elsewhere are facing those dangers every minute. Many have sacrificed their lives, bodies, careers and families to those challenges and more will do so in the days and months ahead. As difficult and painful as those challenges are, there can also be no question that when we are at our very best, our nation can truly achieve great things. The launch of the Shuttle is just one example among millions.

To honor the sacrifices of those who have given their all, for the sake of our children and grandchildren, for the sake of our nation and the world, we must now meet the challenges head on. We have no other choice and we must not fail.

To succeed together, we must call upon a deeper faith in our nation, a deeper store of honesty, integrity and courage, a deeper commitment to humility and community and deeper sense of responsibility. As individuals, as citizens, as elected leaders, as human beings, we must call upon the highest standards of character. We must face and surmount the current challenges, focus again on the highest aspirations and very best qualities of our people, and lift this nation up again.

2.

DEFICITS AND DEBT

No responsible adult would choose to pass physical pain or illness on to their children rather than dealing with it themselves. Yet, when it comes to financial choices and fiscal pain, that is precisely what we are doing. In order to live beyond our means today, we are passing unconscionable debt onto our children. This has to stop.

The responsibility rests with each and every one of us, both inside government and in the public, because everyone has benefited in some way from deficit spending. We have enjoyed lower taxes that have allowed us to spend more personally and we have benefited from government spending paid for by dollars the government has borrowed from abroad.

Every day we delay makes the task more difficult for us and nearly impossible for the next generation. Kicking the can down the road, blaming others, and defending unsustainable systems will not solve our problems. We need to take responsibility now, have the honesty to tell the people the truth about where we are and how we got here, realistically assess where we are headed, and have the courage to change course.

Not everyone will welcome hearing about our budget troubles, and it will not be politically easy or popular to talk about the solutions. But if we cannot be honest about where we are and what we need to do with the budget, why should anyone believe what we say about anything else?

If the choice is between keeping people happy by telling them comforting lies or risk angering them by speaking truth, which is the responsible course? To those who do not agree with certain of the remedies that will be proposed, let them offer some other realistic and honest solution instead. What is not acceptable or honest is to criticize without offering practical alternatives.

Our National and Individual Financial Problems

Let us begin by squarely facing the problems. When I
began writing this chapter while serving on the House Budget
committee in 2007, the growing deficits and debt were already
substantial concerns. That was before the financial meltdown,
TARP, Stimulus, other new spending, further tax cuts and
declining revenues. Since then, the deficit numbers for Federal
and state governments have exploded. Indeed, it has become
increasingly difficult to keep this chapter updated because it
seems every week some new, and usually worse, numbers
emerge. Hence, I acknowledge that some of the numbers that
follows may not be current, but the underlying issues that are
addressed are still valid.

Debt, Deficits and Foreign Dependence

The non-partisan Congressional Budget Office estimated in
August of 2009 that the Federal budget deficit for fiscal year
2009 would total $1.6 trillion, or 11.2 percent of gross
domestic product, which is the highest level since World War
II. If borrowing from Social Security trust funds were
included, which I think it should be, the deficit number would
actually exceed $1.7 trillion. The cumulative effect of such
borrowing up to the present is a national debt that now stands
at more than $13.2 trillion and increases by more than $3
billion every day.

One of the consequences of so much deficit spending and
debt is the large and growing interest costs we pay. That
amount exceeded $383 billion in 2009. All this money only
services interest on the debt for what we have already spent --
it does not help build new schools, or pay our troops, or
improve our health care, or fix our roads.

To fund the debt and deficit spending, we are increasingly
dependent on borrowing from other nations. In fact, the
amount of foreign-held treasury securities now exceeds $3.4
trillion.

Looking ahead, the situation gets worse. Indeed, , President Obama's budget for Fiscal Year 2011 proposed $3.8 trillion in spending against receipts of $2.6 trillion, resulting in a projected deficit of $1.3 trillion. Over the next decade, this budget projects deficits totaling $8.5 trillion. For more about the budget details, a valuable source of non-partisan analysis is the Center for A Responsible Federal Budget.

On the positive side, the President's budget included a proposed freeze on non-defense discretionary spending and calls for some revenue increases from taxpayers with incomes above $250,000 per year. However, these deficit reducing measures are countered by proposed spending increases in defense and further tax cuts for middle income families.

I disagree strongly with certain aspects of the President's approach. It is simply not realistic to expect to achieve balance while increasing spending and cutting taxes. Contrary to the President's proposals, I believe no area of spending should be off limits for a freeze or reductions. Further, campaign promises notwithstanding, in a time of high unemployment and record deficits anyone who has a job and is making more than a hundred thousand dollars a year should perhaps be paying somewhat more taxes rather than passing debt on to everyone's children and grandchildren.

Debt and Deficits as a Percentage of GDP

To put the current situation into historical context, it is important to note that the Federal budget was in balance with a modest surplus at the end of the Clinton administration. In the eight years that followed under President Bush, the deficit grew rapidly, with the debt more than doubling and the nation becoming more dependent on foreign credit than all of the combined prior borrowing under every presidential administration from George Washington through the end of Bill Clinton's terms in office. In fact, while President Bush inherited a surplus from President Clinton, President Obama inherited a deficit of $1.3 trillion dollars from the last fiscal year of the Bush administration.

As deficits and debt mounted under President Bush and the Republican Congress, some, including former Treasury Secretary John Snow, argued that the deficit and debt were not as significant as they might have appeared in absolute numbers because, as a percentage of Gross Domestic Product, we had faced similar debts before.

In truth, the GDP percentage argument was not sustainable at the time and is even less defensible today. As noted earlier, the numbers have gotten much worse as a result of the financial collapse, tax cuts, unfunded spending on wars, and other factors. At the same time, a host of other key conditions are different and, far worse, today than they have been in the past. These differences include our aging demographic picture, international economic and employment competition, trade imbalances, national security concerns, energy costs and other challenges that make comparisons to prior debt to GDP levels dangerously misleading.

Stated bluntly, unless we act responsibly today, this generation of children will be saddled with unprecedented debt burdens even as they are asked to support an aging and ill older generation. To make matters worse, our children will have to meet these fiscal demands while competing against billions of other workers and growing economic powers around the world.

Demographics and "Entitlements"

Exacerbating many of our financial problems is the imminent retirement of the baby boom generation. That generation started with babies born in 1946 and, though people have talked for years about preparing for the day when the baby boomers begin to retire, that day arrived in 2008. This is because people can begin to draw early OASDI benefits, at age 62 and become eligible for Medicare at age 65.

The arrival of the baby boomers is no longer in the future, they are demanding benefits now, and millions more are soon to follow. In total, more than 77 million baby boomers will be joining the Social Security and Medicare rolls and they will expect to receive full benefits from each program. Because of the way the programs are structured, the burden of paying for those benefits will be placed, along with the current debt, on the younger generations.

The number of workers per Social Security beneficiary will soon fall from 3.3 workers per beneficiary in 2006 to 2.1 workers per beneficiary in 2032. By comparison, in the 1940s, there were 41 workers per beneficiary, and in the 1950s the ratio was 16 workers to each beneficiary. The more workers per beneficiary, the lower the payroll taxes required from each of them; the fewer the workers, the higher the tax per worker to pay benefits.

Aging Americans will also place increasing demands on health care expenditures. The most recent available statistics estimate that the Federal Government spent $511 billion in 2009 on Medicare alone.

Many in the younger generation, who will be required to pay for the entitlements, will themselves be struggling to pay off student loans, start families, and will be facing increasing competition for jobs and wages due to international economic changes. Passing debt, plus entitlement payment demands, plus international economic competition will not be sustainable by or fair to this generation.

Long-Term Federal Spending if Nothing Changes

As daunting as the current deficit and debt are, the long-term horizon is far more troubling. This stems from the demographics just mentioned and from the fact that our promised "entitlement" spending has dramatically increased in recent years.

What is more, there are demands from constituents every day for Congress to further expand these entitlements. In most cases, Congress has no real plan for paying for any of the requested expansions.

The magnitude of the problem is shocking. The 2008 Annual Report of the Social Security and Medicare Boards of Trustees[1] stated, "We are increasingly concerned about

---

[1] *See* http://www.ssa.gov/OACT/TRSUM/index.html

inaction on the financial challenges facing the Social Security and Medicare programs. The longer action is delayed, the greater will be the required adjustments, the larger the burden on future generations, and the more severe the detrimental economic impact on our nation."

The Trustees projected Medicare costs, which were 3.2 percent of GDP in 2007, would reach 10.8 percent of GDP by 2082. Social Security benefits were 4.3 percent of GDP in 2007 but were projected to increase to 6.1 percent of GDP in 2035, and then recede slightly to 5.8 percent of GDP by 2085. The combined costs of Social Security and Medicare in 2082 would represent 16.6 percent of GDP.

To get a sense of what this means, in 2007 total Federal receipts from all sources was just 18.8 percent of GDP. In other words, unless substantial changes are made in entitlement spending, the two major entitlement programs alone would eventually consume nearly the same percentage of GDP as all Federal receipts today. Obviously, that would leave little or nothing for any other Federal government activity, including defense, education, health research, disaster preparedness and so forth.

Similar alarms are sounded by The Financial Report of The U.S. Government (FRUSG)[2]. Required by the Congress and produced by the Treasury, the Financial Report is virtually unknown to the public or most Members of Congress. That lack of awareness is like ignoring a weather forecast that Hurricane Katrina is bearing down on an unsuspecting populace.

In contrast to the Federal Budget which looks at revenue and spending with cash accounting, the Financial Report uses accrual accounting like that required by law of most businesses, corporations, and state and local governments.

According to the Financial Report, if revenues are held constant at around 18 percent of GDP, the anticipated growth of spending on entitlements, plus interest, plus other Federal spending would exceed revenues by three-fold and would reach nearly 60 percent of GDP by the year 2080.

---

[2] *See* http://fms.treas.gov/fr/07frusg/07frusg.pdf

Under the same scenario, the publicly-held debt would more than triple by 2040, double again by 2060, and reach six times the GDP by 2080. This is not remotely sustainable and would result in disastrous economic consequences long before 2080.

To make matters worse, remember that publicly-held debt is only about half of the Government's gross debt. The remaining debt is in the form of intra-governmental borrowing, primarily from the Social Security "trust funds." Although this total debt is seldom mentioned in government press releases, it is nevertheless real debt which, if not repaid, would have real consequences for the seniors who depend on the repayment.

The Government Accountability Office (GAO) has expressed similarly grave concerns about our fiscal situation.[3] In the year 2000, the GAO estimated that the present value of our financial commitments over the next 75 years was $20 trillion. That figure had grown to more than $52.7 trillion by then end of 2008. This unimaginable number represents more than the total net worth of all households in this country. To put this into context, this is $175,000 per person, $410,000 per full-time worker, or $455,000 per household. In other words, if every American liquidated everything they own and gave all the money to the government, that money would not be enough to pay for just the entitlement commitments that await us in the future.

Federal Environmental and Disposal Liabilities

All children are taught they must clean up after their own mess. In theory, the Federal government should follow the same rule but, in practice, the costs of unattended clean ups have continued to grow. Just as we are leaving a financial mess to our children, we are also bequeathing them a host of costly environmental messes.

Leftover nuclear and hazardous waste from World Wars, improperly disposed-of munitions, spent nuclear fuel and other

---

[3] *See* http://www.gao.gov/cghome/d08465cg.pdf

legacy hazards carry a total outstanding liability estimated at
$342 billion according to the Financial Report.

State and Local Government Fiscal Challenges

Adding to the fiscal challenges of the Federal government
are comparably negative forecasts for state and local
governments. The costs of state pension funds plus state-
funded health care programs, including Medicaid and retiree
benefits, are all projected to increase substantially in the
coming years. Estimates back in October 2008 pegged
combined state deficits at more than $100 billion for the
coming year alone. Those estimates, as has been emphasized
before, were made before the financial meltdown worsened and
unemployment figures climbed ever higher.

The GAO forecast in 2008 said that, beginning within the
next decade, states would face a "fiscal gap" that would require
actions equivalent to either a 15.2 percent increase in taxes or a
12.9 percent reduction in spending.[4] Calculated in 2007 dollars
this fiscal gap was estimated at $10.6 trillion. Again, that
number has grown far worse since the financial collapse placed
growing demands and steep revenue declines on state budgets.

Infrastructure and Hidden Deficits

While Federal financial deficits and the debt level are
publicly reported and monitored, other hidden deficits must be
accounted for and addressed at some point. For example, the
American Society of Civil Engineers has estimated that our
nation's infrastructure deficit -- the costs of just maintaining
existing bridges, roads, ports, and water and sewer treatment
facilities -- is $2.2 trillion. This amount would be needed over
five years to bring the nation's infrastructure up to minimum
standards of safety and efficiency.

A recent study by the National Surface Transportation
Policy and Revenue Study Commission estimated that the

---

[4] http://www.gao.gov/new.items/d08317.pdf

nation's roads and railroads require $225 billion per year for the next fifty years just to meet projected maintenance and demand.[5]

The Financial Report estimates that deferred maintenance within Federal government agencies totaled more than $109 billion in 2007. Within the National Park Service alone, the maintenance backlog is as much as $12 billion. The beloved Smithsonian Institution faces more than $3 billion in needed repairs and upkeep. Other agencies have similar maintenance deficits and backlogs.

Our military also faces substantial financial challenges due to the protracted and costly conflicts in Iraq and Afghanistan. Recent estimates of the costs of those conflicts alone suggest they will exceed $3 trillion.

The Trade Deficit and International Competition

If our economy were growing rapidly and we were selling to other nations more than we are buying, it might be easier to manage some of our fiscal problems. Unfortunately, that is not the case.

Our monthly trade deficits for the past several years averaged between $55 billion and $65 billion for a total annual balance in 2006 of negative $811.5 billion. To some degree the weak dollar and recession have helped reduce this deficit but we are still importing far more than we are exporting.

In September of 2009, for example, the net deficit in traded goods was $47.6 billion. When offset by a trade surplus in services of $11.1 billion, the resulting goods and services deficit was $36.5 billion. On an annual basis, this is still more than a $400 billion trade deficit.

We also face international competition that is more substantial than any time in our recent history and likely to get worse. While much of our population is aging, leaving the productive workforce and beginning to draw heavily on social insurance funds, many other nations, such as China, India,

---

[5] *See* http://www.transportationfortomorrow.org/

countries in the Arab world and Latin America have very large populations of young, educated, hard working individuals.

These younger workers are quite capable of performing jobs at every level from basic services to the most advanced scientific and technical. I sometimes point out to high school students that they are about to enter a workforce in which they will compete with 1.3 billion people in China, more than 1 billion in India, and billions more in other developing nations. This will inevitably put continued competitive pressure on U.S. workers, wages and employers.

Personal Financial Challenges

Our fiscal situation at the Federal level is, in many ways, mirrored by the financial circumstances of individual citizens. Let us start with personal debts.

Without going into a discussion of all the factors that led to the financial collapse, it is indisputable that a significant contributor was the tendency of too many people lured by the promise of low interest and easy money to carry far too much personal debt. People across the nation took out mortgages or refinanced at historically low interest rates and used the "excess" equity to buy even more things on even more credit. When housing values stopped climbing, people found themselves "upside down" or "underwater" in their home mortgage by owing more than the value of the home.

The other major debt challenge facing many people is from credit cards. Here too, the attraction of apparently easy spending and low introductory rates, plus desires for immediate gratification rather than long-term savings, has caused many people to burden themselves with large debts and exorbitant interest.

Since the financial collapse credit card debt has actually shown a decline, but the Federal Reserve reported in October of 2009 that Americans still held nearly $888 billion in revolving credit card debt (excluding mortgages).

To be sure, the lending institutions, banks, credit card companies and others have contributed to, taken advantage of (and, in some instances are now suffering from) the situations described above. To its credit, Congress has recently begun to address the conditions that let this happen, but individuals themselves must ultimately take responsibility for their own decisions and choices. It is far too easy to simply blame government, blame the lenders, or look to someone else for a quick fix or bailout.

While debts in the form of home mortgages, car payments, and credit card balances have been worsening, there has been a corresponding decrease in personal savings.

For several years leading up to the financial collapse, our nation had a negative overall savings rate. In 2006, personal savings rate was negative 1 percent; in 2005, personal savings rate was negative 0.5 percent. The savings rate was last negative for a full year only twice before – in 1932 and 1933, during the depths of the Great Depression.

With increasing debt and decreasing savings, more and more people are living from paycheck to paycheck without the resources to carry through any significant and sustained downturn in personal finances. Layoffs, medical emergencies, and other unexpected expenses can very quickly exhaust most people's meager savings.

The long-term picture, in terms of retirement and long term care expenses, is even worse. People of working age can reform their spending and saving choices, but retirees may find it impossible to go back to work.

According to the 2006 Financial Services Forum National Retirement Survey, nearly a third of all working Americans saved nothing for retirement in 2005. One out of four Americans in their peak earning years, and nearing retirement (age 50-65) saved nothing for retirement in 2005.

Nearly three out of five younger Americans (35-49) saved less than $10,000 for retirement in 2005 – too little to sustain an average middle-class lifestyle in retirement. Clearly, many people who are approaching retirement will find it hard to make ends meet. Those problems become exponentially worse if expensive long-term care is needed. They have also been dramatically worsened by the huge decline in the value of whatever retirement investments people might have had.

Future Costs of Long Term Care

More than half of the population will require long-term care at some point in their lives and one out of five Americans over the age of 50 is at risk of needing long-term care in the next 12 months. For couples 65 and over, there is a 75 percent likelihood that one partner will need long-term care and 60 percent of people over age 75 will need long-term care. Alzheimer's disease alone strikes 13 percent of the population (one in eight) age 65 or over, while other illnesses and diseases - strokes, heart disease, diabetes and so forth will put millions more into assisted living facilities or nursing homes.

In spite of the high percentages of people who will eventually need expensive long-term care, fewer than 30 percent of Americans over 45 have purchased a long-term care insurance policy and, of that group, the insured amounts are often too low to fully cover the costs. The average monthly cost of a long-term care facility is $6,266 (for a private room in a nursing home; $2,968/month for care in an assisted living unit).

Stories Voters Love and Politicians Love to Tell

The situation I have described is not imaginary and is not exaggerated. It is cold, hard reality and if space permitted additional statistics would make the reality look even worse. We cannot get out of this by doing more of what got us here to begin with. Politicians on all sides must summon the courage to stop telling voters what they think they want to hear and start telling the truth.

The truth is that to bring our financial house back to responsible balance, we must change entitlement and discretionary programs and spending, we must raise more revenues and that means through taxes, fees and tariffs. We must also stimulate, streamline and expand the economy. We have to stop wasting money and individual citizens must be more accountable and responsible in their personal lives.

In practical political terms, we need to get beyond our traditional political silos and litmus tests and start working together to solve problems. The questions should not be whether a certain proposal is "conservative" or "progressive," "Democratic," or "Republican." The real questions should be: Is it fair, is it honest, is it responsible and will it work? Ultimately, we need to put our love for our children and nation above our love for our ideology, party rhetoric or political power.

Some years ago, an advertising phrase "Where's the beef?" became part of a political campaign. Today, we should ask every elected official and, for that matter, everyone who demands lower taxes or higher spending, "Where's the math?"

To solve our financial problems, Democrats need to stop promising to never touch entitlement programs. At present rates of growth and demographic trends, we simply cannot keep all the promises people think have been made. We certainly cannot keep expanding those promises, and problems, even further.

Democrats also have to stop pretending that we can solve all fiscal or social problems through government spending and that our concern is best shown by how much money we appropriate for it. On the revenue side, Democrats need to accept that we cannot solve our financial problems by just increasing taxes.

Democrats must also understand that some taxes have social and fiscal effects that are contrary to core Democratic values and a healthy economy. Democrats also need to consider that regulations and litigation, however well-intentioned and potentially beneficial, also carry significant economic costs that must be considered.

For their part, Republicans need to stop promising never to raise any taxes and need to stop perpetuating or basing policy on the myth that all tax cuts increase revenues. When current deficits exceed all discretionary spending combined, "cutting waste fraud and abuse" cannot possibly come close to ending the deficit.

Republicans also need to stop making our entitlement problems worse, such as with their Medicare drug benefit -- the largest entitlement expansion since the creation of Medicare in 1965. Republicans need to recognize that in some instances, what appear to be savings, in the form of elimination of programs, rolling back regulations, contracting out services and so forth, may actually have long-term costs that exceed any short-term savings.

Republicans must understand that while government spending cannot solve all our problems, government does have a legitimate role in addressing key social issues and that role often does require money. Finally, Republicans need to acknowledge that, in many instances, if taxpayer money is wisely spent, the benefits to the economy and to our society are oftentimes highly worthwhile.

Saying what the political parties and politicians need to do does not let individual Americans, businesses and families off the hook. Setting aside politics and government, each of us as individuals also has to accept greater personal responsibility in our own lives. We must stop believing that we are owed something by other people or that the government is responsible for making our lives easier or bailing us out of the consequences of our own actions or decisions. We must all learn again to live within our means, and we must pay down our personal debts and increase our savings.

We must also understand and embrace the reality that our quality of life is not determined by how much stuff we have or how much fossil fuel we burn. All of us must distinguish between want and need, between responsibility and desire. We must consider the effects of our actions or government policies on the common good, on others, on the future and not just on our own self and selfish interests.

Of course, no one has to do any of what was just described or adopt any of the recommendations that follow. If we wish, we can continue doing what we've been doing and watch our people and our nation slip ever deeper into debt with no real plans for how to pay for it, with our dependence on foreign nations increasing, with our economy and national security suffering and with the problems simply getting worse and worse as we pass them on to our children and grandchildren.

3.
TAXES

Recognizing that comprehensive, integrated reform is essential, let's start the needed reforms with something easy -- transforming the tax system.

A responsible tax system should tax consumption more than savings, speculation more than investment, and reward work more than wealth. The system should be simple to comprehend, fair in its impacts, easy to comply with, not easy to avoid, and predictable. It should generate sufficient revenues each year to fund that year's spending and future commitments so we do not accrue debt, but it should not be so burdensome in its levels or structure that it stifles innovation and growth.

The current income and payroll tax system does not meet any of these criteria well -- it should be abolished and replaced.

No system of taxation will be perfect, most can be "gamed" or manipulated in some ways, and whatever proposal is offered will generate winners and losers relative to certain provisions of the present tax code and system. The goal, therefore, is not to offer a perfect alternative. It is to offer a much better one.

In place of the current system, Federal revenues should be generated from a combination of a progressive national sales tax, a progressive time-indexed capital gains tax, and a substantially modified estate tax. Additional revenues should be obtained from selective tariffs and targeted user fees.

Under the proposed reform, there would not be separate payroll and income taxes as under the current system. The so called "entitlement programs," which will be discussed in the following chapters, would be funded from the same source as other programs. In contrast to the current practice, their total costs would be fully counted in tallying the nation's expenditures and deficits or surpluses for both the near term and the future.

In general, for all forms of taxes the rates charged should be based on a gradual and steady progressive continuum rather than just a few distinct levels. This will maintain the progressivity of taxation while more evenly distributing taxation rates across the spectrum of wealth and spending.

Structure and Benefits of a National Sales Tax

Consistent with the principle of taxing consumption more than savings or work, a national sales tax should be established and levied on the end sale of new and used goods as well as services, with the percentage tax rates increasing progressively with the price of the goods or services being sold. Simply put, those who spend more will pay more in taxes with the most expensive luxury items or services being taxed at progressively higher rates.

There are many advantages of shifting to a sales tax system, including simplicity, immediacy of payment, and the rewarding of thrift and responsibility. Under this plan, there would be no annual filing of income taxes, thus saving individual and corporate taxpayers the billions of hours, dollars and frustrations that currently go into filing and processing income taxes. Each year, some 134 million tax returns are filed by taxpayers and must be processed by the IRS. All this would be obviated by eliminating the income tax and replacing it with a sales tax.

Additional savings will result because the huge IRS infrastructure dedicated to processing income taxes can be substantially reduced. The IRS estimates it currently spends about $10.8 billion to collect taxes each year.

It is a myth to suggest, as some have, that the IRS could be entirely eliminated with a sales tax. Some government entity would still be needed to monitor the collection of sales taxes. Perhaps it would not be called the IRS, but there would still be some such agency needed. The difference, and it will be substantial, is that the size and costs of the agency could be dramatically reduced by eliminating the income tax and the complexities of the tax code.

Shifting from income to sales tax would also help reduce the "tax gap," which the IRS estimates costs about $345 billion each year. This amount reflects the difference between what is collected and what should be collected if individual tax returns were filed honestly and accurately. It does not, however, reflect the taxes that should have been paid, but were not, by corporations. Neither does it reflect income from illegal activities that evade income tax reporting entirely.

Just as important as the direct savings in time and money, eliminating the income tax code would mean the system could not be manipulated by those who can afford the best accountants or lobbyists. In the process, so called "tax expenditures," targeted tax benefits for certain groups, would be eliminated. The total "costs" to the treasury of these features of the current tax is estimated at more than $900 billion annually.

If government wants to encourage or discourage certain economic activities, there are countless more transparent, fair and direct ways to do so without complicating and biasing the tax code in favor of one group or activity over another.

Benefits of Eliminating Payroll Taxes

Along with elimination of income taxes, payroll taxes which now go to support OASDI and Medicare would be eliminated. This will accomplish several things.

First, it is consistent with the principles of taxing wealth over work. Our current tax structure assesses payroll taxes on the first penny to the last dollar earned for most workers. By comparison, those who do not work for wages or salaries but gain money solely through investments do not pay such taxes. This is just not right. People who work for minimum wages should not pay higher overall tax rates as a percentage of income and wealth than multibillionaires who make money from investments.

In conjunction with other reforms to be discussed in the next chapter, ending payroll taxes will also help promote personal responsibility and eliminate the illusion that money is being paid into some form of account that is set aside for individuals.

Ending payroll taxes also discourages the "off the books" accounting that allows the government to say on the one hand that it has set aside money in a "trust fund" even as it borrows from that very fund and writes IOUs to pay for the rest of government spending.

Capital Gains Taxes

To keep sales tax rates reasonable, and consistent with the principles of taxing wealth more than work and encouraging investment over speculation, additional revenue will be obtained from time indexed capital gains taxes. The longer someone has held an asset, the lower the capital gains rate they would pay on sale of that asset. Rates would range on a continuum from zero for long term savings to substantially higher levels for speculative trading.

Long term retirement and other savings will be taxed much lower or zero rates and sales of primary single family homes should be tax free up to the median home value when the proceeds are reinvested in purchase of another home.

Estate Tax Reform

Families that wish to pass their businesses or farms on to their children should be able to do so. At the same time, our society has an interest in guarding against the excessive accumulation of vast wealth in the hands of very few individuals.

To achieve both goals, the current estate tax should be scrapped and replaced by an inheritance tax paid by the family recipients of the inheritance not against the estate itself. Small businesses and farms should be protected through reasonable exemptions for modest inheritances, for example, $10 million in net assets, with the exemption level to be adjusted on an annual basis to account for inflation.

As with sales and capital gains taxes, the rates of inheritance taxes would be set on a continuum proportionate to the taxable value of the inheritance at the time of transfer or liquidation.

Beyond the exempt inheritance levels, the generational transfer of tangible assets directly used in a business or farm should be tax-free providing the transfer is to family members who continue to use the assets in the business or farm activity. This is particularly important for businesses or farms that require costly infrastructure in buildings, land, equipment, and so forth, but may not have ready liquid capital. If the assets of such businesses or farms are liquidated, the net income above the exempt limits would then be subject to taxation under sales or capital gains rates and rules.

To limit the opportunities for circumventing inheritance taxes through direct gifts, current gift taxes should be substantially reformed with much stricter limits placed on the types and amount of gifts that would be allowed.

User Fees and Tariffs

To help fund specific government services or resources, those who make use of such services and resources should be charged reasonable fees. Those fees would then either be deposited in the general fund or dedicated to particular uses related to the source of the fees. In addition, selective tariffs should be charged as trade policies and agreements allow.

Specific fees may also be applied to certain activities or resources to promote or discourage certain practices. For example, as a way to influence consumer behavior, reduce consumption of fossil fuels, fund infrastructure improvements and generate revenue to help reduce the debt, fees should be placed on the use of gasoline or diesel for passengers, but with lower rates for fuels used for commercial trucking, barges, mass transit or farm vehicles used in the production of food stocks. Carbon taxes combined with overall carbon caps (rather than a "cap and trade" system) should also be established to place the true overall costs of consuming fossil fuels and to stimulate more competition for alternative, cleaner energy sources.

Tax Rates, Revenue and Spending Amounts

To bring our budget back into balance and pay down the existing debt, by law all tax rates for the combined revenue sources described above should be set at levels that will, in combination with changes in spending, lead to a zero budget deficit within five years and thereafter begin to pay down the debt to responsible, sustainable levels.

The precise levels of each of the taxes described in this chapter will need to be determined by the Congress, but, at least in the near term, restoring balance may mean an increase in total taxation because we simply cannot get back to balance simply through spending cuts or economic growth.

Because of the benefits of the changes proposed in this chapter and throughout this book, any increases in out of pocket spending may actually be rather small, but political leaders who pledge to never raise taxes are just as unrealistic and irresponsible as those who pledge to never touch entitlement spending.

Congressional procedures, which will be discussed later, should also be modified so that spending on all programs, both new and existing, must be accompanied by specification of precisely where the money will come from. In other words, we will begin to match our revenue structure with our spending levels just as average American families and businesses must. This must be a two way street however, with increases in revenue matched by corresponding decreases in overall spending, and with any proposed decreases in revenue matched by explicit specification of corresponding cuts in programs and expenditures.

Why This Chapter Is So Short
and How To Make Reform Happen

Before concluding this chapter, a word is in order about why it is so short relative to others. The reason is simple – the tax code should be simple.

With a simple, fair and understandable tax structure in place, our economy will realize immediate savings and stimulus through removing the costs of compliance. The economy will also be stimulated by removal of all the distorting effects of the current tax code.

In spite of these benefits, it will still be difficult to get members of the Congress to make such a dramatic shift in tax policy. The solution to this problem, like the proposed tax system itself, is actually simple - require every member of Congress and all other elected officials and candidates for office to do their own taxes for their families and their business without any help from accountants of tax preparers. Then make those returns public.

After just one tax season with this requirement in place and enforced, resistance to tax reform would evaporate.

But this is only one of the key ingredients to solving our fiscal crisis. We must also look at how government spends the money it collects. That is the subject we turn to now.

4.

ENDING THE ENTITLEMENT/ MANDATORY MINDSET

Reforming the tax code and increasing revenues will only address part of the equation that brings our country back to fiscal strength and responsibility. There must also be profound and comprehensive reforms to all spending, including what are currently called discretionary and entitlement programs.

I start the spending discussion with entitlement programs for two reasons. First, they are the largest blocks of Federal spending today and will be the biggest drivers of deficits and debt in the future if they are not reformed. Second, entitlement programs are the "third rail" of political discussion and policy makers. People are afraid to touch them (unless it is to promise increases) because doing so is thought to be certain death. Yet touch them we must and it need not be fatal if managed properly.

Discretionary and "Mandatory" Spending

Congress considers spending as falling into two broad categories, discretionary and mandatory. Discretionary spending refers to programs which get specific amounts of money each year depending on annual appropriation votes taken in Congress.

This spending, which amounted to over a trillion dollars last year, represents just a third of our overall annual budget. It includes everything from funding for defense, Federal prisons, NASA, research at the National Institutes of Health, National Parks, highways, border security and countless other programs. How these spending decisions are made, and how they should be reformed, is discussed later in this book.

The other form of spending, so-called "mandatory" spending, represents in total about two thirds of our overall annual budget. Unlike discretionary programs, once so-called "mandatory" programs, like OASDI (Social Security), Medicare, Medicaid, Veterans Benefits, Federal and Military Retirement and others are established, anyone who meets certain qualifications such as age, income, disability and so forth, is considered "entitled" to specified amounts of money and that money must be spent by Congress.

It is important to understand that Congress typically does not actually set finite limits on mandatory spending each year. Rather, mandatory spending is on a sort of budgetary auto pilot. The trouble is this auto pilot only knows how to climb, it was not programmed to land or even stay level.

Once such programs are created, there is usually no corresponding enforced "mandate" that the funds for this spending must actually be raised either today or in the future. Our current and growing debt is, to a great degree, a result of this imbalance. In the longer term, as people age and their health care needs and costs increase, these "entitlements" pose the greatest challenge to our financial solvency.

Reassuring Those Currently in Need

Before discussing any reforms to current "entitlement programs" I believe there must be a strong up-front reassurance that, under any reform scenario, people in genuine current need, and I emphasize genuine need – low income seniors, children who have lost parents, and the truly severely disabled, would not lose needed benefits or be left destitute.

No one is going to "take away" Social Security, Medicare, or other essential benefits people truly need without assuring that those genuine needs will still be addressed. Any one of us could find ourselves in dire circumstances and needs through no fault of our own. It is neither responsible nor fair to pull the rug out from under people in genuine need with no alternative to meet that need.

Respecting the needs of current beneficiaries also means that those who have lived under certain assumptions and commitments the longest should be sheltered to the greatest extent possible from substantial changes that would impact their lives or circumstances. A senior citizen, for example, currently depending on Social Security and Medicare benefits to make ends meet should not experience changes that make life unbearably more difficult for them or create excessive uncertainties or anxieties.

Changing Mindsets and Policies

Now comes the hard part politically. Promising to meet a commitment to help those with genuine and urgent needs does not mean we can or should continue with business as usual. Our commitment should be to helping those in greatest need, not to maintaining specific programs as they currently are.

We must consider two facts. First, the present and future course of entitlement spending is unsustainable financially. Second, not everyone currently receiving entitlement benefits is equally in need.

Considering that much of our current Federal spending is funded by borrowing and passing debt on to our children, it is hard to justify paying continued entitlement benefits to persons who have no real need for them. Why, for example, should everyone's grandchildren pay off debt in the future in order to provide Medicare benefits and OASDI payments to those who have many millions, or even billions of dollars in wealth or income?

The honest answer is - they shouldn't.

To put our fiscal house in order, we must emphasize and encourage personal responsibility, savings, investments and insurance. We must also distinguish between meeting genuine needs from the practice of encouraging everyone to simply take it for granted that they should receive something regardless of their need or the costs and impact on the rest of society.

How do we change this mindset?

First and foremost, all of us, average citizens and elected officials alike, must stop thinking of ourselves as somehow "entitled" to receive something from the government, especially if that money is ultimately coming at the expense of our children and grandchildren. In Congress and the Administration, elected leaders need to stop considering certain spending as "mandatory" and thereby both untouchable and unlinked to revenues. In fact, I believe policy makers and the public need to do away entirely with the very concepts of entitlements and mandatory spending.

If we recognize that the social programs we now call entitlements are better thought of as needs-based social insurance, and if we acknowledge that the funding of these programs depends on the willingness and ability of others to pay for it, then it should follow that need, not mere desire or status, should govern both eligibility to receive benefits and the amounts of benefits that are received.

Insurance is something we all invest in hoping we will not actually face the conditions that force us to draw upon it. Insurance is not a guaranteed investment with a promised return regardless of need.

We must also recognize that while many people legitimately need and benefit from "entitlement" programs, it is also true that in far too many ways our current system of taxation and social entitlements rewards people for not taking responsibility and penalizes people for acting responsibly. Those who choose not to work or save are too often rewarded while those who set aside money for savings or personal insurance are effectively penalized for their prudence because they will pay higher taxes and receive fewer benefits than the irresponsible.

This is not healthy for individuals themselves or for the society as a whole. That is why the tax reforms I have already proposed focus on taxing spending rather than savings and speculation rather than investment. But, again, tax reforms without reforms of other spending are not enough. To really solve our problems we must address both discretionary and "entitlement" programs and spending.

5.

OLD-AGE, SURVIVORS AND DISABILITY INSURANCE – SOCIAL SECURITY

Most Americans, especially older Americans, are deeply concerned about the future we are leaving to our children and grandchildren and most do not want to pass on huge debt to the next generations. That desire to do the right thing is powerful, real and should not be underestimated.

If policy makers meet with their constituents honestly and put forward fair proposals that truly solve problems, most people are willing to make the right choices for the good of their country and their children.

For this to happen, however, we must begin by restating the prior chapter's commitment that any reforms maintain current protections and support for those in greatest genuine need. Without this assurance, resistance to any thought of reform would, for good reason, be insurmountable and even the most creative and constructive proposals would likely fail.

I want to, again, state emphatically that any reforms in or alternatives to OASDI, Medicare, or Medicaid should be designed and implemented in such a way that those truly in need and currently dependent on these programs would not be harmed even if the programs themselves are significantly changed. But, let us also then acknowledge that the programs must change.

The Current Status of OASDI

Because it was the first of the social insurance programs, and because in many ways it is the easier of the major programs to fix, OASDI is a good place to start.

Old-Age, Survivors, and Disability Insurance, abbreviated OASDI, is the full name for what most people know as Social Security. I purposefully used OASDI rather than Social Security in order to emphasize as strongly and often as possible the Insurance aspect of the program. The I, in OASDI stands for Insurance, not "[I]ntitlement."

Presently, funding for OASDI comes from payroll taxes, assessed at a rate of 6.2 percent of wages paid by the employer and 6.2 percent paid by employees. The self-employed pay the entire 12.4% themselves.

Until recently, it had been estimated that each year until 2017 the amount taken in from payroll taxes was projected to exceed the amount being paid out. That has changed however due to the recession and now payroll tax revenues are actually already less than what is being paid out in benefits.

In the past, the surplus revenues were put into a "trust fund" which was supposed to be set aside to help pay the benefits for the now arriving baby boom generation. In fact, however, the "general fund" of the government has borrowed this money to pay for other expenses. The general fund then effectively writes an IOU to the Social Security Administration by giving it treasury bills (actually special paper certificates) to cover the debt.

Social Security benefits comprised 4.3 percent of our Gross Domestic Product in 2007, but they are projected to reach 6.1 percent by 2035.[6] The combined OASDI deficit for the next 75 years is estimated to be $4.3 trillion dollars in present value terms.

Most people do not see OASDI as an insurance program for current rather than future beneficiaries, but that is in fact, by its very title, what it is and how it operates. Contrary to what many people believe, payroll taxes paid by those who are presently working do not go into a set aside personal retirement fund for each current worker.

Rather, those taxes go to pay for the benefits of the current generation of OASDI recipients, not the future generation of retirees. A significant portion of payroll taxes also goes to help

---

[6] http://www.ssa.gov/OACT/TRSUM/trsummary.html

children who have lost parents, and to provide support for persons with disabilities.

The most accurate and honest way to think about OASDI is not as a future retirement system at all. Those of us who are paying into OASDI now are actually doing so as a way to help out our parents' and grandparents' generation, the disabled and young children who have lost their parents.

We benefit from this individually and socially because it reduces what many of us might otherwise have to pay to help sustain parents, and because we and our children are helped by having this social insurance in case we should die prematurely or become disabled and need the assistance.

The key fact remains, however, that through our payroll taxes we are not actually setting aside anything for own personal retirement. Not one dime of what we pay personally into Social Security today will actually be there for ourselves in the future because it has already been spent. Instead, we are depending on future generations of workers to pay for our needs just as we are paying now for the needs of previous workers and the disabled.

It is important to emphasize too that this also applies to current retirees who are receiving OASDI benefits. Though today's retirees may well have paid into the program during their working lives, what they paid at the time went to support retirees who preceded them, not to set up a guaranteed retirement fund for themselves. What is more, in many cases, especially for the oldest beneficiaries, what people are receiving in benefits has vastly exceeded the total amount they ever paid into the program.

The truth is, every penny that has ever been paid into Social Security through payroll taxes has already been spent and we are counting on future workers to pay for our retirement and health care through their payroll taxes.

That statement bears repeating - every penny that has ever been paid into Social Security through payroll taxes has already been spent and we are counting on future workers to pay for our retirement and health care through their payroll taxes. There is, in fact, no real money set aside in a retirement account for future retirees.

"What about the trust fund?" some may ask. Again, the truth is the so-called "trust fund" is simply paper IOUs representing money borrowed by the general treasury that will eventually be "paid back" to Social Security by the very people who are also paying all the other taxes needed to run the rest of government.

The "trust fund" is not really an IOU where one person of the same age owes another person. It is actually more like a "we owe we" note, or, worse, a "you owe us", with the you being our children and grandchildren and the us being those who imposed the debt on them and will receive the benefits of their labors.

It is not inaccurate or unfair to say that there really are no funds in the trust fund, there is, at present, only trust. That trust might be sufficient if it were based on a realistic plan to make good on it, but the truth is that no such plan exists today in law or in our financial practices. The truth suggests that not only are there no funds in the trust fund, perhaps there shouldn't be any trust there either.

When people feel they are "entitled" to a payment under Social Security, the basis of that payment is coming from a generation of younger workers who never had a say in creating the entitlement and who will face a host of other serious challenges largely created by the actions of the supposedly "entitled" generation which is demanding their payment.

The system of current workers paying for current retirees worked in the past as long as the life expectancy of retirees was shorter and the demographics of younger population growth and economic expansion sustained it. But those factors are now working against, rather than for, the system and it cannot be sustained in its current form for the future.

Need-Based Benefits — Not "[I]ntitlements"

I should emphasize here that I strongly believe there is merit to having some form of social based insurance, such as OASDI, and I would strongly defend that principle.

What I disagree with about our present system is how we pay for it and how people have been encouraged to think they are entitled to receive everything they put into the program (and more) regardless of their personal needs or the financial impact on the nation and on future generations. This expectation of entitlement has become so engrained in much of our citizenry that people become irate at the mere suggestion that the benefits "the government has promised" might not be forthcoming.

At some of my own town hall discussions of the budget constituents have angrily risen to their feet to condemn "you people in the government" who have spent all the money, then demand that "the government is just going to have to pay us what we've been promised! That's all there is to it." Often these demands are then followed by equally insistent demands that we stop deficit spending and eliminate the Federal debt. Oh, and by the way, you have to cut taxes while you do all this.

Blaming someone else or demanding that "government" fix things is easy, but the difficult reality is that all of us as citizens, not just the people in the government, have spent the money. Citizens have demanded lower taxes and increased spending, including on entitlement benefits, and that is how we got here. Voters too often and too happily put into office people who made easy promises and rejected those who told hard truths and demanded tough choices.

It may be true that politicians have demagogued the issue on one side of the equation or the other by promising never to raise taxes or touch entitlements. But it is the voters in the end who have encouraged and rewarded such deception.

As Walt Kelley's cartoon character Pogo said years ago, "We have met the enemy and he is us."

The most difficult mental shift from the current practice to the changes I would propose is this: regardless of what people think they have been promised, we must begin to adjust benefits from OASDI and other so called entitlements to base them on real need, not just on prior amounts contributed, age, or other elements not necessarily linked to genuine needs.

Let me say that again, if OASDI is truly an insurance program, which it is, then benefits from that program should be based on need. This should begin immediately and should be central to the program from here out.

This means that those fortunate enough to never have a need to draw on the insurance would never draw payments from the program regardless of how much they paid into it through sales and other taxes. That is how insurance works and it does not mean people will not or have not received benefits from what they have paid into the program.

Paying into an insurance policy does not mean you get back everything you paid regardless of events or need. With car insurance, for example, if you never have an accident you may never draw upon your insurance. You certainly do not expect to get back a check for everything you paid to insure your car when the time comes to sell it and buy a new one.

On the other hand, if the need ever truly arises, if your car is totaled and someone is seriously injured, you stand to receive far more in benefits than you may ever have paid into the program. The benefit of insurance comes first and foremost from being insured and knowing that if disaster strikes there will be some level of support provided.

"Wait a minute," many will likely say, "That's fine for car insurance, but when it comes to Social Security I paid into the program and I deserve to get my money back, every penny I paid."

I hear this often. It is certainly understandable and is perpetuated by political rhetoric and current policy. But it is based on misunderstanding and is simply unsustainable in reality. This demand neglects both the fact that current payroll taxes are being spent to support current retirees and, again, that insurance (the "I" in OASDI) does not work that way. What is more, as appealing and understandable as such a mindset may be it cannot be honored financially. Those who insist that this unrealistic belief and desire must be met are insisting on that belief at the expense of their children and our nation's future.

Stating this matter so bluntly might well be politically difficult, but it also happens to be true. More importantly, denying this truth may avoid political suicide but only at the expense of committing the equivalent of political fiscal homicide with our children as the victims.

Given that choice, what should responsible politicians and citizens do?

The Impacts of Eliminating Payroll Taxes

Elimination of payroll taxes, as described earlier in this book, and emphasizing the insurance role of OASDI will lead to a number of changes in how OASDI functions.

With funding coming from consumption and other taxes rather than payroll taxes on wages, it will no longer possible, or necessary, to know how much any individual paid into the system in order to calculate their "guaranteed future benefits."

This is because there would be no "guaranteed benefits." Money would only be received if one genuinely needed it. All program benefits would be funded through the general fund and would be based on need, not on the amount the recipient paid into the program.

This is such a profound change in how we understand OASDI today that it merits explanation. Consider first that most workers pay into the current system by being taxed on everything they earn in wages or salary from the first dime to the last. By comparison, those who make very large incomes only have payroll taxes taken from what they make up to a certain threshold. In 2008 that threshold was $102,000. Everything after that is exempt from OASDI taxes.

Those fortunate enough to have incomes that do not come from working for wages or a salary do not have to pay a penny into OASDI. Everything they earn is exempt from payroll taxes because they are not on a payroll.

This differential in taxation on wealth versus work and on middle income earners versus the very wealthy explains much of why effective total tax rates as percentages of incomes are often higher for middle income workers than for the very wealthy.

In fairness, it should be pointed out that when it comes time to receive OASDI benefits, those in lower income brackets tend to receive a greater percentage of "return on investment," i.e. higher actual benefits relative to their contributions compared to the benefits received by higher income workers. In this regard benefit payments are progressive.

It is also true that under the current system those who have not paid into Social Security at all do not earn benefits from the program and, hence, do not have any right to its benefits if their personal financial world collapses. Some may have difficulty feeling sympathetic to a multimillionaire who loses it all, but if we are to truly have a social insurance program, it makes sense that everyone, including millionaires, should pay into it and everyone should be eligible for basic benefits if tragedy strikes them or their families.

Conditions For Accepting Changes

In a moment I will outline other changes needed in OASDI and similar "entitlement" programs. Before I describe these changes, I want to note that I have spoken with a great many people who, rather surprisingly, are in fact perfectly comfortable with, or at least recognize the necessity of, the proposed changes. This is in spite of the fact that many of these individuals would end up receiving less money than they do now.

That willingness to accept changes, however, depends on three conditions:

- First, that if a person's circumstance changed and they truly began to need the support of a program, they would be assured of receiving that support without difficulty.
- Second, that the money saved as a result would actually go to reducing the deficit and debt rather than to other spending increases.
- Third, that we establish some way in which we are not punishing those who have done the right thing and saved while rewarding those who have spent their lives spending rather saving for the future.

All of these concerns are absolutely legitimate and I share them. They must and will be addressed as part of the overall policy changes described in this book. In fact, without these conditions, I could not in good conscience put forth the proposals that follow.

With that commitment, let's consider the proposed changes in more detail and how those concerns will be resolved.

Determining Need-Based Benefits

As promised from the outset of this chapter, those seniors, survivors and disabled who have legitimate and significant needs for OASDI payments should not see their current checks reduced and, in some instances, might actually merit increased payments.

At the same time, those who are currently receiving OASDI payments, but whose income and wealth are sufficient that the benefits are not in fact necessary, should begin to receive reduced payments and, at the highest levels of wealth and income, should receive no further payments.

If, however, someone's financial circumstances changed and genuine need arose, they would again be eligible and would have their payments restored promptly. This addresses the first concern mentioned earlier as a condition for accepting the change.

Notwithstanding the reassurances just offered, I recognize that this change will of course upset a number of people who believe they paid into the program and are therefore entitled to get back what they paid in. Again, everyone who has paid into the system has in fact received benefits, whether or not they have received a check. They have received the benefit of having insurance for their children if a parent dies, they have received the benefit of having insurance against disability, and they have received the benefit of having the financial needs of the prior generation taken care of.

The proposed change cannot take any of those benefits away because they have already been received. What the change would mean is that the Insurance function, the real intention of the I in OASDI at its inception, is now being applied and people will not receive payments at the expense of current workers or future generations unless there is a real need.

Under the new approach, no one will have to live in fear that they will be left destitute and unable to meet basic needs, but neither will those who do not have legitimate needs continue to receive payments at the expense of current workers or future generations.

Changing How Future Benefits are Calculated

Adjusting current and future benefits to reflect actual needs will immediately begin to reduce spending on OASDI and other "entitlements". That will help lower both current deficits and future debt accumulation. To realize future savings, we must also review how projected future payments are calculated.

Presently, future Social Security benefits are calculated based on the wages of beneficiaries and are adjusted each year based on a formula that estimates wage growth. Many people, myself included, believe a more legitimate basis for adjustment of future benefits is price-indexing.

Under this approach, rather than calculating future benefits based on wages and payroll taxes paid into the system, future benefit levels, for those who need them, would be based on calculations of what is necessary to meet basic needs, not what was paid in through separate taxes and not as an attempt to keep benefit growth commensurate with growth in wages.

The key goal of a social insurance program should be, again, to insure against anyone facing truly desperate circumstances. The responsibility for insuring a higher standard of living upon retirement in the event of disability or death of a parent falls to the individual to set aside sufficient savings and personal insurance to achieve that goal.

Why Not Just Raise Taxes to Pay for OASDI?

Many will argue, particularly on the Left, that the proposals to change our tax system and base OASDI benefits on need are not necessary. They say it is actually possible to pay for future benefits by making adjustments to the payroll tax rate or increasing or eliminating the top level of exempted income. On the other side of the political aisle, the Right may be more likely to advocate changing the age of retirement, lowering retirement benefits or both.

Mathematically, both arguments are defendable. For example, the Social Security Board of Trustees estimates that if payroll taxes were increased immediately by 14%, bringing them from 12.4 percent to 14.1 percent, or if there were a reduction in benefits of 12 percent, balance could be achieved over the next 75 years. Eliminating the cap on payroll taxable earnings would also generate substantial revenue and help reduce the future shortfall.

If OASDI were the only problem, any of these changes would likely be better than simply passing on more debt to our children. But keep in mind two things.

First, as noted earlier, payroll taxes hit working families from the first dollar earned to the very last and do not generate any revenue from people who make money simply because they have money. Second, remember all the other financial challenges facing our country described in Chapter 2.

We begin from a point of a $13 trillion debt and more than $1.6 trillion dollar annual deficits. On top of that we must also deal with looming deficits in Medicare, which are far higher than those of Social Security. In addition are all the other hidden deficits we face, including infrastructure, long term care, defense and so forth.

Contrary to what some have suggested, simply proposing to raise taxes to solve our entitlement and other spending problems is insufficient, inefficient and impractical. At some point, the combined increases in taxes would cripple individual family budgets and the nation's economy.

That is why a more targeted effort that provides a safety net for those truly in need but does not promise benefits to those without real need is a better solution.

Promoting Individual Investments and Savings

While I believe it is good and responsible public policy to have some form of social insurance, I also believe strongly in personal responsibility. OASDI should come to be viewed as a safety net rather than a promised entitlement. People should not "count on" this as their primary or sole source of either retirement income or insurance. They certainly should not count on Social Security to give them more money than they put in to begin with or to maintain some desired standard of living simply because someone has become accustomed to or feels entitled to it.

The existence of OASDI as a need-based insurance system should not imply to anyone that they do not need to take the personal responsibility to set aside savings for retirement and have other forms of personal insurance against unexpected events. Instead, government policies should encourage and reward individual savings and personal insurance.

If we are going to change the mindset of our country to consider OASDI a social insurance program, and if we are going to base payments from that program on real financial need, individuals will need to understand and plan for the fact that their long term financial well being and outcome depends on their personal choices and decisions today.

In recent years, a number of proposals have been put forth to put Social Security funds into private investment accounts. However well-intentioned these proposals may have been, most suffered from several shortcomings. The first and most important was they failed the test of honest mathematics.

Most of the proposals for privatization of Social Security tried to suggest that we could allow current workers to put a portion of what they pay in payroll taxes into private accounts instead of paying it in payroll taxes. The promise was that such investments would pay higher returns over the long run and, hence, improve people's retirement incomes.

As appealing as this may have been, consider first of all what has happened to the stock market in the past year. Where would people be if their entire retirement savings were in the market and with no social safety nets as backup?

Also remember that all of what is presently paid into the payroll tax system is being spent. The bulk of the money is going to fund current beneficiaries. The remainder that is supposedly going into a trust fund is also being spent on programs not covered by the general fund with unfunded IOUs left behind.

Given that all of what is currently being paid into the system is being spent, where is there any money to give back to people to invest on their own unless we simultaneously increase the debt, which, of course, simply means writing more IOUs?

Personally, I believe there is merit to encouraging private retirement accounts. What I oppose is trying to justify it with false math and increasing the debt to do so. I also oppose making this the sole source of retirement security and doing away with the safety net provided by social insurance.

The second major problem with the private accounts suggested in the past is that they failed to recognize the insurance component of OASDI that currently goes to help surviving children and the disabled. Most of us do not anticipate that we will need such support, but life doesn't always work out that way and the fact is many of us will. If personal misfortune strikes early on, there is simply no way most people will have put aside enough money themselves to cover the needs of survivors or help them deal with the financial losses from a disabling condition.

There is an alternative that provides the necessary insurance function and does not rely on phony or misleading math. Several key elements will help make this successful.

First, and most importantly, if we are going to encourage people to invest in private savings accounts for retirement, disability or other functions, we must make honest calculations of the costs of such programs and include those costs fully in annual and long term budget projections and revenue targets.

Remember also that I have proposed we do away with payroll taxes entirely and fund retirement, disability and survivors benefits for the most in need from the general revenue funds. Those funds will, in turn, come from sales, capital gains, estate taxes and selected fees. This means that the money employers and employees currently pay into Social Security will now be available directly as wages or salary.

When this happens, it will be tremendously important to help employees understand that while their take home pay may appear larger, they will have to personally budget for, and pay other taxes, notably sales and perhaps capital gains, to supplant what they formerly paid through income and payroll taxes. Workers will also have to understand that they are no longer automatically paying into what they may have believed was a guaranteed personal retirement account through payroll taxes.

One way to help individuals deal with this responsibly is to require a portion of all wages or salary to be automatically deducted for all workers and placed in personal long term savings/investment accounts of their choosing. In many cases this is happening voluntarily already through workplace sponsored retirement plans.

The key change here is that mandatory deduction and investment in personal accounts would apply to all workers and these would be placed in personal investment accounts. Annual personal investment accounts should also be required of those whose income doesn't come from wages or salaries.

To supplement the amounts that individual workers in the lowest income categories can afford to set aside, their personal investments in savings accounts should be matched to a significant degree by government contributions. This approach encourages and rewards savings and helps create sufficient individual reserves to reduce the need for future dependence on social insurance programs.

At this point it is fair to ask how this plan differs from Social Security privatization proposals of the past?

To begin with, as noted before, this plan will be paid for in full from the general revenues. That would be part of the requirement for its creation, i.e. that current and future revenues from taxes be sufficient to fully pay for the costs of the program. This may require revenue increases, but, unlike prior proposals, there is no duplicitous assertion that one can spend money twice, once for the trust fund and at the same time for private accounts without increasing debt.

Because payroll taxes will be eliminated as part of overall tax reform, there will be no illusion of a trust fund from which to borrow the money to pay for private investments. At the same time, it should be kept in mind that substantial savings will be realized, both through need-based benefit eligibility and by fundamentally changing how future benefits are calculated. As a result, the net costs of the basic OASDI insurance payments will be reduced, thereby significantly limiting the potential or size of any required revenue increases.

Ideally, along with encouraging personal retirement accounts, several other types of savings or insurance accounts should be created for specific needs and with specific exemptions from capital gains taxation for each. The four most important such funds would be for retirement, disability, education, and long term care. Again, for those most in need, funding for personal contributions and government match to these individual savings accounts would come from a combination of money that is now being paid through payroll taxes and from the general treasury. Current "tax incentives" written into the income tax code to stimulate such investments would be eliminated in favor of direct payments into the relevant accounts.

Reducing the Reward for Irresponsibility

Earlier I emphasized the importance of establishing some way in which we are not punishing those who have done the right thing and saved while rewarding those who have spent their lives spending rather saving for the future. I believe this is perhaps the most vexing challenge facing any form of social insurance program.

On the one hand, as a society we are uncomfortable seeing our fellow citizens left destitute. At the same time, it is not fair or right that some people make vastly irresponsible, selfish, shortsighted and reckless decisions and then expect those who have been more responsible to bail them out. This happens far too often in our society and it should not continue.

Frankly, there is no perfect resolution to this dilemma, but I believe the tax changes discussed in the prior chapter are an important step in the right direction. By collecting revenues from sales taxes rather than income taxes, those who choose to consume heavily in the short term rather than saving for the long term, will pay taxes on that consumption. So too, those who make money through illegal activities and do not file income taxes at all will nevertheless be taxed to at least some degree when they make purchases. On the savings side, long term investments and retirement accounts will face low or zero taxes. Further, providing matching funds also encourages savings by lower income workers.

These programmatic changes will, in combination, penalize profligate spending and reward thrift. At the same time, however, it is important to also emphasize the points of the first chapter of this book.

No program, no matter how well intended or designed, can be fully successful unless certain core qualities exist among the people. If honesty, integrity, responsibility, and a strong sense of community are instilled throughout our society and embodied in our policies and conduct, many of the current abuses of social insurance will be reduced and, to a significant degree, the need for the insurance itself will be lessened.

Saving the Money that is Saved

The third essential condition for changing how benefits are calculated and received is providing assurance that savings will actually go toward reducing the debt burden on our children and not toward new spending programs. One cannot in honesty say to people that for the sake of their children and the nation they must forego receiving benefits to which they thought they were entitled unless the money is actually going to be used wisely. How government spending overall should be reformed will be discussed in Chapter 13.

For now, let us turn our attention to the most difficult and costly of all government spending – health care.

6.
HEALTH CARE

Like much of this book, this chapter has been in the works as a written project for nearly four years now. In the case of health care, however, what follows has grown from more than a twenty-three years delivering health care as a clinical psychologist specializing in not only mental illness but the effects of brain injury, cancer and other illnesses.

From that background, and in my prior capacity as a university professor and researcher, I have spent a fair bit of time not only studying our current health care system but working in it as a professional service provider. At the same time, of course, I also come to this as a consumer of health care services for myself and my family.

Although this chapter was started before the debate and associated furor over health care reform that dominated the Congress and public discussion in 2009 and on through spring of 2010, that debate and the resulting legislation must be addressed from the outset.

"Less Bad"

People often say that the health care system in the U.S. is the best in the world. It should be, but it is not. Health care in our nation suffers from three key shortcomings – cost, access, and quality of outcomes.

We spend more per capita on health care than any other nation, yet 47 million people in America lack health insurance. Moreover, our health care outcomes on a host of different variables and illnesses rank well below many other developed nations. Furthermore, as discussed earlier in chapters on the debt and entitlement reform, health care costs and their rapid growth are key challenges to the immediate and long term financial stability and competitiveness of our nation.

In the context of these unpleasant realities, it is admirable that the Congress and Administration have made a serious effort at implementing health care reform. I disagree, however, with how this effort was approached and much of what has emerged as the result.

Appraising the overall result, I am reminded of a useful phrase I learned while living in Spain, "Menos Mal" or, "Less Bad." In my judgment, what has emerged would make health care "less bad" in many ways, but it would miss and in some ways prevent an opportunity for real comprehensive reform.

What Should Have Been Done

Given the state of the Nation's economy, the first priority of Congress and the new administration in 2009 should have been economic recovery, not health care reform. When more than twenty percent of people in some areas are without jobs, when millions of Americans are losing their homes, when countless businesses are going under, and with the deficit and debt expanding, the economy should have been Job One.

In fairness, the substantial stimulus package and the financial rescue efforts of the TARP did help stop the freefall of the economy, but then we moved on to energy, health care and other matters as if the job of restoring jobs was finished. That was a mistake.

Elsewhere I have described some of what can and should be done to get the economy moving again. Among other things, infrastructure investments, energy conservation, tax simplification, regulatory streamlining, and improved capital access would have been good places to start and would likely have been welcomed by most Americans.

The key point here is that when people are worried about losing their job, home or business, it's understandably difficult, and frightening to ask them to consider complicated legislation (more than two thousand pages) with uncertain impacts on one of the most fundamental aspects of their lives – their health. Add to this the growing concerns about the Federal budget

70

deficit and debt, and it should not be surprising that strong feelings have emerged in response to the health care debate.

This is not to say that health care reform had to be neglected in favor of economic issues. In fact, I believe it would have been good policy and smart politics to initiate reforms immediately with things that most people, regardless of party affiliation or ideology, would have supported.

For example, there is broad agreement that insurance discrimination against preexisting conditions should end. This is especially important as people who have lost a job, and often the insurance that went with it, seek to find new health care coverage but are denied because of prior conditions. The same applies to the indefensible practice of "rescissions" in which insurance companies, which have accepted the premium payments of subscribers, suddenly begin to deny coverage for promised treatment payments when the subscriber actually becomes ill.

As a starting point for health care reform, it may have been wiser to introduce a stand-alone measure banning these practices.

As a second step, individuals, families and businesses should be allowed to purchase insurance from nationwide insurers that would include both for profit and not for profit insurance organizations. This would immediately have the desired effects of lowering costs, as a result of competition, and would reduce the uninsured because everyone could become part of much larger risk pools.

Here again, this reform has been championed in various forms by members of Congress and advocates from across the political spectrum.

With these measures in place, and while keeping the economy as Job One, Congress and the Administration could have shown the American people that people are interested in and capable of moving forward together to solve long standing problems in responsible, understandable ways. From there, other comprehensive reforms might have been possible with greater support.

Unfortunately, that is not the path that was chosen. Instead, Republican members of the House and Senate set out for political purposes to block any health care reform, seeking to defeat reform to create a "Waterloo" for President Obama. At the same time, an extraordinarily complex combination of measures emerged from the Democrats which, while making things "less bad" in some ways, still keeps in place many of the fundamental structural flaws of our present approach to health care.

Again, a step by step approach of dealing with preexisting conditions and nationwide plans would likely have been the smartest political and policy approach, but if we were instead going to propose a comprehensive reform, then we should have been truly bold and made real reforms, not built upon an already flawed system.

What follows are my own proposals for tackling and truly transforming health care and its impacts on the budget and economy.

Problems With Health Care Reform

The most important reason the health care reform bill was so long and complex is that it built upon an overly complicated and costly web of underlying programs. No one, starting from scratch, would have created a "system" by globbing programs one on top of each other the way we now have Medicare Parts A, B, Advantage, D, Medicaid, Social Security, S-CHIP, Flexible Spending Accounts, Community Health Centers, Disproportionate Share Hospitals, private and employer insurance, fifty different state programs and so forth.

As if that were not complicated enough, we fund and incentivize much of our health care through the most complex, inefficient and reviled of all Federal programs, the income tax code. Rather than trying to repair such a rickety and expensive house of cards on a fractured foundation, we should have been bold and built something truly new and much more efficient on a solid and lasting footing.

What Real Reform Should Do

From the outset we must assure seniors, the truly disabled, and others in genuine need that their health care needs will still be met even though specific programs will change or be replaced. Second, we must assure individuals and employers who have non-government funded health care that they are perfectly free to keep their existing plans.

With those assurances, and, again, assuring those who already have policies that they can keep those policies, we should phase out and replace all of the current Federal and state government need or age based health programs with the following:

1. Basic prepaid health care that covers routine medical, dental, vision and mental health and requires no insurance forms. Such programs could be for-profit or not-for-profit and individuals could choose which basic health programs to participate in, but everyone without employer-based or individual insurance would be required to enroll.

2. Catastrophic insurance would then cover low risk but high cost occurrences, expensive pharmaceuticals and devices as medically necessary, plus long term care. Individuals could choose these plans from a range of options that meet specified coverage and financial soundness requirements, including for-profit or not-for-profit plans.

3. To expand risk pools and assure that people will not lose care if they move or change jobs, basic care and insurance plans would be state-based, regional or national. A single and simple form would be used by all insurance plans and a Congressionally-established national health and insurance commission would assure financial soundness, quality of care, and provide redress for concerns.

4. Individual payments for basic care and catastrophic insurance would be based on financial means. Everyone participating, regardless of age, would pay as their financial resources allow. Those who can afford to, or whose employers choose to on their behalf, would pay for the full costs of basic care and insurance directly. Those who need financial assistance would receive needs adjusted support from the government for their coverage.

5. Discrimination against pre-existing conditions or genetics would be banned, but there would be incentives for positive health choices and illness prevention.

6. Student aid and loan assistance, plus increased compensation rates, would encourage general and family practice and other high need health care providers. A Federal licensing process would standardize professional licensing for health care practitioners nationwide.

7. Comprehensive malpractice reforms would preserve patient rights and improve quality of care but provide alternatives to litigation and reduce defensive medicine and abusive lawsuits.

8. Veterans, the Guard, Reserve, and active duty personnel and families would be able to continue existing VA or DOD provided health care, or have the option of participating in the alternative program with the government funding their costs as the terms of enlistment and personal circumstances allow or require.

9. The program would be paid for by money now spent on all the existing Federal and state programs and bureaucracies that would be replaced; through cost savings from malpractice reforms, paperwork

reduction, national risk pools and improved preventive care; and through direct payments and premiums from individuals and employers (but no new taxes would be placed on existing insurance).

That's it. Simple, affordable, individual choices with existing insurance and health care plans preserved. There would be no discrimination for pre-existing conditions, basic health would be met through prepaid plans that cover medical, mental dental and vision, and people could choose insurance from state, regional or nationwide private or not for profit insurance choices. Support for those in need would be provided on a sliding scale with everyone required to purchase basic care and insurance. Paperwork would be reduced, malpractice laws reformed, long term care would be included, provider shortages resolved and there would be no addition to the debt or deficit.

More will be said about each of these elements in a moment, but first another word about the tax code as it relates to health care.

Replace the Tax Code and De-link Health Care

While replacing government health programs with something better, we should, as discussed earlier in this book, do the same with the tax code by eliminating all income and payroll taxes along with all of the current health care tax exemptions, deductions, credits, etc. This would "de-link" our health care system from the income tax system and end all of the distorting and unequal tax subsidies that contribute to costs and complexity of health insurance and health care delivery.

In contrast to the status quo and the recent reforms, the new health care and tax programs I am proposing should require just a few hundred pages to describe yet that would replace tens of thousands of pages and massive bureaucracies associated with all the existing tax and health care laws.

Health and Tax Reform FAQs

1. Why is this proposal better than what we already have or what has just been passed into law?

Answer: First of all, this is much simpler. The reason the House and Senate bills were so long and complicated is they tried to modify multiple programs, each of which was designed to remedy problems left or created by what came before, but each of which created its own new laws, bureaucracy and problems. This complexity adds to the confusion and to the costs but it does not improve health care.

Replacing all other government insurance programs with one needs-based Federal program and expanding options for private insurance will dramatically reduce costs and complexity. In fact, rather than the thousand plus pages of the House version, the new proposal should require just a few hundred pages and that would simultaneously replace all the additional thousands of pages that currently describe the Medicare, Medicaid, SCHIP, FSA, DSH and other programs and bureaucracies. The same is true of the tax reform proposal, which would dramatically simplify how taxes are paid and collected and would replace more than twenty thousand pages of current tax law.

A second advantage of this proposal is that it much more clearly and honestly protects those who have existing insurance or basic care and wish to continue with what they already have. Apart from ending pre-existing discrimination and rescissions, existing plans would be unchanged. In addition, by allowing nationwide basic care and insurance plans, individuals and employers can participate in much larger risk pools and therefore have lower costs. At the same time, people who change jobs, move, or travel will not have to lose or change their coverage if they are part of a cross state plan.

Another very important difference is that the new proposal includes medical, dental, mental, and vision health care plus long-term care insurance. This is not the case with existing programs or the reform bill, which largely neglects dental and vision and does not adequately address the looming crisis and costs of long-term care.

Finally, this proposal ends the linkage between the income tax code and health care. It replaces the tax code with a much simpler, fairer system that rewards savings and eliminates tens of thousands of pages of complex law and associated paperwork and bureaucracy.

 2. What happens to people who are already receiving care through existing Federal or state government programs?

Answer: Any citizen or legal resident whose income and assets are such that they are in genuine need will receive government support to purchase basic health care and wraparound insurance, but this will be based on financial means, not age, state of residence, or any other category. This assistance will be provided on a continuum with those in greatest need receiving the greatest help, while those who can afford to pay more on their own bearing that responsibility themselves.

This will apply to people of all ages equally. Hence, a two year old child whose family needs assistance to afford health care will receive that assistance as will a 98 year old from the same Federal government program. However, if the 98 year old or the family of the two year old can afford to pay the bill themselves, they will do so without government assistance.

 3. Why "means test" this program?

Answer: Our national debt exceeds $13 trillion and the deficit for the past year was more than $1.6 trillion. The present value of our 75 year entitlement commitments exceeds $52 trillion, more than the net worth of all the American people combined. Given that we are passing that burden of debt on to our children, who had nothing to do with creating it, we cannot honestly justify having the government borrow more money to pay for the health care of people who can afford to pay for it themselves.

If people who don't need the financial help had to literally tear the money from the hands of their children and grandchildren to avoid paying their own way, they would recognize that doing so is immoral and irresponsible.

4. How much would this cost per person and how much would it cost the government?

Answer: To estimate the costs of the proposal, we can look to real world examples already in place. One such example is the Qliance program from Seattle, Washington.

Qliance is a company that offers basic care through what it calls "Direct Primary Care Medical Home" at a per-patient cost of between $39-79 a month. This is not an insurance policy but prepaid basic care through which most routine medical visits are covered for a simple monthly fee with no need for complex insurance paperwork, co-pays, and so forth.

The elimination of insurance and associated paperwork, bureaucracy and such produces large cost savings while allowing more quality time with health care providers who are salaried rather than paid on a fee-for-service basis. Qliance also negotiates pharmaceutical and other contracts directly on behalf of their patients so these costs are kept to a minimum.

To cover higher expense and specialty services that cannot be offered within their own clinics, Qliance participants purchase separate wraparound insurance. For high deductible policies, Qliance participants typically pay about $250 per month per patient. Combined with basic care, total monthly costs (not counting deductibles) total around $325, with annual costs at $3,900. Contrast this with estimated annual per capita expenditures of $7,400 in the U.S. and it is evident that substantial savings can be realized from a different approach to health care.

Because the model I have proposed also includes dental, mental, and vision plus long-term care insurance, I researched a number of existing plans to estimate these additional service costs. If we go beyond the Qliance costs to cover additional services at $125 per month plus wraparound care at $500 per month, on an individual basis, the total monthly cost for this care plus insurance would be $625, with annual costs of $7,500 per person. In actuality, it is very likely that costs could be substantially lower, but this is a useful upper end estimate.

This proposal does not call for everyone in the country to be covered under these sorts of plans unless they choose, but if our population of roughly 300 million people were covered by such plans the estimated cost would be approximately $2.25 trillion, which is about what we spent on health care as a nation in 2007.

The difference, however, is that the calculations of the new proposal assume coverage of mental, dental, vision and long term care while current expenditures leave more than 47 million with no medical insurance, more than 100 million with no dental insurance and more than 70 percent of adults without long term care insurance. The recent reforms and their underlying House and Senate bills are insufficient on the issue of dental and vision care or long term care. What is more, the alternative proposed here does not require an additional trillion dollars of expenditures, nor have we factored in the likely savings from malpractice reform, national risk pools and health promotion.

The bottom line is that for what we are already spending as a nation, we can provide comprehensive basic health care including medical, dental, mental, and vision plus wrap-around insurance including long term care for those in need. This would do away with costly and complex bureaucracies, preserve and expand patient choices, and slow the growth of health care costs.

5. How would this be paid for?

Answer: The first source of funds would come from all the existing programs that would be replaced. This includes Medicare A, B, & D, Medicaid, SCHIP, DSH Hospitals, the FSA tax deductions and all of the state run programs. Money would come both from what is now spent on health care through these programs and through savings from eliminating much of the bureaucracy and overhead that goes with these programs. That will cover the bulk of the costs.

In addition, because financial assistance is on a sliding scale commensurate with need, premiums paid by participants who can afford to pay a portion of the costs will help hold costs down and provide funding. Further cost savings will be realized by cutting out the costs of insurance paperwork for basic care. Savings on the costs of wraparound insurance will be realized by creating national insurance pools that all Americans can participate in, whether they are purchasing insurance on their own, through their employer, or as part of the government assistance program.

Finally, malpractice reforms, cradle-to-grave wellness and prevention, reduction of costly emergency room visits, and other measures will further lower costs. Remaining expenses, if there are any, will be paid for from general revenues which by law will be set to levels sufficient to pay for the full costs from year to year without passing debt on to the future.

6. What would malpractice reform look like under this proposal?

Answer: Separately in this chapter, legislation is described which I introduced that sets inflation adjusted caps on non-economic damages, provides mediation alternatives to litigation, improves the quality of health care licensing and review boards, limits "frivolous" lawsuits, and reforms how medical liability insurance is regulated. All of these elements would be included in the reform.

7. How would existing individual or group health insurance policies be affected?

Answer: People would be perfectly free to keep their existing insurance if they or their employers choose to do so. Discrimination against preexisting conditions would be prohibited for all insurance and health care, and the practice of "rescission" that denies people coverage they have already paid for would be eliminated.

Replacement of the income tax with a sales tax would do away with the various tax exemptions, deductions and so forth

80

that factor into current insurance, but because there would no longer be any income tax there would be no income taxes imposed on insurance either. There would, as for all services, be a modest sales tax applied at the time of purchase of insurance and health services.

8. Where would we get the general practitioners and other providers to treat people?

Answer: Regardless of which health care reform is enacted, be it the one I am proposing or the recently enacted reforms, we face an imminent shortage of family practice doctors, nurses, general surgeons and medical specialists, along with a looming shortage of gerontologists. We must immediately address this through a combination of educational support and incentives in schools of medicine, dentistry, nursing, psychology and other disciplines. Compensation rates must also reward these professions to sufficiently provide ongoing incentives throughout the professional careers of these practitioners.

9. How is the individual mandate enforced?

Answer: First of all, it is important to explain why there should be an individual mandate. If we are to prohibit discrimination against pre-existing conditions, we cannot let people wait to buy insurance until they discover they are sick.

This is unfair to everyone else and distorts the shared risk upon which insurance is based. We require all drivers of automobiles to have insurance because it is not acceptable to let irresponsible people place the burden on everyone else while they pocket savings themselves. Furthermore, because people drive cars across state lines, and could thereby subject residents of other states to unacceptable risk, every state has some form of mandatory auto insurance.

The same is true in health care. To meet the mandate of basic care and insurance, those with existing coverage could keep that coverage as is. Those who lack coverage now, either through personal choice or lack of resources, would be required to choose a plan and pay for it according to their means with government assistance for those in need. Those who do not enroll in basic health and insurance would be penalized with fines, much as those who do not have auto insurance must pay fines. The level of the fine would need to be substantial, sufficient to make it unrewarding financially to dodge one's personal and legal responsibility.

For those who have constitutional or other concerns about a mandate and fine model of requiring insurance purchase, there is still a need to deal with the problem of free riders who delay insurance purchase until they get sick or injured. One way to deal with this is to set a fixed period for purchase of basic care and insurance, then, after the period expires, protections against preexisting condition discrimination would end for those who have not purchased basic health and insurance plans

The key to this is a social willingness to let people accept full responsibility for their choices. Thus, if someone who had an opportunity and needs based assistance in purchasing insurance chose not to do so, they could not later be guaranteed a policy or care if they became ill or injured.

This would mean that no providers, hospitals, ERs, insurers, pharmacists or any other source of health care delivery would be required, legally or morally, to provide care to those who made the choice not to purchase coverage when they had the opportunity and assistance. We do not require that any other profession, service or product be given free to those who have made irresponsible choices. Health care should be no different.

People who chose to shift costs and risks on to others would have to bear the responsibility for that decision. In some unfortunate incidents, this would mean they might lose their cars, homes or other possessions to pay for care. In other cases, some would bear the ultimate responsibility of not having access to care and the loss of their own lives as the result of their own choices. This may sound harsh, but it is no less harsh to let everyone else bear the costs of care so irresponsible or intransigent people can have choices without consequences at the expense of the rest of society.

10. What holds down costs in this model?

Answer: Cost control is included in virtually every element of this plan. Simplification of government programs and elimination of multiple Federal and state bureaucracies will produce substantial savings as will need-testing of benefits at all ages. Providing basic health care without the overhead of insurance paperwork has been proven to dramatically lower costs.

Creation of nationwide basic care and insurance programs will expand risk pools and increase competition, thereby lowering the costs of insurance. Requiring that everyone have basic care and insurance will reduce costly ER visits and uncompensated care.

Comprehensive malpractice reforms will improve patient care, reduce medical errors and lower the costs of litigation and insurance. Incentives for health behaviors plus cradle-to-grave coverage will help reduce preventable illnesses and promote healthy decisions and treatment compliance. Insurers would have the right to encourage and reward healthy behaviors such as weight reduction, exercise, smoking cessation, medication compliance and other preventive actions.

Recent estimates indicate that preventable illnesses alone may be costing our nation more than $100 billion per year. Health care providers would also be required to provide direct information to patients about treatment and diagnostic options along with the empirical evidence of effectiveness and costs of those options. Individuals who insist on choosing more expensive options that do not bring corresponding improvements in proven outcomes would pay higher co-pays.

Proposed reforms in taxes will also produce savings by obviating the billions of hours spent on income taxes each year and eliminate the hundreds of billions of "tax expenditures" that are lost in the current code.

11. Why reform the tax code at the same time?

Answer: It is not absolutely necessary to reform both health care and taxes simultaneously, but the current system that enmeshes health care payments and incentives in the tax code is a mistake that leads to higher costs, inequities and excessive expense. Further, the current tax code itself carries with it huge costs and inefficiencies that hamstring our economy and waste billions of valuable human hours and dollars. If we are going to grow our economy, we ought to take this opportunity to fix both health care and the tax code.

12. Isn't this just another big bureaucracy?

Answer: No. First of all, this proposal would eliminate multiple existing programs each of which has its own bureaucracy and underlying laws, overhead and inefficiency. Medicare A, B, D, Advantage; Medicaid, Flexible Spending Accounts (FSAs), SCHIP, and all state run health care programs would be eliminated. What would take their place is far simpler and more straightforward.

Consider this: Right now we have a Medicare program that sets different compensation rates for thousands of different medical procedures at different levels for different locations across the country. Every year countless interest groups – doctors, patients, insurers, hospitals, and others descend on Washington asking for specific changes to one aspect of this law.

We also have Medicaid, which requires negotiations and intergovernmental agreements that can differ from each state and requires both Federal and State agencies to administer. Because many people want more coverage than Medicare provides, there are Medicare supplemental policies, all of which must be regulated and monitored in some way.

Then we have SCHIP, that covers children not covered by Medicare and Medicaid but which also can vary from state to state. On top of all that, we have FSAs, which first withdraw money from people's salary so they can avoid taxes but then requires all sorts of paperwork and encourages additional spending if people want to get their own money back. We can and should do away with all of this.

What I have proposed would involve just one agency to administer all government funded need-based health care and one agency to oversee cross-state basic care and insurance plans. This agency would manage the distribution of supplemental funds that go to basic care and insurance plans. The agency would not set compensation rates for doctors or determine payment rates for specific procedures. That would be left up to the basic care and wraparound insurance plans and the marketplace itself to determine as their model of care and financial structure determined.

The second agency would function much as state insurance commissioners do, but on a national scale to regulate and monitor the rates, financial soundness and quality of care provided by cross state plans and to provide an entity to manage claims or grievances filed against a cross state or national plan.

Again, that's it as far as bureaucracy goes.

What Gets Paid For and How

Whatever approach is taken to achieve universal coverage, it is absolutely essential to address the issue of rising costs. Cost containment is included throughout the proposal I have offered, but we must also recognize that the greatest contributor to the rising cost of health care is the fact that the financial incentives for health care providers and patients alike lead precisely in the wrong direction. There is far too little relation between the efficacy or appropriateness of care and compensation. If this is not corrected, rising costs will be unsustainable while the quality of care and outcomes will continue to be substandard. In some cases, what passes for care will in fact be iatrogenic.

Most Americans probably assume that medical practice is guided by sound scientific research that indicates what diagnostic and treatment procedures have been proven to be the most effective. Once again, that should be the case, but too often it is not.

Research has shown that in far too many instances best practices, as demonstrated by controlled research and clinical evidence, are not being followed. Diagnostic procedures and treatments are performed for which little or no quality research exists to demonstrate that their efficacy or benefits are superior to more affordable alternatives or, in some cases, to no treatment at all.

Dr. Guy Clifton, the author of "Flat-lined: Resuscitating American Medicine,"[7] cites estimates suggesting that as much as fifty percent of "what is done in hospitals is a waste." He then describes how many of the most common, and costly, diagnostic and surgical procedures applied today lack a solid base of research support to justify them in comparison to alternatives.

While unnecessary or ineffective diagnostic and treatment procedures increases health care costs, those costs and poor outcomes, can also be increased by failure to utilize appropriate and proven interventions and diagnostic assessments. One example Dr. Clifton cites suggests that the prompt use of "clot-busting" drugs given within three hours of a stroke can substantially improve the chance of survival and lower subsequent morbidity. In spite of this evidence, less than ten percent of eligible patients ever receive such treatment.

Evidence-Based Practice and Compensation

In order to reduce both errors and improve the quality and appropriateness of diagnoses and treatments, health care providers must employ the latest data on treatment and diagnostic efficacy. I should emphasize that most responsible practitioners already do their level best to keep up with the latest developments through journals, conferences, continuing education and so forth. This is admirable but not sufficient. The evidence that such procedures are not sufficient is seen in the wide deviations in practice from the best available evidence and in discrepancies across providers, institutions and regions.

To reduce such discrepancies in practice, evidence-based standards of care must be established and disseminated to all providers and insurers. These standards must be updated regularly as new information becomes available. Most

---

[7] Rutgers University Press, November 2008.

importantly, they must be followed unless compelling evidence argues otherwise.

A comprehensive review of how evidence can better inform clinical decision making was recently published by the Institute of Medicine of the National Academies. The authors recommend creating a program within the U.S. Department of Health and Human Services for evaluating and disseminating clinical effectiveness information.

I support this recommendation and a comparable proposal is actually contained within the legislation currently before Congress, but more is needed. In order to encourage practitioners to utilize and adhere to practice standards, they should receive data indicating the degree to which their actual procedures compare to the evidence-based standards. To ensure that financial incentives are aligned with best practices, payments should be linked directly with adherence to best practices.

In England, a model for how this might be done is provided by the National Institute for Health and Clinical Excellence (NICE). This independent organization provides guidance on public health, health technologies, and clinical practice. This information then helps inform practices within England's National Health Service.

Adopting an evidence-based approach does not mean that all autonomy will be removed from individual providers, but it does mean that the autonomy and professional judgment must be informed by the best available research. It also means that compensation for health care providers and shared costs of patients should be heavily guided by the appropriateness of care and the outcomes, not simply the number of procedures performed or patients seen.

Technology and Electronic Medical Records

One of the positive measures enacted by this Congress and supported by the Administration has been the increased emphasis on electronic medical records. Anyone who has tried to read a physician's handwriting on prescriptions can appreciate that prescription errors are far too common and costly. Writing a marginally legible script on a paper slip to be hand carried for delivery to a pharmacy is unnecessarily inefficient.

A far better method is for health care professionals to enter data electronically and then transmit that directly to the pharmaceutical provider to be filled. A RAND study of the potential economic benefits of electronic medical records suggests annual savings of more than $81 billion. This technology not only reduces errors caused by misreading, it saves time, reduces fraud, and simultaneously enters the data into a patient's medical record.

Prescription information filed electronically should be part of a comprehensive electronic medical records system in which all data is entered, stored and shared digitally with appropriate safeguards for data security and storage. This is already starting to happen, but incompatibilities in hardware and software, costs of implementation, and the need for staff training and technical support are slowing the widespread adoption.

In addition to improving efficiency, electronic medical records are also beginning to improve health care by providing vital information to practitioners. For example, intelligent computer systems can track all of the medications a patient is taking and notify the physician, the pharmacist and the patient if there are potentially dangerous interactions or side effects.

Consistent with principles of evidence-based standards, electronic records can also provide real time updates about best available evidence pertaining to treatment outcomes, costs and alternatives. With reliable and standard information, practitioners can also receive accurate and timely feedback about the degree to which their patterns of practice adhere to or deviate from best practice standards.

Who Pays and Who Benefits from Savings

It's easy to understand that people are more likely to do things for which they are paid and the more they get paid for doing certain things the more likely they are to do them.

Under our current models of compensation, health care practitioners will be drawn to procedures and specialties that pay the highest rewards. They will also tend to prescribe more procedures and treatments when they are compensated more for doing so.

On the other hand, if compensation is linked to only proven procedures and quality of outcomes, providers will be more inclined to be focused on those outcomes as opposed to simply doing more of what pays the most.

The same principles also apply to patients. One of the common problems with proposals for universal coverage is that having insurance in and of itself can tend to disconnect patients from a sense of the true costs of care. Indeed, as long as "someone else is paying for it," patients tend to have little incentive to limit costs and, in fact, may be biased toward seeking the most advanced and expensive diagnoses and treatments on the assumption that what costs the most must be better and, besides, when someone else foots the bill cost is no object.

In light of these quite understandable behaviors, in order to control costs and improve quality of care it will be absolutely essential that both patients and providers have "skin in the game" in ways that link efficacy and appropriateness with the personal economics of their decisions. As Dr. Clifton states on the matter, "All the information and standards of practice in the world won't reduce health care costs unless payment incentives are aligned to reward efficiency."

One way to do this, as suggested earlier, is to tie what basic care organizations and insurers pay practitioners to the kinds of research-based best practices that we have been discussing. At the same time, patients should be required in some way to pay some personally meaningful amount for both their insurance and their own care.

Further, if patients demand diagnostics or treatments that are not warranted or for which lower cost alternatives are equally effective, the patients should be given information about their options and relevant research data, then required to foot the bill for any additional cost beyond the proven practices.

Such structures that link providers and patients to cost and efficacy decisions would go a long way in themselves to improve efficiency and lower expenses. Further gains can be achieved by rewarding more effective care and sharing the savings gained from better practices.

Insurers should have the ability to provide incentives to patients who help reduce costs by engaging in healthy behaviors and who choose the most cost-beneficial treatments or diagnoses when given information and choices. So too, health care practitioners who follow best practices in their delivery of care should also be rewarded and able to share in any savings resulting from their adherence to evidence-based standards.

Prescription Drugs

Much of what has just been said about health care practices in general applies to the costs and efficacy of pharmaceuticals as well. Every American owes a tremendous debt of appreciation to the benefits of pharmaceutical drugs and vaccines. Thanks to these products, diseases that once ravaged generations have been largely vanquished, infections that were once death sentences have been countered, and excruciating procedures or injuries can be managed with lessened or no agony and more rapid recovery.

Increasingly, Americans also owe a different sort of debt related to pharmaceuticals – hundreds of billions of dollars of Federal borrowing plus comparable amounts of personal financial indebtedness. To bring our overall health care costs under control, and to improve health care outcomes, we must address the ways pharmaceuticals and related products are developed, tested, marketed, prescribed, used and paid for. One of these realities that must be recognized is that if individuals and companies are going to invest the time, money and other resources needed to create and produce new products, there must be an opportunity for a reasonable return on that investment. At the same time, the returns that are realized should come from sales of products that actually have demonstrable and beneficial effects rather than from sales of products that were marketed heavily and demanded by people who do not really need them or who will realize little benefit. As is the case with how health care providers are compensated, the incentives for pharmaceutical companies are largely opposite from what they should be. It is quicker and easier to make money by heavily marketing a drug, regardless of its appropriateness or efficacy, than it is to research and develop something that will be proven effective and used only where appropriate. This needs to change.

Perhaps the most immediate thing that can be done to reduce the cost increases associated with pharmaceuticals is to end the practice of direct-to-consumer advertising. Doctors and pharmacists alike report that patients not only request but demand prescriptions for drugs they have seen advertised on television even if the medication in question is not related to or appropriate for the patient's individual condition.

This puts health care professionals in difficult dilemmas and drives up the use, expenses and risk of inappropriate medication usage. Ending or substantially limiting such advertising would help solve this problem and would shift the incentives from marketing to research and development.

Ending direct-to-consumer advertising is only part of the problem. Direct-to-Doctor marketing is a multimillion dollar endeavor and is, first and foremost, intended to sell medications, not convey objective benefits, costs, and side effect information. Just as there is a need for best practice standards to guide medical procedures, and just as there needs to be a direct connection between compensation and adherence to evidence-based practice, the prescription and use of pharmaceuticals needs to be aligned in the same way.

Researching New Cures

While there is a need to lower prescription spending, there is also a real and urgent need to encourage the pharmaceutical industry to make substantial investments to develop new, more effective medications to combat existing illnesses and potential future diseases. Quite understandably, the pharmaceutical companies will not do this unless there is a potential for a return on their investments.

In an effort to address one aspect of this need, the potential of pandemic disease outbreaks, I have introduced legislation that would provide several incentives for vaccine and pharmaceutical companies. These incentives are important because virtually all of the financial, legal and regulatory considerations work against, rather than for, new drug or vaccine development for pandemics.

To reverse this situation, a "fast-track" FDA review and approval process should be created to shorten the approval time for potential pandemic fighting agents. At the same time, the patent length for such medicines should be extended and, as an added financial incentive, companies that develop successful vaccines or medicines for the most dangerous pandemics would be allowed to extend their patents for certain other existing medications as well. As a further incentive, tax benefits or direct subsidies can be provided to help offset the costs of investing in new manufacturing capacity to produce the new agents. Special liability protections can also be implemented to protect against the risks if medications must be brought to market and applied on an exceptionally wide scale.

These measures will not be without cost and some will be controversial, but history tells us that pandemics happen. If we have done nothing to prepare for them, and everything to prevent companies from investing in such preparation, the consequences could be horrific.

Health Care Education

When I meet with physicians and other health care providers one of the most distressing things I hear is that many would not recommend that their children follow in their footsteps. In part, these statements are often related to concerns about issues that are addressed in this chapter – the fear and costs of litigation, the high costs of treating the uninsured, frustrations with insurance plans, paperwork and so forth. Many of those issues would be substantially reduced or eliminated by some of the changes suggested thus far.

One other issue that must also be addressed is the high cost of medical education. A 2005 report by Gail Morrison in the New England Journal of Medicine revealed that the average medical student graduating in 2004 carried more than $105,000 in debt if they had attended a public school or more than $140,000 in debt if they attended private medical school.

On top of this debt, most medical students spend three or more years in postgraduate training, continuing to accrue interest, before entering full paying employment as a physician. The study's author points out that it can easily take 10 to 25 years to pay off these loans.

Other health care professions, including psychologists, nurses, and others must also deal with increasing tuition costs and the challenges of obtaining and paying off student loans. One of the results is a troubling shortage of personnel in many critical health care fields. This shortage is particularly acute in primary care and in low-income or rural areas.

If we are truly to tackle the problems of health care access and make sure every American has adequate basic care and catastrophic health insurance, we must immediately begin to correct the shortage of primary care providers and other essential professionals. Otherwise, we will be promising millions more people they will have access to care without having the health care professionals needed to provide that care.

In order to address these problems we must provide additional financial support for education across the health care professions. We must also provide meaningful financial and other incentives for those who chose to go into critical shortage areas such as primary practice and practice in rural or low income areas. Increasing scholarships, lower student loan rates, and loan forgiveness incentives should all be part of this solution.

Health Research and Research Practitioners

Another important, yet largely overlooked, challenge posed by high education costs is the impact of these costs on research practitioners, i.e. practicing health care providers who also participate actively in research.

Some of the brightest minds and leading innovators in areas such as cancer research and treatment, neuroscience, and other fields have told me that it is increasingly hard to participate in both hands-on treatment of patients and active research. This is not only due to the costs of education, it is also a consequence of the complex bureaucracy and paperwork that is required of researchers today.

The result of this is that as the current generation of research practitioners begins to retire, fewer and fewer individuals are following their career paths. Instead, those who might be drawn to careers in both practice and research are being lured to the higher paying, less demanding, careers in specialty medicine. This is leaving a dangerous gap in mentors and in practical, hands-on knowledge of how diseases and treatments play out in patient groups.

To stem this tide, the previously mentioned measures of scholarships, lower loan rates and loan forgiveness should carry special incentives for those who combine research and practice. There are also critically needed changes, which are beyond the scope of this book, that must be implemented to simplify, streamline and reduce unnecessary bureaucratic and paperwork burdens on research practitioners.

Mental Health Parity

Too often, discussions of health care in America neglect the importance of mental illnesses and their treatment. This is unfortunate for many reasons. In my own experience, I have never met a person who has not had a family member, close friend or coworker who was affected by mental illness.

The fact is, every one of our lives has in some way been impacted by mental illnesses, but it is not something we talk about. This active neglect can be especially tragic because mental illness can be every bit as disabling and lethal as any form of physical illness.

The good, but too little known news, is that there are successful, research-based and cost beneficial treatments for a great many such illnesses. Unfortunately, in spite of the morbidity and mortality of mental illness, and in spite of proven treatment efficacy, many insurance policies provide no mental health benefits or offer diagnostic or treatment coverage that is far inferior to the coverage provide for physical ailments. There seems to be an ironic assumption that the brain is not a physical organ and, therefore, mental illness is not eligible for treatment under health insurance.

Consistent with the need for evidence-based standards, it must be emphasized again that many of the leading treatments for mental illness are in fact based on well documented and designed scientific research. It must also be reiterated that in many cases this research has shown treatments for mental illnesses to have superior outcomes to many of the most commonly performed treatments in the rest of health care.

Some have argued that the costs of including mental health care as part of insurance are too great. The evidence argues convincingly in the opposite direction. The best available studies indicate that at most premium costs would increase by less than one and a half percent and there would be multiple cost savings that would more than compensate for this. The Congressional Budget Office suggests an increase of just 0.4% in average health care costs as the result of parity legislation.

Reductions in lost time from work, improvements in school behaviors, fewer psychologically related medical visits and other social and economic benefits would far outweigh the negligible increase in premiums. In fact, costs of absenteeism, lost performance and other workplace impacts have been estimated to exceed $150 billion per year.

Fortunately, Congress took a major step toward reducing disparities in Mental Health coverage by passing landmark Mental Health Parity legislation at the end of 2008. As important as that measure is, however, it only requires plans that include a mental health portion to ensure that mental health benefits and payments are on par with those of other illnesses and treatments. The law does not require that mental health benefits actually be included as part of all insurance policies. That is the next essential step as we move toward universal coverage.

Dental/Oral Health Parity

Much as mental health coverage is often omitted or inadequate under many insurance policies, the same is true of dental health. It is almost as if anything that happens inside ones head is considered to be outside one's body or at least outside one's health insurance policy. This defies common sense and is foolish policy.

A 2000 report by the Surgeon General[8] stated strongly that "oral health is essential to the general health" and well being of American, but that many Americans are not benefiting from appropriate prevention or treatment of oral health disease and disorders. This report indicates that more than 108 million people in our country have no dental insurance. The report also found "striking disparities by income" in access to the prevention and treatment of oral health diseases.

The remedy for this glaring omission in our health care is to include a requirement that oral health care be included in all basic care and wraparound policies, such as the reforms I have proposed earlier in this chapter.

Liability Reform

Liability reform measures must be part of solving our overall health care challenges, but no one should be under the illusion that "fixing" our medical liability system will solve all our health care cost problems. Let us start by recognizing the limits of what liability reform might achieve, and then address why it matters and how it can be done.

---

[8]*See* http://www.nidcr.nih.gov/DataStatistics/SurgeonGeneral/sgr/

A recent comprehensive analysis of U.S. health care costs by McKinsey and Company estimated that each year about $20 billion is paid for malpractice insurance, far more than in any other nation. However, the report also concludes that overall, compared to other factors, malpractice is "only a small contributor to higher health care costs" in the U.S.

This does not mean, however, that we cannot and should not improve upon how things are done right now. In spite of being the most litigious society on earth, and in spite of all the medical malpractice lawsuits, medical errors are still far too common and costly in lives and dollars.

I believe unjustified lawsuits do in fact drive up the costs of health care and health insurance. It is also true that the practice of "defensive medicine", i.e. diagnostics and treatments that are driven primarily as a defense against litigation rather than medical need, are simultaneously increasing the costs of health care and, in many instances, leading to poorer outcomes for patients.

Once again, a comprehensive, coordinated and common sense solution is needed. The goal and standard for success should be improving access, lowering costs and improving the quality of care.

Central to any liability reform must be ways to reduce the costs and frequency of unwarranted litigation while protecting the rights of patients who have been harmed. I have introduced legislation to achieve this dual goal. One element of this proposal is to set limits on the amount of non-economic damages that can be awarded in liability cases.

Many liability reform proposals that have come before Congress previously would set limits based on a law passed in California in 1975 and known by its acronym MICRA (Medical Injury Compensation Reform Act). Opinions differ about the degree to which this law or other factors were responsible for reducing the costs of malpractice claims and insurance. Even if one argues that it did contribute to lowering costs, the $250,000 damage cap which California adopted at the time has since become degraded due to the effect of inflation. When indexed for inflation, a comparable cap in today's dollars would be around $950,000. My belief is that if we are to impose a limit on non-economic damages, this inflation adjusted number would make the most sense.

Establishing limits of this size today, which could later be adjusted for inflation, would still be substantially lower than many uncapped damage awards and, hence, would reduce the virtually unlimited financial risks that can accompany lawsuits. At the same time, however, allowing close to a million dollars in non-economic damages over and above the other compensations that can be awarded, would still provide for reasonable compensation for victims and their attorneys.

Another way to lower the costs and frequency of lawsuits is to provide alternatives to the litigation process itself. This is especially valuable when a hospital, doctor or other professional recognizes that a mistake has been made and would like to have a way to help make things right for a patient but is blocked from doing so by fears of lawsuits.

Successful models of voluntary malpractice mediation programs have shown that mediation is a cost-effective and timely way to settle many such cases. Expansion of these programs nationwide would further reduce malpractice costs while protecting the needs of patients and providers. In order to promote and expand the use of such approaches, Federal grants and training programs should be made available to encourage states and health care institutions to create or enhance malpractice mediation programs. Mediation has been proven successful in cases where the providers and patients recognize errors and have a goal of resolving the situation to the benefit of all concerned.

As beneficial as mediation can be, there is nevertheless a small subset of patients and attorneys that file suit, often repeatedly, without justification. It should be emphasized that this is by no means the norm. The vast majority of patients have justified concerns and most plaintiffs' attorneys carefully select cases and reject those without basis. Professional ethics demands this and the economic costs of taking unfounded cases provides further incentives to only take legitimate complaints. Still, a small number of unscrupulous attorneys and predatory patients are a reality. They drive costs up for everyone else and weaken both the medical and legal systems.

To help discourage this, courts should have the authority to enforce a "3 Strikes and You're Out" law, suspending from practice for no less than one year lawyers who file their 3rd meritless lawsuit. Again, this should not be a concern for most responsible attorneys, but it would help remove those few bad actors who abuse the system at everyone's expense.

Limiting malpractice lawsuits and providing alternatives to litigation is clearly necessary, but it is not enough. To further lower malpractice costs we must act to reduce the medical errors that harm patients and also contribute to litigation and health care costs.

Most health care providers are well-motivated and trained and sincerely want to do their best to help patients, but a small percentage of providers are responsible for the greatest number of medical errors and resulting lawsuits. Some providers are incompetent, others are corrupt, and still others work while impaired in some way. Unfortunately, identifying and removing these individuals is far too difficult and, hence, far too uncommon.

To demonstrate this, I sometimes ask physicians who are passionately committed to malpractice reform if they know colleagues whose practice and competence they question. Then I ask how often they have taken proactive measures to do something about those colleagues?

In general the answers to these questions are yes to the first, followed by equivocation, then no to the second question, followed again by equivocation.

To remedy this, improve quality of care and ensure that physicians and other professionals who are incompetent or impaired are removed from practice, substantial improvements are needed in how state medical and professional review boards function.

State medical boards would benefit from the development and distribution of national performance standards and best practices for such boards. Such standards should address areas including maintaining adequate and qualified independent staff on review boards, improving the screening procedures for new license applicants, enhancing the ease of use and validity of procedures for filing complaints, establishing mechanisms for tracking patient complaints, setting procedures and time periods for handling disseminating disciplinary information to the public, and codification of consequences for providers found culpable of violations of performance or ethical guidelines.

State laws should also implement "whistle blower"-like protections against litigation for individuals who, without malice, sincerely and accurately report concerns about the practices of colleagues or institutions. As an incentive to adopt such best practices, any Federal constraints on liability should only apply in states that have implemented best practices.

An additional and innovative way to improve quality of care and reduce medical errors can be found by emulating the Federal Aviation Administration's successful Aviation Safety Reporting System. In aviation, this system allows aircraft manufacturers or maintenance personnel to report problems they have discovered so that others can be warned about those problems and future accidents prevented.

The key to making this work is that those who report such problems in good faith are protected from liability that might otherwise result from such reporting. Applied to health care - practitioners, researchers and institutions would have the opportunity, for the good of overall practice, to anonymously report on incidents or procedures in which medical safety or quality was inadvertently compromised. Those making such reports in good faith would then be protected from any liability related to such reports.

All of the measures discussed so far could, in combination, go a long way to lower liability costs, but evidence suggests there is a corresponding need to deal with the malpractice insurance industry itself. This point is buttressed by evidence from state legislative experience, and, rather surprisingly, has been made repeatedly in testimony under oath by representatives of the insurers themselves even as they advocate liability caps.

To directly address and constrain the rising costs of liability insurance, the insurance industry itself must be more closely monitored and regulated. Specifically, any proposed increase in malpractice rates should be justified before a regulatory agency empowered to examine actuarial and experiential data of claims made and paid, expenses and profits of the insurer, and ensure that unreasonable or exorbitant rate increases are disallowed. As part of this process, if the reforms recommended above produce savings in malpractice settlements, insurers should be required to pass those savings on to health care providers though lower premiums.

A final area of needed liability reform pertains to liability protections for emergency care. Under the Emergency Medical Treatment and Active Labor Act (EMTALA) of 1986, hospital emergency rooms and ambulances must provide anyone needing emergency treatment with care regardless of their ability to pay, their legal status or citizenship.

The costs of this care is not provided for by the Federal government, yet estimates suggest that as much as half of the total costs of emergency room care is not paid for by the patients or insurance. Adding to the expense of providing the care itself, those receiving care under EMTALA requirements are free to sue for malpractice with no restrictions.

I do not believe it makes sense, nor is it fair, to demand that hospitals, ambulance services and the people who work there must give essentially free treatment while at the same time bearing unlimited liability risks for their troubles. I cannot think of any other profession or economic activity in which it is mandated that people give away their services without compensation but in exchange expose themselves to substantial economic risks.

One way to address this is to substantially limit malpractice suits and damages for care provided under EMTALA. Another alternative would be to provide Federally-supported malpractice insurance specifically for EMTALA-related treatment. These measures would not absolve caregivers of their ethical responsibilities, nor is there evidence that they would lower standards of care, but the government would at least say to those who are being ordered to provide their time, expertise and resources without compensation that their liability risks would be taken care of.

Fraud

Estimates suggest that fraud may be costing the Medicare system alone as much as $60 billion every year. Schemes for fraudulently billing Medicare range from individuals who invent illnesses to sophisticated crime rings that create false companies that repeatedly bill Medicare for products which are never actually sent to patients.

It may never be possible to completely eliminate all forms of health care fraud, but, as the described costs demonstrate, it is in every honest person's interest to do so. To a large degree, many of the measures described in this chapter can contribute to that goal.

For example, if individuals purchase policies from private insurers, those insurers will have every incentive to closely monitor the practices and costs of their participating health care providers. Fraud will drive up expenses and reduce competitiveness so insurers will likely conduct their own quality control and fraud prevention activities.

Under the proposals I have offered, individual consumers will also have incentives to eliminate fraud because they will bear some of the costs of their insurance and share in paying for the expenses of treatments. Greater transparency and required evidence of diagnostic and treatment efficacy will further empower consumers and help reveal providers, vendors or institutions that engage in questionable and unjustified practices. Electronic medical records and data keeping will facilitate this process as well and make monitoring practices easier.

In spite of these measures, unscrupulous individuals will continue to seek to find ways to make an easy, dishonest buck at the expense of everyone else. Because such people are driving up costs for everyone and, thereby, depriving those truly in need, severe civil and criminal penalties should be established at both the state and Federal level and special investigative and prosecutorial personnel should be dedicated solely to this purpose.

This is already happening within the Center for Medicare and Medicaid Services (CMS), which requested $1.4 billion for 2008 to help fight fraud and abuse. The Chief Financial Officer for CMS has estimated that overall this investment in countering fraud has yielded a 13 to 1 return on investment, helping to return nearly $9 billion to the trust funds from 1997 to 2005.[9] As impressive as that $9 billion figure is, it obviously pales in comparison to a $60 billion annual loss.

Much more is needed to combat this problem and one of the positive aspects of the recent health care reform bill is the provision of substantial increases in funding plus changes in law to help combat fraud and abuse across multiple areas of Medicare, Medicaid and other government health care spending. The message should be absolutely clear – if anyone engages in health care fraud they will be caught, they will be prosecuted, and the consequences, both civil and criminal will be severe.

Disability Reform

While systematic health care fraud against Medicare and Medicaid may involve organized crime and sophisticated scams, the health care system and our economy are also suffering increasing costs as a result of individual abuses. What I am about to say is not easy and will undoubtedly make some people angry, but it is, unfortunately, true. Our disability compensation system too often encourages people to exaggerate or feign disability rather than making every effort possible to return to productive work.

I believe it is thoroughly appropriate for a caring society to provide financial support to those who are truly disabled, but not everyone who receives disability payments today is, in fact, disabled. Many are perfectly capable of performing some form of work or service and a significant number should not be receiving any disability insurance payments at all.

Let me cite just two examples that I have encountered recently. The first occurred while I was campaigning and

---

[9] *See* http://www.cms.hhs.gov/apps/media/press/testimony.asp?Counter=2369).

going door to door to talk to voters. As I approached a nice, upper middle class home I saw that a man who appeared to be in his early thirties was carrying an armload of boards that he was using to build a new fence. After introducing myself and talking briefly about the campaign, I asked by way of small talk where the man worked and what he did for a living. His answer was that he didn't have a job at all, he was on disability payments.

The second example was even more striking. This individual was a volunteer ski patrolman I met while riding up the ski lift at our local area. We made a quick run together down an expert slope, then on the next ride up the lift the patrolman learned that I was in Congress and said he wanted to raise a concern. It turned out his concern was that his disability payments from a job injury were only paying a part of his college education expenses and he thought they should pay the entire amount. As he explained it, his "unique" disability did not prevent him from skiing or working as a patrolman, but it did keep him from doing the job he had wanted and he felt he was "owed" the full amount of his education so he could get retrained for something new.

Maybe I was missing something about these examples and others, but it certainly seems that somewhere along the line far too many people in our society have gotten the idea that they are "entitled" to other people's money and "deserve" to get paid without working for a living. Many of these same people, by the way, are the first to protest against "the government" spending their money or intruding in their lives. I have witnessed this time and again at town halls and other events.

Wherever this idea may come from, it needs to end. There is a tremendous difference between providing a social insurance safety net and people feeling they are owed or entitled to it.

In the case of disability, the key social and policy focus should be in helping people maximize their abilities and their economic and social contributions. Our explicit and implicit values as a nation and as a society should insist that each person carry their own load the greatest extent possible. Our policies should reflect that value.

To be sure, there are many people who, through misfortune at birth or accidents do lose many of their capacities to work or function on their own. These people need and deserve society's support. But that is much different than someone who is capable of building a fence, ski patrolling or standing up to shout at town halls receiving benefits at the expense of others.

To a substantial degree, remedying this abuse of the disability system can be achieved by a return to the principles of character that were discussed at the outset of this book. If honesty, personal responsibility, integrity and community are restored, individuals will not seek to game the disability system because they will realize they have a responsibility to contribute to the maximum of their ability, not feign illness or need at the expense of others.

Counting on character alone, however, is not enough. The Social Security Administration has indicated that Continuing Disability Reviews (CDRs), which are periodic reevaluations of medical eligibility for disability, have been shown to have a ten to one return on investment. Although less than one percent of beneficiaries are found to be receiving benefits improperly, identifying those who are could save as much as $2 billion annually. This savings is something we must pursue.

Replacing Medicare and Medicaid

Many seniors I represent have sincerely asked why it is that under our present health care system those nearing the end of life now have insurance while the youngest and most vulnerable in our nation are often without insurance or care. Other seniors have noted that it makes little sense for a senior citizen who is financially well off to receive heavily subsidized care while a young worker just starting a family may put in sixty hour work weeks with no health insurance benefits, a mortgage (if they can afford a house at all), education costs for their kids, and no retirement benefits.

"Something is really wrong with that picture," said one older constituent at a town hall meeting. The constituent went on to say, "If anyone needs the help, it's that young working guy, not me."

This is by no means to suggest that a great many seniors do not need support to afford health care. Indeed, many do and, again, they would receive that support under the terms of the proposal I have offered. But the support that is given by the government should be determined by the level of support that is needed based on the individual's financial status, not by someone's age alone.

Including everyone in a health care program that offers insurance coverage from pre-cradle to grave also has the advantage of providing powerful incentives to promote healthy behaviors across the life span. Under the present approach to insurance, people change insurers multiple times during their lives as they change jobs. This provides insurers, and to some degree beneficiaries, relatively little economic incentive to promote healthier behaviors because the economic benefits of those behaviors, in the form of health care savings, are likely to be realized after the person has left the initial insurer and gone on to receive benefits from some other program.

What is more, by shifting the costs of the most expensive treatment period of our lives, i.e. old age, to the government rather than the individual or prior insurers, there is even less economic incentive for the individual or business to support healthy behavior and long term cost prevention.

Another major benefit of changing from the current system is that doctors and other providers would be more likely to follow patients through their lives. When providers know their patient's full medical history and have built trust and communication, medical errors are much less likely and subtle changes in health status are more likely to be recognized early.

Such continuity in care would also mean that senior citizens would no longer be left to search in vain for doctors willing to accept Medicare patients. In my home state of Washington, inadequate and inequitable Medicare payment rates have led nearly half of doctors surveyed to indicate that they will no longer accept new Medicare patients into their practice. I have personally spoken to seniors who have had to contact as many as a dozen or more physicians before finding one who would accept them as a patient. Under the proposed changes this would not happen.

Considering these and other benefits, it should be clear that transitioning away from the current Medicare and Medicaid systems to an alternative system would have multiple benefits. Costs would be lowered, quality and continuity of care would be improved, and seniors would no longer have difficulty finding providers.

End of Life Care and Decisions

I end this chapter with perhaps the most difficult part, acknowledging that each of us will eventually die; me, you, the ones we love, all of us. No matter what health care model or government program we put in place, no matter how much we spend, we all must die. That is the hard reality of life.

My father died in my arms a few years ago from Idiopathic Pulmonary Fibrosis, a disease which has no known cause or cure, is typically fatal within two years of diagnosis, and is growing in prevalence, killing some twenty to forty thousand Americans every year. The only real treatment that holds any significant hope of survival is a lung transplant, but that procedure has a high mortality rate during the operation itself and, as a result of complications, many patients will die within several years of the surgery.

My father, at age 73, made a conscious decision not to seek such treatment because, in his words, "I have had a good life. Sure I'd like to live longer if I could, but not if it means being sick and hooked up to hoses the whole time. And really son, I just can't justify spending all that money on someone my age to live another few years when we've got millions of kids in our own country and billions around the world who don't have anything. That just isn't right."

The most painful and difficult experience of my life was holding my father as he died, but, as wrenching and heartbreaking as that was, I could not argue with his reasoning then or today.

Approximately 25 percent of total Medicare spending goes to beneficiaries in their last year of life, but there is not compelling evidence that greater spending on patients leads to better outcomes. In fact, some recent research from Dartmouth suggests that in regions with the best quality and outcomes fewer resources are actually used. According to this study, had the best practices been followed universally across the nation, Medicare spending for patients could be reduced by nearly a third with no reduction in quality of care or survival rates.

In many ways, these findings suggest that end of life care suffers from some of the same kinds of problems and inconsistencies in quality and costs that afflict health care as whole. End of life care is expensive in part because it is an extraordinarily resource-intensive task to keep a very ill person from dying. It is also costly because our current ways of paying for health care incentivize and reward the most costly interventions and provide disincentives, even penalties, for cost savings. Ways to treat those systemic afflictions have already been offered in this chapter. What is different about end of life care is the element of finality and the role of volition and choice in that finality.

Because health insurance draws money from a risk pool to which we all in one way or another contribute, each of us must wrestle with the personal and social morality of how much will be spent to prolong our own lives or the lives of loved ones.

Many would prefer to avoid this question. But it cannot, in fact, be avoided because resources are finite and choices must be made about how best to allocate them. If a 73 year old man demands a procedure costing many hundreds of thousands of dollars with a relatively high risk of mortality and morbidity, that money will not be available to provide quality pre-natal or well-baby care, vaccinations, nutrition, hearing and vision screening, and all the other services that can enhance the lives of the very young for many years to come.

Throughout this book I have emphasized the essential importance of Character - honesty, integrity, responsibility, judgment, courage, community and humility. When it comes to end of life care and decisions, these qualities are put to a severe but ultimately important test.

Each of us, as individuals, must ask ourselves what the consequences of our choices are and must bear in mind how our own decisions affect others. At the same time, in setting health care policies, government must show similar courage, comparable integrity and create the conditions that allow responsible, reasoned judgments to be made for the maximum benefit of the society as a whole.

7.

THE ECONOMY

For millions of Americans, the U.S. economy is not working. Jobs are being lost and exported, health care costs are rising, retirement savings are not secure, energy costs can rapidly reach crippling levels and the gap between what it costs to get by and average wages is growing larger. At the time of this writing, one out of five American men between the ages of 25 to 55 was out of work. In some areas, this number is much higher.

In response, the new Administration and Congress have taken important measures to turn things around, but as yet there has not been a fully coordinated, practical and effective national strategy to truly transform the economy and make it work for all. Unfortunately, too much of the recent discussion and action has been about doing more of what got us into this situation to begin with. That applies equally to Democratic proposals for more spending and to Republican proposals for more tax cuts.

The plain truth is an economy based on credit and consumption cannot sustain itself indefinitely.

This is especially true when the credit comes from foreign nations and so does much of what is consumed. For far too long, the American economy has been driven by consumption of foreign goods enabled by credit from foreign nations. An economic collapse was bound to happen eventually, but, as bad as this downturn has been, unless we address the underlying fundamentals a collapse of even greater scale awaits us. We simply must end the cycle of buying things we cannot afford with money we have no real way of paying back.

The Right Stimulus

Earlier chapters discussed the problems of deficit spending at the national level and for individual Americans. For many

reasons, in response to the recent recession the primary effort
to stimulate the economy has come from injections of money
through a combination of tax cuts and direct spending. All of
this is borrowed money.

Most economists argue that such borrowing is necessary in
economic downturns, but the wisdom of that justification
depends on three things - how the money is spent, what
alternatives are available, and how we will pay the money
back.

In my judgment, a stimulus of some form was absolutely
essential to rescue the economy and prevent a slide into full
blown depression. At the same time, however, too much of
the money in the stimulus bill went to tax cuts, producing
relatively few new jobs and leaving no lasting tangible results.
Indeed, although 37 percent of the stimulus, some $288 billion,
went to various individual and business tax cuts, including
reductions in payroll taxes and the allowance of longer loss
carry backs for business, most Americans are unaware that they
actually received a tax cut and it is difficult to point to any
specific tangible products or jobs that resulted.

I believe the better investment would have been to put a
greater proportion of the stimulus into infrastructure, including
transportation, schools, energy, water treatment and sanitation
and so forth. This should not have solely been for so called
"shovel ready" projects. The focus on 90 day shovel ready
pushed too much of the money into immediate projects
whether or not they were the best investment. Infrastructure
jobs do not just come from the end of shovels or backhoe but
include planning, engineers and surveying among other tasks.
Allowing a longer time frame for projects and investing a
greater percentage of the funds into infrastructure would have
resulted in better investments, with longer impacts and would
have produced more beneficial project outcomes.

This did not happen because many of the same economists
who failed to spot the collapse coming to begin with insisted
that infrastructure investment would not create jobs. Ironically,
their preference for tax rebates had been tested in a smaller
stimulus package a year earlier (remember the rebate checks?)
with no lasting economic benefits and no roads, schools, wind

farms, or water treatment facilities to show for it. Nevertheless, they opposed infrastructure and, hence, the ninety day shovel ready provision was pressed to placate them.

Beyond the debate about tax cuts versus infrastructure spending, there is also the question of alternatives that would not have added to the deficit. This, to me, is where we should have begun the discussion of how to restore the economy, but it has received too little attention from Congress, the Administration or pundits.

In contrast to that neglect, much of the rest of this chapter will be devoted to precisely this question: How can we get the economy moving again in the short run without making the problems worse in the long run, and what core changes in government or the economy will be necessary for long term financial growth?

What it takes to create jobs

While it may indeed be necessary to spend more in the short term to stimulate the economy, long term economic growth cannot be sustained by repeating infusions of deficit financed spending or tax cuts. Instead, we must take a system-wide look at how to grow the economy for the long term without increasing the deficit.

When I meet with and listen to the employers who create jobs I consistently hear shared concerns about what it takes to make businesses work.

This is what employers tell me they need:

- A workforce that is skilled, motivated, reliable and that is willing and able to adapt to changes.
- A tax code that is simple, predictable, fair to all participants, reasonable, not confiscatory in its amounts, and that rewards innovation.
- Affordable health care that does not unfairly and inequitably penalize businesses.
- Affordable and dependable energy.

- Efficient and reliable infrastructure including transportation, energy, water, and communication networks.
- Regulation that is fair, predictable, and efficiently administered.
- Access to capital for startup and expansion.
- Access to domestic and international markets and a level playing field with international competition.

Reforms to educating the workforce, taxes, health care, and energy are discussed in detail in separate chapters of this book. In addition, as just mentioned, I believe we must invest in our infrastructure of all types, including transportation, water, energy, schools and other public resources.

Together, those changes would go a long way toward stimulating and sustaining economic growth again, but growth is also hobbled by other constraints that must be addressed. If Congress and the Administration would demonstrate a solid commitment and tangible results toward addressing these constraints, the stimulus impact would be both prompt and lasting.

Cutting Drag and Streamlining the Economy-Regulatory Reform and Simplification

The number of ways and places we have found to put "drag" onto our economy through unnecessary or counterproductive regulations are incalculable but the effect is easily seen. As we try to restore our nation's economic strength and international competitiveness, we must look for every way we can to streamline growth and encourage innovation and investment.

Let me give just a few examples. Every month or so I receive a letter explaining in small print and much detail the privacy policies of my bank, credit card company or some other financial institution. Who actually reads these things? The answer is virtually no one, but the collective and cumulative costs of sending the notices must be substantial.

Like so many other well-intended laws, these privacy policy notifications are required in response to abuses and violations by a relatively small number of companies and individuals. As wrong as those abuses were, the annual letters themselves do very little to stop them. Rather than sending hundreds of millions of letters each year, it would make far more sense to simply inform customers what the privacy policies are when they first sign up and only require further contact if policies changed in some significant way?

Consider another example. In an effort to save energy and money I recently sought to replace the windows on our home in Washington, D.C. with more energy efficient double-pane, Low-E windows. This seemed like the right thing to do, but our home is in a historic district so I had to get permission from the city's office of Historic Preservation.

Getting this permission entailed taking time away from work to go to a special office, then having them tell me what their best judgment said constituted the most historically accurate style of window frames and panes. Keep in mind that this was for a house on top of which sits modern heat exchanging air conditioning units, a TV antennae, and in front of which there are modern automobiles, streetlights, recycle bins and so forth. All these other visible anachronisms aside, it was apparently vital that the window panes be historically accurate in the minds of an expert.

As if that were not enough, I then had to go to the DC building planning department, where I waited no less than four hours to simply submit my application for permission and then be told to return again in several weeks to again wait several hours to see if my building permit had been approved.

Several weeks, more than ten hours wasted waiting in lines, and it goes without saying various fees later, I finally had my permit. As I write this I can hear in my mind hundreds of thousands of builders, contractors and others saying, "Now you know how we feel pal!" Yes, I do.

Such costly, unnecessary and economically counterproductive nonsense and inefficiency cannot continue if we want to compete in a global economy. Waste and drag on the economy could perhaps be tolerated when we were the economic leaders of the world, but in this new century, as we compete with 1.3 billion people in China, 1 billion in India, and hundreds of millions more in other nations, we cannot afford the luxury of unnecessary or inefficient regulation.

This is by no means to imply that all regulations are bad or should be removed. Quite the contrary, as the recent financial meltdown has demonstrated, well designed and prudently enforced regulations can be essential to economic health and quality of life. So too, the value of responsible regulation is evident in the striking difference in destruction and loss of life from earthquakes in Haiti, with lax building codes, compared to Chile, which has stronger codes and weathered a much more severe quake. Still more recently, the massive oil spill in the Gulf reveals the risks of inadequate regulations and monitoring.

Such examples notwithstanding, the creation and maintenance of laws and regulations, regardless of actual impacts or costs and benefits has to stop. What is more, Members of Congress and the Administration who make an earnest effort to end wasteful programs and regulations should receive just as much political attention and credit as those who create them.

Common Sense Regulatory Review and Reform

To correct the thousands of legal and regulatory inefficiencies that hamstring our economy without tangible benefits, government officials and agencies at every level should conduct annual reviews of regulations, laws, and procedures to identify which can be modified or completely eliminated. Throughout this process, public input should be solicited to help identify and improve the reforms but not in a way that further obstructs needed changes.

There should be created within both the Legislative and the Administrative branches specific offices of "Regulatory Ombudsman." An alternative title might be "The Office of Common Sense".

This office would be the point of contact for citizens to communicate their experiences dealing with rules, regulations, bureaucracies and bureaucrats that function inefficiently or do not make any real sense. The role of the office would be to gather information about what or who is or isn't working, then convey that information to representatives and the administration so it can be acted upon as part of annual reviews of laws and regulations.

In addition to these measures, voters and the media would do well to ask not just of politicians, "Which programs or agencies have you created through legislation?" but, just as importantly, "Which programs or agencies have you examined carefully and which have you identified or voted for elimination or reduction?"

Benefit/Cost Considerations Before Enactment

While the creation of more regulatory ombudsmen and ombudswomen combined with annual reviews of regulations could help identify and change existing problems, there is also a need to prevent the establishment of new laws, rules or regulations that would not make sense or would impose unreasonable costs to begin with.

Various legislative and administrative attempts to deal with this have been made in the past. The "Paperwork Reduction Act" is one example, as is the Office of Information and Regulatory Analysis within the Office of Management and Budget (OMB).

In many instances, unfortunately, these efforts have become yet another part of the very problems they were designed to overcome or prevent. Filing paperwork to demonstrate one has complied with the paperwork reduction act is perhaps the best example of all.

This experience suggests there is no magic bullet or easy solution to this problem. As I set out to write this chapter, I had originally considered proposing establishment of a Congressional Regulatory Office, comparable to the Congressional Budget Office (CBO). The CBO is a non-partisan entity that provides objective estimates of the financial costs of proposed legislation. This process, known as "scoring" a bill, tells members of Congress how much tax or spending legislation might cost the treasury if passed into law.

A "Congressional Regulatory Office" (CRO) would function similarly but would focus on the procedures involved in complying with proposed laws and regulations. "Scoring" these costs should include estimates of how much government bureaucracy would be needed to implement and enforce the regulations, how much time it would take those affected by the regulations to comply with them, how much it might cost in dollars to comply with a regulation, and some estimates of the net benefits. Informed by this knowledge, members of Congress and the public would have a better opportunity to determine if a proposed measure would actually achieve its desired goal and what the total costs and benefits of would be.

It turns out that the Congressional Budget Office has actually conducted a comprehensive study of this issue and produced an illuminating 1997 report "Regulatory impact analysis: Costs at selected agencies and implications for the legislative process."[10]

As that report indicates, regulatory impact analyses (RIAs) are already required for rules that would cost more than $100 million per year or adversely affect the U.S. economy or budget. CBO's study revealed that these analyses are not easy or inexpensive to produce, with costs ranging from a low of $14,000 to a high of $6 million per analysis and a median of $270,000. Neither were such analyses quick to complete. Times reported in the CBO study ranged from six weeks to twelve years and an average of three years.

The CBO notes in its analysis of analyses that Congress, if it chooses, can vote on a bill on the same day it is reported by a committee and with very little time for members to read or consider the impacts of the legislation. I have commented on this in the chapter on Congressional reforms, but it takes special relevance in light of the three year average that is

---

[10] *See* http://www.cbo.gov/doc.cfm?index=4015&type=0

required for agencies to conduct comprehensive analyses of the impacts of regulations.

Thus, while it makes sense to find ways to expedite the time and lower the costs of regulatory impact analyses, it may well be that such analyses will save substantial amounts in the long run by helping prevent unnecessary or poorly written regulations from coming into being.

Reducing Redundancy and Improving Agency Communication

If foolish regulations or inefficiencies at individual government agencies are not sufficiently frustrating, the problem is compounded exponentially when multiple agencies have shared jurisdictions but each must operate under different sets of rules and with different staff. This problem exists vertically, as local, county, state and then Federal agencies all play a hand in certain activities. It also exists horizontally within each level of government as different agencies share, or perhaps more accurately, compete for jurisdiction.

These sorts of problems can be found in everything from regulations concerning health care delivery to workplace safety, environmental protection to banking. I want to emphasize that I think all of these activities warrant some regulation, but they do not all warrant all of the regulations or the regulators that have been piled on to them.

What is needed, again, is a top-to-bottom review that identifies redundancies, duplications and conflicting rules and instead produces more coherent, streamlined and consistent procedures. Having dealt with this on a number of fronts, I am absolutely convinced that we can actually achieve better protection of workers, consumers, the environment, public safety and a host of other goals with much simpler, quicker and more affordable processes.

If businesses and employers could spend more of their time and money on growth and job creation and less on compliance with complex and conflicting regulation, the effect on economic growth would be extraordinary. Again, most responsible employers and businesses I know do not seek to do away with regulation, they just want it to make sense and be done efficiently.

Which raises one final point on this topic. Too much of the attention of regulations and regulators goes toward those businesses that reliably do the right thing, while those who don't are overlooked. In our overall approach to regulation we ought to follow the examples of community policing, which forms collaborative working relationships with responsible members of communities and tends to put the greatest number of enforcement officers where the crime rates are highest. In the regulatory realm, those entities that have a consistent and reliable record of honest compliance with regulations should be monitored less frequently in order that those which avoid or flaunt the law.

This approach recognizes and rewards the good actors while identifying and penalizing the bad. The result is that those who have made the investment and commitment to follow the rules are no longer at a competitive disadvantage compared to those who do not.

Training and Selecting Government Employees

Along with preventing and eliminating bad laws and regulations, it is also essential to do a better job of implementing and enforcing the laws and regulations that are in place and necessary. Just as in the business world, one of the greatest challenges facing government is finding qualified, motivated employees to perform these and government jobs. This challenge is becoming especially acute as a current generation of government employees retires, taking their knowledge, experience and insights with them and without an adequate number of equally knowledgeable or skilled replacements.

Finding strong applicants to fill essential government positions is complicated by strong competition and higher compensation from the private sector plus public criticism of government and government employees in general. Until recently, for example, a graduate with a degree in finance could make six figure salaries plus generous bonuses for working on Wall Street. Government pay would have been much lower and the government job would likely be seen as much less glamorous. This makes it very difficult to regulate the financial industry because the private sector may be seen as having more to offer potential employees who understand the industry.

What does this have to do with stimulating the economy, one might ask? The costs to society of vacant positions or inexperienced government workers are many and substantial. They include inadequate oversight and enforcement, delays and mistakes in promulgating new rules or regulations, errors in the interpretation or application of existing laws and regulations, delays in processing of permits, applications and other paperwork due to insufficient staffing, and idiosyncratic applications of laws and rules.

On the one hand, bad actors and law breakers are not identified or punished while, on the other hand, those who are trying to play by the rules face costly, lengthy and frustrating delays or idiosyncratic interpretations.

We cannot afford to do the people's business this way anymore. Better selection, training, monitoring and retention of top quality people to fill government slots would, especially if combined with the previously mentioned regulatory reform efforts, have a significant and positive economic impact.

Access to Capital

Businesses cannot grow and create jobs unless there is reliable access to sufficient capital. This problem has always been present, especially for rapidly growing businesses, but it has reached crisis levels since the financial meltdown.

To a significant degree, the capital access problem reflects and results from regulatory issues as they apply to the financial industry. On the one hand, the lack of regulation of investment banks contributed to the financial collapse, on the other hand mixed signals from regulators of local lenders has made it nearly impossible for many to actually get money out to businesses to create jobs, even when the businesses and loans are sound.

I have met on numerous occasions with local lenders and their borrowers who describe frustrations at having fully performing loans called into question merely because they were in categories of real estate or retail that were determined as a class to be high risk. This needs to change.

Regulators of local and regional banks have a responsibility to ensure their financial soundness, but one size fits all scorekeeping and micromanagement by formula is not the way to do it. Instead, interactive discussions and accurate assessments of each specific institution and their specific debt and asset portfolio is required.

At the same time, if Federal taxpayer money is going to be spent to bail out large financial institutions, which did far more than local banks to cause the bubble and subsequent collapse, then at least a much more significant portion of those funds should also be made directly available to local and community banks, credit unions and other responsible lenders to make available to local businesses.

Another way in which capital access can be increased is to promote greater cooperation between government funding for business development and venture or other private capital. For example, a joint funding program would involve private and public sector collaboration to identify promising high growth businesses that need capital for expansion and job creation. These businesses would then be granted low interest loans or grants, with proceeds from successful investment shared between the private investors and government.

In contrast to most existing government loan programs, such as the Small Business Administration loans, which tend to focus on new businesses that historically have high base rates of failure, the alternative proposed here, which has been used successfully in Israel and other nations, focuses the investment on businesses that are more likely to succeed and grow toward greater job creation.

Another possibility is reflected in legislation I have previously introduced to allow fast growth companies to reinvest money they would otherwise owe as income taxes. Essentially, this amounts to a loan of what would be tax liability for several years, after which the initial liability would be paid back with modest interest from the proceeds of the growth that was stimulated by the prior reinvestment. Initial scoring by the Congressional Budget Office suggested this approach could create hundreds of thousands of new jobs but it would actually generate, rather than cost additional revenue for the treasury.

There are many other creative models for getting more capital to business, and perhaps still better approaches have yet to be invented. To be certain, the days of excessively easy credit are likely over, but we will not escape a jobless recovery unless we make it possible for local lenders to lend and local businesses to have the capital to create new jobs. So far, we have not solved that problem, in large part because the focus has been elsewhere. It is long past time to shift the focus back to local job creators and away from international money speculators.

Access to Markets

Doing all that we can to make capital available, streamline regulations, reform the tax code, ensure affordable energy and health care and have a skilled workforce are all essential but not sufficient measures unless employers also have access to markets, both domestic and international.

In general, the evidence suggests that international trade has the potential to produce great benefits, but only if the trade is truly fair and all nations play by the same rules. For too long, the U.S. has negotiated trade agreements with foreign nations but then given little if any attention to monitoring and enforcing those agreements.

What is more, while any hint of protectionism in U.S. policy immediately elicits howls of protest and alarm from the global community, clear and egregious violations of all sorts, when practiced by other countries are tolerated with a wink and a nod by our trading partners. These abuses range from currency manipulation to mercantilist subsidies, from theft of intellectual property to bribery and corruption.

To get the economy going again we must move forward with key trade agreements on bilateral and multilateral bases, but this must be done with a much greater commitment to laws for worker, environmental and human rights protections. Just as importantly, we must then follow up to investigate and enforce compliance of those terms.

A National Industrial and Economic Strategy

While preserving the free enterprise, entrepreneurial economy that has made our nation so successful, I believe there is also a need for a national industrial strategy that looks at our strengths and challenges today and in the future and takes proactive measures to capitalize on the strengths and meet the challenges ahead of time.

Two examples illustrate the importance of this. Heavy manufacturing, for example steel smelting and fabrication, is necessary for the economic independence of major nations and for their national security. If a nation cannot build its own military hardware or provide basic material for buildings, transportation and other infrastructure, it will be left to the will of other nations and, hence, vulnerable to those nations.

A second example comes from high technology. As our nation's defense and economic security increasingly depend on high technology, outsourcing the development and manufacture of that technology makes us vulnerable at least as surely as does the loss of steel or other manufacturing capacity.

Some may argue that this is protectionist thinking. I would counter that failure to preserve certain core industries is irresponsible. Nations must be granted the right to maintain some core capacities or insistence on completely free trade will be tantamount to insistence on defenselessness and dependency.

This is not to suggest that the solution to our problems will be found in crass protectionism that defends antiquated or overpriced industries. It is, however, to argue that we need a coherent national strategy that looks on a sector by sector basis and strives to keep our own research, development and manufacturing strong, especially in certain essential areas of our economy.

At present, this sort of review is lacking and we lose critical capacity in many areas before we even realize they are gone and long after it is too late to get them back.

Demographics and the Need for Jobs for All Workers

As a final point to a discussion of sustained economic recovery, the issue of demographics and population should always be kept in mind. As the global population increases, there will be increasing competition for employment at all levels and across all sectors.

The risk this creates is that people become disposable and interchangeable in the workforce. With more and more people able to do the same job, and with international markets and production open, the potential for a race to the bottom on wages and benefits is real and growing.

Several measures can help reduce this risk. First, we must strategically evaluate economic policies and development with a mind to not just financial returns but the implications for all sectors of society. Some have suggested, and I agree, that an alternative to GDP should be used to measure the real health of economies for their people. What good does it do, for example, if there is strong GDP growth but jobs remain stagnant or are lost? How responsible is it if GDP grows but at the externalized cost of long term environmental destruction?

The second thing that must be done to address this issue is to substantially lower the rate of population growth to zero or less. It is already a daunting challenge to consider how we will meet the job demands of the hundreds of millions of young people already approaching the age of employment. Looking ahead to exponential growth beyond that is virtually unimaginable.

Finally, within our own nation, we must implement the educational changes suggested elsewhere in this book but we must do so with full awareness that in an overpopulated world even well-educated individuals will still face stark competition from global workers who may be just a smart, just as hard working, just as educated and willing to work longer hours for lower wages and benefits. Education, alone, will not solve this problem except perhaps in so far as education in foreign countries has been shown to generally lower rates of population growth.

8.
ENERGY

The most immediate economic stimulus of all is to Stop Burning Money! Rather than borrowing money we don't have for short term stimulus, and rather than exporting and combusting our wealth, there should be a national commitment to stimulate savings and the economy by using less energy immediately.

The simple fact is that it makes sense to save energy because that saves money for other things. This basic truth should be the starting point for our national economic recovery and our energy policy.

The surprising thing about this is how easily it can be done, how immediate the savings are, how those savings go straight to the people most in need, and how we ignore or even resist those savings.

Consider this. In October of 2009 (the most recent data at publication) the U.S. consumed over 360 million gallons of gasoline per day, plus 137 million gallons of diesel and nearly 11 million gallons of home heating oil. As we all know only too well, the price of petroleum can vary substantially, but for ease of calculation let's assume an average price of around $3.00 a gallon for these fuels. If prices go higher, which they likely will, the points made here all only gain in strength.

This means that nationwide we spend about $1.5 billion per day on these fuels alone, not counting natural gas, jet fuel and other products. If we could save just twenty percent on transportation and heating fuels, through such easy measures as changing driving habits, car-pooling, tire inflation, and simply obeying the posted speed limit, that would save consumers more than $300 million every day, more than $100 billion dollars a year without adding a penny to the deficit.

To appreciate how much money could be saved by individuals, suppose for simplicity that someone commutes about twenty miles per day and gets twenty miles per gallon.

With gas at $3.00 a gallon, they spend about $6.00 a day, $30.00 per week, $1,500 a year on gasoline alone, not counting maintenance, parking and other expenses of driving. A twenty percent savings from reduced speed, better tire inflation, more conservative driving and car pooling just once a week would save at least $300 per year per consumer.

Of course many people commute much longer distances and would save much more by making these changes. What's more, if we all do these simple things the price of fuel itself with drop because the supply/demand ratio will get right again, thereby saving everyone even more money. As an added benefit, greenhouse and ocean acidification emissions will also be lowered much more and much more rapidly than at current rates. For those who care, incidents like the Gulf oil spill will also become less likely.

Turning from vehicle fuel consumption to home usages, try this simple experiment and consider the savings. Most people take showers that are longer than needed, hotter than needed and with water pressures higher than needed. To appreciate this, close the drain next time you take your usual shower and mark how high the water level rises.

Then see what happens if you turn down the water pressure somewhat and take a military-style shower by turning off the water while you soap and shampoo and then turning it on again to rinse. My hunch is that most people will see they can easily reduce water consumption by over fifty percent and if they also turn the temperature down on their water heater and at the spigot itself the savings in energy will be even greater.

Water heating alone can account for between 14% -25% of energy consumed in the home. Saving more than fifty percent on this one activity does not require cold showers, simply shorter showers with slightly less water pressure and maybe slightly less hot water. Is that a "sacrifice" compared to what most people in the world live with? Not really. And even if it were, isn't it worth it for the sake of the nation and for our children?

Again, this measure costs absolutely nothing and adds zero to Federal spending yet it can produce substantial savings in energy costs and greenhouse emissions especially when multiplied by the 300 million Americans doing this every day.

Look at the rest of our lives and ask where other savings could be found to hit or beat the twenty percent savings mark. We can lower the settings on our refrigerators and clean the cooling elements. We can turn off our computers, printers and so forth when not in use and unplug all the chargers in our homes until we need them.

We can make sure no rooms or buildings are lit at night unless someone is in them. We can turn the thermostat down just a couple of degrees or so in the winter and raise it a couple of degree in the summer. We can set smart appliances to run in off-peak hours. Is it really too much to ask that we wear sweaters for the sake of preserving the oceans for our children? Does it really make sense to cool our homes so much in the summer that we sleep under blankets to stay warm in the air conditioning?

None of what was just described requires an act of Congress, none of it costs anyone a penny and all of it saves money and reduces pollution. These changes simply require us to make the right decisions and do the right thing and we can start that right now, today in our driving habits, our own homes and at the workplace.

What is the difference between inconvenience and suffering, between doing something out of habit versus doing something because we know it is the right thing to do? What is the difference between asking government or everyone else to make changes versus taking personal responsibility to join those who are in fact doing the right thing for the nation? What do we mean when we speak of the importance of Integrity?

Just as individuals can do much more to save energy and lower prices, governments and businesses can do the same. Let's take a few simple examples that, collectively, would add up to extraordinary savings. We'll start with steps local, county, state and Federal governments can take that require no legislation, just responsible actions.

I recently returned from work at 2 am and passed by an airport parking garage that was lit up inside as if it were broad daylight or Yankee Stadium. Looking into the multistory structure I was astonished how many lights were inside and how brightly they were burning. Surely that garage could function just as well with half the lights or even fewer with no real compromise in the safety or convenience of the users. Right there a fifty percent savings would be realized, and if the remaining lights were replaced with energy efficient bulbs, the savings would be grater still.

Much the same is true of countless city streets, roads and highways that have far more lighting than is necessary for traffic or personal safety. Certainly at key intersections and other locations lighting may contribute to safety, but pay attention to lighting in city streets and highways and it is easy to see where savings far greater than twenty percent can be achieved immediately simply by turning off one fifth or more of the lights.

The same is also true of government and other buildings. The Rayburn House Office building, where I work, had every single light in every hallway fully illuminated on Christmas Eve, a Federal holiday during which all offices were officially closed. Even during normal work days there is no need for more than half the lights in that building, but there was no legitimate reason or excuse for having them all on during a holiday. Turning half of the light fixtures in each hallway off immediately saves fifty percent, turning all but a very few off on weekends, evenings and holidays saves even more.

As evidence of further possible savings, most hotels and countless other businesses are too cold in summer and hot in winter. Again, lowering the winter heat and reducing the air conditioning just a couple of degrees would have no adverse effect on real quality of life or safety, but it would realize substantial savings on energy consumption and carbon production.

When one looks at examples like this, and you will find them everywhere as soon as you start to look in your own community and business, you begin to see that at no real sacrifice or inconvenience, many governments and businesses could easily cut their expenditures on lighting, heat and other energy consuming functions by twenty percent or more in very short order.

Who would benefit from the savings if these changes were made? You, the taxpayer and consumer, that's who. It is astonishing that with so many people calling for tax cuts we do not demand energy savings by government that would lower costs and make those tax cuts more affordable. Does anyone believe that if we were at wartime, and the leaders of the nation insisted that we implement such measures immediately, every patriotic community, from the tiniest town to the largest metropolis would not do this?

Our current economic woes, and to some degree our present international and security challenges, have come about in part because of our dependence on fossil fuels and rising energy prices. We have a chance to cut that dependency and lower energy prices by reducing demand immediately. If we do we realize the double savings because we will purchase less in total and what we do use will cost less.

This does not take a scientific miracle, a new government program, new drilling or an extraordinary change in our quality of life. Neither does it require complex new programs, incentives or taxes. It simply takes common sense, sound judgment and the will to act and do what is right together for our own good and for the good of the nation. That is not too much to ask and it is time we had real leaders who are willing to make that ask and lead by example.

Too many people will be tempted to reflexively reject this suggestion because there is a desire for someone else - the government, scientists, or private inventors to solve the problem for us. Someone else has to come up with limitless energy that is free and non-polluting so we don't have to change anything at all about what we do. Sure, and while we're at it let's have free beer for everyone too.

As I have said repeatedly in this book, such a response is simply not honest or responsible. The "someone else" we turn to for solutions has to be each and every one of us. Reducing energy consumption is not actually so difficult and the benefits are more than many realize. Technology already exists that will help solve our energy challenges if we only choose to use it wisely. Such simple measures as changing light bulbs, installing and actually using programmable thermostats, adjusting settings on hot water heaters and other such actions can all help reach the twenty percent savings goal.

Again, achieving this goal in energy consumption and expenditures would do more than any other proposed or enacted stimulus package to stimulate the economy in the short term and for the future, without adding anything to the deficit and, again, while actually lowering government spending.

Global Overheating and Ocean Acidification

This chapter started by emphasizing the economic benefits and stimulus effect of energy conservation for two reasons. First, given the state of the nation's economy, the high levels of unemployment, and the swelling Federal, state and personal deficits, getting the economy right again has to be our highest policy and political priority. The second reason is that too often energy policies are promoted based on environmental arguments rather than economic ones. I believe the environmental case for transforming our energy policy and practices is sound and strong, but whether or not one shares that judgment, the economic argument alone ought to be reason enough for change.

Having made the economic argument (and it has been made in much greater detail elsewhere, see for example the great work of the Rocky Mountain Institute) the environmental argument must also be considered.

The language we have been using to describe "Climate change" and "global warming" is itself part of the reason we have not solved either the energy challenges or the environmental threats. "Change" can be a good thing and "warming" is a comforting term. Why should we expect people to do anything about a problem if it is labeled with words that imply good things? A more accurate, and hopefully more motivating, terminology would be "Lethal Overheating and Ocean Acidification."

Lethal overheating is the only honest way to describe the effects of a projected four to six degree temperature rise. Set aside if you like what may seem like distant or theoretical discussions of sea level rise, hurricane increases and glacial melting, and just ask what happens if your body temperature increases four to six degrees?

When we run a fever of more than four degrees, we are very sick people. We take aspirin, put on cold packs, use antibiotics and hope things get better fast. We certainly cannot work productively or care well for our families. If the fever persists and gets even a degree or so worse we run the risk of seizures and, eventually, death.

That is what "global warming", which sounds so pleasant, means for countless species. Many fish, for example, perish when water temperature increases just a few degrees. So too, many mammals will also die as will the food and habitat they depend on. This alone ought to get the attention of fishermen and hunters if no one else, but most do not fully grasp what is at stake or how serious the problem is. Speaking of lethal overheating rather than "climate change" would help bring about that realization and the necessary changes.

To the overheating problem we must add acidification of the oceans. This impact of atmospheric carbon increase was largely overlooked in the early discussions of climate change, but it is at least as dangerous.

The chemistry of ocean acidification is not complex and can be easily demonstrated in a lab. Roughly twenty-five percent of the manmade CO_2 that enters the atmosphere is dissolved in the oceans. The dissolved CO_2 forms carbonic acid, which in turn makes the essential minerals in water, like aragonite and calcium carbonate, less available for shelled organisms to build their exoskeletons.

Skeptics of overheating can make all the arguments about sunspots, natural variation in temperature and so forth (even though these have all been compellingly answered), but denying acidification is to deny basic chemistry. It might be impossible to conclusively demonstrate the warming of the entire planet in a lab, but it is easy to demonstrate acidification and measure the effects on mineral availability.

It is also possible to place shelled organisms, like coral, oysters, and certain plankton into that water and watch what happens. This research has in fact been done and the results show impaired growth and diminished survival. Add increased temperature to that more acidic bath and the organisms die more rapidly and in greater numbers.

The bad news, and it is very bad indeed, is that this happens at levels of acidity that we are rapidly approaching even at current levels of CO_2 emissions. At slightly higher levels, coral reefs begin to literally dissolve, thus wiping out that unique ecosystem and all the species of fish, and human communities that depend on them. If certain plankton that form the basis of much of the ocean food chain perish, a great portion of other life in the oceans will also die.

Now do we have people's attention?

A Call To Action and Responsibility

Our nation comprises only about five percent of the world's population but we consume more than twenty percent of the world's energy and produce a comparable percentage of global overheating and ocean acidification gasses. Most of the current policy proposals for addressing lethal overheating and acidification are too little too late.

Government has the capacity and the power to make wise policy reforms and invest in new energy sources and alternatives, but these things take time. The more rapid response begins not in the Capitol or the White House but in the houses, businesses and communities of average people making responsible choices.

The immediate response to our situation should start with the President, along with his former opponent, joining together with Congressional leaders from both parties, plus military, business, social and religious figures, all gathering as a united group to say straight to the American people:

"For the sake of our economy today and in the future, in the interest of our national security and

independence, and for the health of this the planet we live on each and every one of us as patriotic Americans should set a goal of cutting our energy consumption as quickly as possible. We are all in this together, we all have a responsibility to each other and to our children, and we will all benefit together from doing what is right."

With clear and compelling explanations, a unified call to patriotism, shared commitment, and clear guidance for steps to take to achieve the goal, I believe the American people would rally and do the right thing. It has been done before in our country in times of war. The threats we face today may be less apparent than in wartime, but they are no less grave.

Carbon Taxes versus Cap and Trade

If individuals, communities and businesses make the decisions and take the actions that have been recommended, energy prices and pollution will go down immediately. But there is more that can and should be done to realize further savings and that is where government policy can come in.

Let's start with the hardest political steps first.

We should immediately impose a tax on all carbon and other greenhouse and ocean acidifying fuels with the proceeds to be invested in clean energy research and capacity installation, energy conservation, and reducing entitlement debt. To benefit areas of the country that would be most heavily impacted by the tax, investments of the revenues through conservation, research, and renewable energy manufacturing should be targeted to those areas most generously.

For transportation, the Federal general motor fuel tax, which is currently 18.4 cents per gallon of gasoline and 24.4 cents per gallon of diesel has not been increased since 1993. For both fuels there should be an added thirty cents per gallon applied at the pump with provisions made for commercial, freight, agriculture and mass transit to pay only half this increase per gallon.

Each year thereafter the fuel tax should increase by an additional twenty cents. Meanwhile, subsidies for corn or other food crop-based ethanol should be reduced to zero within the next five years and mandated fuel blends should be thoroughly and objectively reviewed to assess total energy input and outputs and lifecycle environmental costs of alternative fuels.

For coal, natural gas and other fossil fuels used to generate electric power an added tax should be applied on a per-ton of coal or per-normal cubic meter of gas basis as 'upstream" in the distribution system as possible and practical. Higher taxes should be levied on "dirtier" fuels and, like the proposed gasoline and diesel taxes, coal and gas taxes should be increased each year.

Some argue that imposing any new taxes during the present economic downturn will cripple the economy. This is not necessarily true.

Three points should be made in response. First, if proper conservation measures are implemented the net financial expenditures will not necessarily be higher, and will likely actually be lower than they are at present. This is because less fuel will be used and what is used will, apart from the taxes, cost less due to supply and demand changes.

Second, the money from carbon taxes will not disappear, nor will it be shipped overseas as happens with our current foreign fuel dependence. Rather, it will be reinvested in our own economy.

Third, lethal overheating of the planet and acidification of the oceans do not care about our economic emergency today and if we fail to act their economic impacts will ultimately be far greater than any carbon tax imposed today. Indeed, failing to act on these challenges today is just adding yet another enormous burden on top of the financial debt we are passing on to our children.

Just as importantly, in response to a tax on carbon new jobs will be created through installation of conservation and alternative energy technologies. Research will create further jobs and inventions that produce further growth, and reduction of debt will lower interest payments and address economic shortcomings that must be resolved.

Anyone who shudders at the mere mention of a fuel tax increase could take some solace from a simple example of how this would work in practice.

Consider again the earlier example of a person who uses two gallons of gas a day to commute twenty miles each way to work in a vehicle that gets twenty miles per gallon.
If a thirty cent per gallon tax were implemented, that would add sixty cents a day or three dollars per week in fuel costs.

At the same time, however, a twenty percent savings in consumption as discussed earlier would save more than $1.20 in fuel costs each day on the initial price. That savings more than outweighs the impact of the tax increase, meaning that the net out of pocket expenses for the consumer would be lower even after the tax increase.

Transportation analysts have suggested that to meet our nation's infrastructure needs a fuel tax of a little more than a dollar a gallon would be necessary. This would require a substantial increase above the levels I have just proposed, but even with such an increase an individual who reduced consumption as described would still be saving more compared to current consumption and costs. Again, keep in mind, too, that the net savings would likely be still greater because the costs of gasoline would likely decline with the reduction in overall demand.

The most commonly discussed alternative to a carbon tax is a "cap and trade" system that limits total CO2 and other overheating and ocean acidifying gasses and creates a market for permission to emit CO2. The theory is that this process will create market forces to create incentives for investments in the most efficient and cost effective measures of reducing output.

There is merit in this model and it has been implemented with some success, though not without shortcomings and setbacks as well, in Europe and elsewhere.

There are, however, a number of reasons for favoring an immediate carbon tax, at least for the present. The carbon tax can be implemented immediately, thereby generating immediate incentives for reductions plus revenue for research and deficit reduction. A cap and trade system would take time to implement and there are complex and as yet unanswered questions about how carbon emissions will be monitored and the possibility that the market could be manipulated.

The latter question is of particular concern given market manipulations in the electrical energy sector at the start of this decade and considering the meltdown of financial institutions in the past year. What is more, to truly function effectively a cap and trade system needs global or near global buy in. The disappointing outcome of the Copenhagen meeting at the end of 2009 shows how difficult this will be to achieve. Carbon taxes, by comparison, do not demand such international agreements to begin producing results.

Even though a full cap and trade system may not be ready or advisable at present, it is still possible to gain further emissions reductions without establishing a cap and trade market. In addition to placing an immediate tax on carbon-based fuels, there should be a strict limit on the amount of fossil fuel energy from all sources that can be used in this nation during any given year.

The total overall consumption cap for each energy source should be structured so that caps on foreign supplies are more heavily weighted in the total relative to domestic sources. The total fossil fuel consumption allowed under this limit the coming year, 2011 should be set at five percent less than total consumption for 2010 and should decline by at least five percent each year for the next ten years.

Anyone who proposes such a substantial increase in fuel taxes faces a likely political backlash. The only response I know to that backlash is this -- the truth.

The two most important truths are these: 1. Our current use of fossil fuels is killing our planet, funding despots and terrorists, and distorting our economy. 2. Making the proposed changes would take effort and involve costs, but if paired with conservation measures and reinvestment of the revenue in new energy technologies and debt reduction, the net result would stimulate the economy, promote investment in new technology, reduce traffic congestion, improve safety, and put our nation at the lead, rather than the tail, of world efforts to reduce climate change and ocean acidification.

A Manhattan or Apollo Project for Energy

As we work vigorously to reduce fossil fuel dependence we must also expand the availability and use of other energy sources. To achieve this we should embark on a national energy research program comparable in scope, scale and urgency to the Manhattan or Apollo projects. Simply put, we should throw every bright mind available at this project and explore every practical clean energy option.

The good news on this front is that legislation enacted in the 110th and 111th Congress, plus investments of stimulus money by Congress and the Obama administration, made real and important strides toward improving our basic and applied energy research.

Based on a blue ribbon commission recommendation contained in the report "Rising Above the Gathering Storm", Congress authorized and funded the Advanced Research Projects Agency for Energy, or ARPA-E.

This nimble, minimally bureaucratic agency, is modeled after the highly successful predecessor known as DARPA, the Defense Advanced Research Projects Agency. DARPA funded some of the most advanced defense applications, several of which, including the internet, stealth technology, and others that have now become well known and essential to our civilian lives and national security.

In just its first year in operation, the ARPA-E program has funded multiple research and applications of new energy technologies that are truly transformative and that cross the spectrum of energy sources. In my judgment, we should continue and dramatically expand ARPA-E funding.

Questionable Investments

While pursuing promising options, we should also avoid costly pathways that are unlikely to generate cost effective energy for many years to come. We simply do not have time or money to waste on avenues that may be dead ends and will certainly not get us where we need to be soon enough.

One recurrent example is the call for nuclear fusion-based energy. For many decades now fusion energy has been most effective at burning taxpayer money and has been completely ineffective at producing anything close to a viable source of electricity. Indeed, it always seems, and has always seemed, that the proponents of fusion say if we just throw enough money at fusion research, within forty years or so it will be viable.

In fairness, scientists have learned a great deal from fusion energy research, and that may justify its continued pursuit. But as a practical solution to our energy challenges it is a dismal failure and likely to be so for at least many, many decades to come. There are cheaper, more practical, more proven methods that could be in place today, not forty years from now, if we took the money from fusion energy research and applied it elsewhere.

The rush to subsidize corn-based ethanol is another example of a politically appealing but bad economic and environmental energy policy. Turning fossil fuel, food, topsoil, water, and fertilizer into a different kind of fuel that burns less efficiently is not sound policy. Corn-based ethanol production heavily uses fossil fuels at virtually every step of production and delivery, depletes aquifers and draws down rivers, exhausts the land, increases and distorts food prices, creates incentives to destroy rainforests and other fragile areas, and, according to most studies, produces little if any net positive energy gain in the end. Subsidizing this endeavor with taxpayer dollars is simply bad policy and should be phased out.

Pointing out the flaws of a corn-based ethanol strategy does not mean ethanol from all sources is bad. It does, however, mean that we should carefully consider the net energy inputs and outputs and the total costs, including financial and environmental, of alternatives.

One alternative that has promise, but is not yet commercially viable, is cellulosic ethanol. Various plant sources, ranging from switch grass to forest products have been studied and we should continue to vigorously pursue those studies. Along these same lines, direct conversion of biomass to more gasoline or diesel like fuels, rather than alcohol, should also be promoted.

As we do, however, the key deciding factors should not be political considerations or where presidential caucuses or primaries are held. Rather the consideration should be based on hard science and practical realities of which sources produce the most efficient fuels and the greatest CO_2 reductions and the most economic benefits for the least total costs, including all financial, energy, employment and environmental inputs and outputs.

Because so much of the current and "potential" energy in our nation and internationally is in the form of coal, much has been made of the prospect of sequestering the carbon from coal combustion as a way to reduce greenhouse gasses.

I fully understand and respect the desire to do this. Our own nation's dependence on coal, the increasing use of coal in places such as China, along with the domestic and international political considerations are driving carbon capture and storage (CCS). I only wish it were financially and practically viable within the time frame we need. I also wish it did not carry such enormous opportunity costs and lock us into a host of other inefficiencies, expenses and hazards.

Unfortunately the astonishing volumes of carbon that are produced each day from coal combustion, the costs and technical difficulties of capturing and then compressing this gas into a form that can be stored, and the costs and technical demands of actually putting the resulting material into the ground for permanent storage are prohibitive. In fact, best estimates suggest that as much as a quarter or a third of the energy generated by a coal plant would be needed just to power the sequestration efforts.

Testimony at a recent Congressional hearing on this topic suggested that commercially viable large scale sequestration is not likely to be available until 2025 or later. Even then, the economics of that project will likely require substantial cost increases in the price of coal based electricity generation. Frankly, we do not have that much time to turn around the overheating and ocean acidification.

In addition to the long time frame and prohibitive energy and financial costs of CCS, heavy investment in coal power plants means investment in centralized power sources which, in turn, demands new transmission lines. Those lines, in addition to being costly to construct and maintain, are also terribly inefficient, losing a great deal of power along the way.

Coal-based energy also means a host of environmental and human impacts that result from mining. Air and water pollution from the mining, transport of the coal, and combustion during the generation process itself must also be considered. Mining is also an inherently dangerous occupation. A 2006 study, for example, reported that nearly five thousand Chinese coal miners were killed that year alone. Here at home, in April of 2010 the lives of 29 coal miners were lost in the explosion at the Upper Big Branch mine in West Virginia.

Once again, there are much better, proven ways to achieve the desired results of energy generation and carbon reduction for far less cost and much more immediate benefit. Rather than pouring a hundred billion dollars into CCS technology, as the House energy bill proposed, that money would be far better spent to develop truly revolutionary technologies that are distributive in nature, more efficient, do not pose the risks to life and health that coal mining and power generation create, and that are cheaper to produce and operate.

9.

EDUCATION

"Preach a crusade against ignorance. Establish and improve the law for educating the common people. Let our countrymen know that the people alone can protect us against these evils, and that the tax which will be paid for this purpose, is not more than the thousandth part of what will be paid to kings, priests and nobles who will rise up among us if we leave the people in ignorance." Thomas Jefferson

The survival of our nation depends on an educated, informed public making reasoned, responsible decisions for themselves, their families, their community and the country. While the U.S. continues to produce some of the most educated, informed and accomplished people in the world, too many of our children are not completing school and too many who do are graduating without the ability to read, write, or do basic math. Indeed, many Americans would likely have difficulty reading and understanding the text of our great national documents - The Declaration of Independence, The Constitution and Bill of Rights. What is more, and worse, core values of personal responsibility, hard work, honesty, and thrift seem to be declining.

These deficiencies do not end at high school. A great many college graduates also lack core skills in writing, math and critical thinking. Far too many seem to believe they should get credit for simply showing up and "trying hard" regardless of their actual skill or performance.

The number one concern I hear when I speak to employers, almost regardless of the enterprise, is difficulty finding skilled, motivated and reliable workers. No wonder our economy is in the tank. We have an economy in which countless skilled jobs are going wanting or are filled by marginally qualified people while, at the same time, unemployment rates are rising.

Do We Really Value Education?

For all the talk of how important education is, for all the speeches and slogans of politicians and candidates, and for all the money we already spend, (much more per capita than any other nation) the fact is our culture does not really act as though it values education and our education system does not work as well as it should.

Most American children and adults spend far more time watching television or playing sports than they do reading, writing, mastering math or understanding what is happening in their own nation or in the world. If we do not change this, our children and our nation will fall farther and farther behind other nations and cultures that really do value education and which put those values into action.

Fortunately, the good news is that there are countless involved parents and incredibly talented, dedicated teachers and administrators. There are also proven programs that dramatically improve educational outcomes. By studying what has worked in our own country and in other nations we can put into place proven measures that will help all our children have a better chance for success.

Parents

The best place to start any discussion of education is with parents. It is the primary responsibility of parents, not the government, not the school district, not the teacher and certainly not the television to make sure children are learning. No government program, no matter how much we spend, and no teacher, no matter how dedicated and talented, can succeed if parents and students do not accept responsibility first and do the work it takes to learn.

As parents, we need to turn off the TV, put limits on the time spent on sporting activities, and insist that our children open the math and English and science books and do the hard but enjoyable work it takes to learn.

Some may argue that it is not the government's role to talk about parental responsibility or that doing so does not constitute a government "policy" or program. This is understandable, but if we act as though the solution and responsibility for educational improvement starts with politicians or government rather than with parents and students, we are starting from a false premise and we are sure to fail.

In many of the nations where children are now scoring higher than American students on tests of math, science and other fields, far less money is being spent per student than in the U.S., but the attitude of parents and students is much different.

Early education

While emphasizing parental responsibility, we must also recognize that the structure of families today is often complex and not all children come from ideal homes. If we wait until children enter kindergarten to begin their education, we have missed some of the most important years of life and learning.

We need instead to start approaching the developmental and educational mission in the earliest years of life and make sure all children have basic nutrition, health care and stimulating supportive environments as a foundation for learning. This effort has two essential elements. First, we need to give all parents the knowledge, skill and support they need to help their children develop. Second, we need to provide improved and expanded day care and preschool to help the children of parents who work outside the home.

Nothing a parent does in life is more important than raising their children, yet we give virtually no instruction or support to help parents do this well. Indeed, we demand more training and testing to drive a car than we do to become a parent. Driver's education has, ironically, become a standard aspect of many high school course offerings, but parent education is rare. This should change. Every student in high school should be given a basic course in parenting.

This course should include information about child development, nutrition and health, plus key parental behaviors and strategies to help deal with the child's emotional, physical and cognitive needs. This training should also include responsible, scientifically accurate information about the importance and methods of family planning.

In addition to training in high school, there should also be outreach to prospective parents beyond school. The government cannot and should not of course force anyone to take training in parenting, but we certainly should make basic information available through health care providers, broadcast media, easily available and widely distributed printed information, plus outreach through churches and other social organizations.

Accessing this information and training should not only be easy, it should become embedded in our culture as an expectation. Every expectant parent should know that it is socially expected of them to prepare for parenting by studying for the responsibilities beforehand.

While helping parents better prepare for their roles, we must also address the importance and challenges of finding quality day care and pre-school for children when parents must work outside the home. Finding well qualified, motivated and nurturing care for children is far more difficult today than it should be. In part this is because the pay for daycare workers is pitiful. Again, it is ironic that nothing is more important than our children but we pay virtually nothing for the people who care for them.

If we truly want to improve our nation and better our educational outcomes, we must make major investments in early childhood education. This includes much improved and accessible training, educating the people who work with children, and paying those people at levels commensurate with the importance of their work and the value of our children. Parents who cannot afford the costs of day care should receive support to do so and all children, regardless of their economic or social status should have ready access to quality care and instruction.

Students

Every child possesses a unique combination of strengths, weaknesses, needs and aspirations. Children also come from extraordinarily diverse circumstances. Some are given every opportunity conceivable while others face seemingly insurmountable disadvantages and obstacles.

In the end, whatever their circumstances, each child must somehow reach adulthood with the core personal qualities, skills and knowledge they will need to succeed in life and contribute to their community. All children need to learn basic values and develop the kinds of character traits we have discussed earlier, such as honesty, integrity, responsibility, community, courage and humility. Children must also understand that learning takes time, effort and dedication and there is no way around that.

The writer Stephen Crane, author of "The Red Badge of Courage," once wrote a brief passage that succinctly states this core principle:

> A man said to the Universe:
> "Sir I exist"
> "However," replied the universe,
> "The fact has not created in me
> A sense of obligation"

While it is the responsibility of parents and society to do everything possible to help children and young people grow and learn, we must also teach children, from a very early age, that they have to make good choices and take responsibility to make something of themselves.

Teachers

When parents place their children in the care of schools and teachers, they have a right to expect that everyone at the school will be dedicated, skilled, prepared, and motivated. It is the responsibility of principals, school boards, colleges, teachers unions and parents alike to ensure that those high standards are met. There can be no excuse for allowing it to be any other way.

Most people who have not been tasked with teaching twenty or more 5 year olds all day long, day after day, have no idea how difficult it is. They would not, or probably could not, do it for all the money in the world.

Teachers, especially good ones, have unimaginably difficult jobs and generally receive far too little support, respect or financial reward for the work they do. Yet good teachers give it their all and do astonishingly good work day after day for very small compensation relative to the importance of what they do and to what many others in our society earn.

Teacher Selection and Training

Improving the quality of teachers and teaching starts with how we select who will become teachers. In the U.S., the traditional model involves letting college students who are interested in becoming teachers select their major, take the requisite education classes and, if they pass the classes, go on to practicum and perhaps eventual employment.

Unfortunately this system does not always attract the very best to the field. Indeed, too often, education departments are viewed as the refuges for students who "can't cut it" in more challenging majors. This impression is accompanied by a parallel observation that too often the expectations and standards placed on education majors are not sufficiently rigorous.

There are certainly many exceptions to this and I do not believe the generalization is fair or accurate, but the fact that the impression exists at all suggests we are doing something, perhaps many things wrong.

If we are to entrust teachers with the lives and minds of children, shouldn't we take a different approach to recruiting, selecting and training teachers? Shouldn't our selection criteria and expectations for teachers be at least as high if not higher than for any other major? If we are to expect future teachers to instill high standards and set high expectations of their students, should we not set equally high standards and expectations for them during their college education and teacher training?

A report by the McKinsey consulting group[11] reveals that other nations, which are dramatically exceeding our educational performance at substantially lower costs, take a much different approach to teacher selection and training.

As described in that report, the place to begin improving teaching is to make entry into the teaching major, and eventually the profession, much more selective. Rigorous screening and higher standards should be required before anyone is allowed to enter the teaching major, not along the way or afterward.

Setting such standards for admission into the major will immediately raise the prestige of the profession and that will have a powerful impact in attracting strong applicants. It will also impact the public impression of teachers and the teaching profession, as people come to realize that teaching is a highly selective and highly skilled profession.

Along with setting high standards for admission into teaching, the education of teachers needs to be much more rigorous both during college and after the teachers have entered the classroom. It is never pleasant or easy to give a student at any level a failing grade, but if an education major is not up to the task of teaching in all respects, they should not be passed. So too, if a college or university faculty member is not up to the task of modeling the very highest standards themselves, that faculty member should be either improved or replaced.

The key questions that must be asked are "Have we rigorously recruited and selected the very best people to be in charge of our children's well being and education?" And, "Has each teacher in training mastered the knowledge and skills that will enable them to provide a quality education to every student in their classroom?"

---

[11] *See* http://www.mckinsey.com/clientservice/socialsector/resources/pdf/Worlds_School_Systems_Final.pdf

If the answers to these questions are anything less than "Absolutely yes!" the student should not be accepted into the major, should not pass the class and should not move forward to become a teacher until they have clearly demonstrated the knowledge and skill. Our children are too precious for it to be any other way.

Attracting New Teachers

To further expand the ranks of quality teachers, experienced professionals in critical fields should have opportunities to enter teaching through expedited, focused training that does not require a full four year education major. This is not to suggest that everyone in a given profession necessarily can or should be a teacher. But it is ironic that, to take a personal example, someone who has actually served in government would not be qualified in most states to teach a high school course in government. The same is true of countless other professions, from architecture or American history to welding or writing.

With a shortage of qualified teachers in such critical fields as math, science, engineering and others, what is needed is both a change in the pay structure and an efficient and effective way to help practicing professionals enter the classroom if they have the skills and knowledge to be good teachers. Some states already have such programs, but they should be expanded.

Maintaining Quality Teachers

Attracting, selecting and training the most capable people to be teachers is essential but not sufficient. Studies suggest that nearly half of the teachers who enter the field will leave within their first five years.

No matter how strong our teacher selection and education systems are in colleges and universities, some of the most important lessons about teaching as a profession cannot be learned or appreciated until one is in the classroom for at least a year or two. This means we must provide top quality mentors and opportunities for continuing education for new teachers after they have been in the classroom for a while.

Indeed, it would be best if we did not really consider that someone is fully qualified as a teacher until after they have not only graduated with a certificate but been in the field with ongoing supervision and summer continuing education course to troubleshoot and help provide practical help with the real world challenges the new teacher has discovered.

One proven approach to improving teacher quality is National Board Certification. This Federally funded program is a rigorous voluntary system of assessment designed to incentivize and identify highly qualified teachers in different areas of teaching specialization. Typically taking one to three years to complete, and with many aspirants failing in their attempts, Board Certification evaluates subject area competence and knowledge along with comprehensive professional skills that emphasizes more strategic, individualized approaches to interacting with students.

Thus far some 64,000 teachers nationwide have been certified. Personal reports of teachers who have achieved board certification offer compelling evidence of how the experience has enhanced, in some cases transformed, their knowledge, methods and attitude. Empirical studies substantiate the effects of this transformation by demonstrating improved student outcomes, teacher satisfaction and teacher retention.

Certified teachers also have a positive effect on their schools through serving as role models for colleagues and mentors to new professionals. Considering these results, this program should be substantially expanded so more teachers have the desire, opportunity and support they need to seek certification.

Pay Increases and Merit Pay

If we truly recognize the importance and difficulty of the work of teachers, if we set high standards for selection and training, and if we demand ongoing training and supervision to maintain professional skills and knowledge, then we must also financially reward teachers. The pay must reflect the importance we place on the well being of our children and our future.

Increased compensation can begin while teachers are still in training by providing special scholarships or loan forgiveness programs to those who make teaching a career and teach in high need areas. Such support was in fact recently provided as part of a loan forgiveness program contained within the Higher Education Authorizing which Congress passed in July of 2008.

Beyond college, there should be substantial across the board increases in pay for all teachers, especially in the early stages of their careers. There should also be merit pay for those teachers who excel, and differential pay rates to attract and retain teachers in the highest demand or most demanding fields.

As in any other endeavor of life, the recognition and reward of outstanding performance attracts the best applicants and encourages improvement across the profession. On the other hand, the failure to recognize excellence, and a system that provides compensation independently of performance, discourages those with the greatest skill and dedication who wish to put in the extra effort to excel.

Some have argued that merit pay for teachers is not feasible or desirable because it is impossible to know who is truly teaching well. This is just not true.

In fairness, it is absolutely true that merely relying on standardized test scores alone to evaluate teacher performance would be a terrible mistake. Aggregate classroom scores do not tell anything about how individual students fare with a given teacher, and basing financial compensation on such measures could easily discourage teachers from tackling classes and students who are most difficult and most in need.

But this does not mean that proper use of a combined set of performance measures cannot distinguish relative strengths and weaknesses of individual teachers and among different teachers. Such measures should include direct classroom observations of empirically proven behaviors; systematic reports and evaluations from students and parents; and direct assessment of the teachers' subject area knowledge and knowledge of pedagogical techniques for those subjects.

Pay should also reflect systematic reports from fellow teachers, consideration of time and effort dedicated to students and classroom, and the use of appropriate adaptive testing that monitors individual progress of individual students.

This sort of monitoring, supervision and mentoring should be especially concentrated during the early years of a teacher's professional development, but it should not end there. Ongoing training and supervision, by accomplished peers, principals or other experts, plus systematic and comprehensive evaluations and feedback should be an essential part of every professional teacher's career from start to finish.

Why does all of this matter so much?..

Several recent research studies have examined the effects of putting students in classes with the very best teachers. The results have consistently shown that having an opportunity to learn from the very best teachers can substantially improve student performance, including students who might otherwise have been struggling to succeed.

Remediating or Removing Those Who Do Not Teach Well

Fortunately, most people have had the experience of being in classes with truly inspired and inspiring teachers. The best teachers manage to bring out the strengths in even the most challenging students and young people genuinely look forward to attending their classes.

At the same time, however, nearly everyone who has been through school has at some point been forced to suffer through teachers who were uninformed in their subject, lazy in their preparation, uninspiring in their classroom, and at times even destructive and abusive to students. In many cases, the fact is well known by other faculty, parents, students, administrators and sometimes even the incompetent teachers themselves. Yet these teachers continue to be allowed into the classroom and to be given the responsibility and power to influence student's lives.

This has to change. We owe it to students and to their parents to ensure that all teaches are the very best they can be and meet the highest standards.

The first responsibility for correcting this falls with the teaching profession itself. As professionals who want and deserve respect, teachers' organizations and unions should be the first to insist that unqualified, ineffective or harmful people do not enter the profession to begin with or are removed once their shortcomings are identified. This is in the best interests of the teachers as professionals but, most importantly, it is in the best interests of the students.

If teachers' unions and associations demonstrate that their highest commitment is to quality instruction and the well being of students, their esteem in the eyes of the public will increase dramatically. Simultaneously, arguments in favor of increased compensation, greater course preparation time, and other legitimate needs will also then receive greater support.

Along with teachers' organizations, academic administrators and principals bear the responsibility for monitoring teacher qualifications and performance, rewarding those who excel and removing those who do not meet standards. To make this possible, principals and other administrative leaders must have the training, tools, time, and the authority to truly monitor teacher performance and take effective corrective action.

There also need to be changes in the laws and rules that tie the hands of administrators who would set the high standards and make the tough choices to reward the best and remove the worst teachers.

One of the key obstacles that should be changed is academic tenure. As someone who has taught in a tenure-based university culture, I am well familiar with all the arguments in favor of tenure. Academic freedom, intellectual independence, creativity and so forth, are all supposed to be protected by tenure.

In my experience, it is exceptionally rare that tenure promotes any of these virtuous qualities. All too often, tenure promotes the opposite characteristics. It provides protection for faculty who are out of touch, lacking in creativity, burned out, and sometimes downright pathological.

Once tenured, faculty can scarcely be removed. They know it, their administrators know it, and their students know it. What is more, in many institutions it is these individuals who decide the fate of their junior colleagues and determine which of these will also become tenured. Those who have the security of tenure but are burned out themselves can all too easily become threatened by truly creative or capable younger members and obstruct, rather than encourage, their progress. The result is damaging to the profession, demoralizing to the truly competent and motivated teachers and administrators and, most lamentably, harmful to students.

How could any enterprise be expected to succeed if the people engaged in it were not required to be fully competent and motivated? When the well being of our children is at stake, how we can justify a system that protects people who have no business being in a classroom or in administration.

It makes perfect sense and is only fair that all employees, teachers or otherwise, have an assurance of due and fair process if there are questions about their competence or performance. It also makes sense that we want to ensure diverse ideas and methods are allowed and encouraged within our educational system. But it does not make sense that the process and protections involved in removing truly ineffective teachers are so onerous that the enterprise of education and the success of our children are compromised as a result.

To those in the teaching profession who would be alarmed by this proposal, I understand and respect their concerns. I also believe, however, that if we are to ask taxpayers to pay higher salaries and give greater support to teachers in general, which I believe we should do, we must assure them that the very best teachers will be recognized and rewarded while those who do not measure up will be removed.

Most importantly, we must all ask ourselves how we can look at our children and feel good about saying anything to them other than, "We did everything we could to make sure you had the very best possible teachers and that no one who was in charge of your education and well being was not fully up to the task of advancing your growth as a human being."

Principals

If you visit many schools, you can recognize almost immediately the influence of the principal. Skilled, dedicated leaders show great pride in their institutions, support and inspire the teachers, know and care for the students and respect and involve parents. When an active and engaged principal enters a classroom the students and teacher welcome them and the principal can point with pride to what the teacher and the students are doing in the class.

By comparison, principals who are ineffective or disengaged do not know what is happening in the classes, do not set high expectations for the teachers, students or the parents, and do not seem connected or committed to the day to day life and flow of the institution.

As the academic leader of the school, it is the principal who sets the standards and provides the model for everyone else. Unfortunately, far too little attention is given to the education, training, selection, supervision, support and recognition of principals. And far too much of the principals' time is taken up in activities that have very little to do with their role as academic leaders.

With all the other things they have to do, many principals spend less than a few hours per year in the classrooms of their teachers. How can principals be effective in supporting and evaluating the quality of teaching if they rarely actually watch teachers at work?

Principal Selection and Training

Just as we need to set high standards for teacher selection and training, we must be even more rigorous in choosing and preparing principals. Administrative talent and the ability to recognize and mentor teachers are not skills that people are born with and not everyone who wants to go into administration is qualified or suited to do so. Just as the place to start to improve teacher quality is through pre-selection and screening, the same applies to principals.

We must be far more selective in determining who enters training as academic leaders, and, once in such programs, there must be high standards and very close supervision. At present, no national standards exist by which to assess and recognize highly qualified principals.

One proposal to address this involves establishment of a program for principals modeled along the lines of the National Board for Professional Teaching Standards. This entity would establish national standards based on empirical studies of administrator effectiveness then implement comprehensive rigorous measures that motivated principals could seek to achieve. As with teachers, the program would be voluntary but there would be incentives to participate including support for the costs of program involvement and the possibility of financial benefits if one achieves national certification.

Empowering Principals

If Principals are to be able to do their jobs as academic leaders, they must have the time, resources, authority and support to do so. This means tasks such as basic financial matters and building maintenance are delegated to staff who are specifically trained and assigned to do them.

Principals must then be given, and must use well, the time necessary to observe, monitor and mentor their teaching staff. As leaders, principals must also have the authority to take necessary actions to reward outstanding performance and remediate or remove faculty or other staff who are not meeting the highest standards. This does not mean due process and necessary accountability should be abandoned. However it does mean that the extraordinarily long and wrenching process required to dismiss low quality teachers or to reward high quality teachers must be made more efficient and fair to all concerned.

Empowering principals also means they should not have to live in fear of lawsuits for exercising reasonable and responsible disciplinary actions. Too often a few extremely disruptive or even dangerous students create havoc in schools and it can be unreasonably difficult for principals or others to determine that those students cannot remain in the school. While we should make efforts to provide services to children in need, doing so at the risk and expense of everyone else is not prudent or fair and we have to give principals the authority to make decisions about removing students when necessary.

Schools

Most schools are too big and too expensive. If we have a choice between investing money in buildings or in the people who work there, we should spend the money on the people. If we have the choice between building a large school for thousands of children or a smaller, local school for fewer students, we should choose the smaller school.

Good teachers can find ways to teach and inspire students in almost any setting. Bad teachers will not succeed in even the most expensive and sophisticated environments. Throwing money into large, ultramodern, architecturally inspiring structures or the latest high tech gadgets will do far less to educate our kids than will investing money in the training, support and pay of quality teachers, administrators and staff.

Smaller Schools

Some years ago a comprehensive study was performed to look at the differences between "Big Schools and Small Schools." At the time, there was a movement, which continues today, to build very large schools holding thousands of students.

What the Big School/Small School research and numerous similar studies have since found was that students at smaller schools were much more likely to be involved in school activities and to be involved in more activities. What is more, the kids at the smaller schools felt more connected to their peers and to their teachers.

This finding really should not be surprising. If we think for a second about the challenge facing teachers or administrators, in a school with several thousand students, it is simply not humanly possible to get to know or even recognize all of the students. On the other hand, in a school of a few hundred students, the teachers and administrators have a much better chance of building a relationship with the students and their families. Students in small schools also have a better chance of playing a role in extracurricular activities because each person in a smaller school is needed for the teams, bands, clubs, choirs and other opportunities.

School Uniforms

To make the jobs of teachers, parents and students easier, we need to promote simple, modest and affordable student uniforms for all schools. I would almost certainly have rebelled mightily against this idea myself when I was young, but I have visited every high school in my Congressional district on many occasions and I can tell you first hand that, frankly, far too many of our young boys are coming to school dressed like gangsters or slobs and too many young women are dressing in scanty, extremely revealing clothing.

This sets a bad example, puts pressure on parents who cannot afford the latest styles, and it distracts from the real reason students are there to begin with. Modest, affordable school uniforms would make everyone's job much easier.

To those who argue that this would stifle the individual creativity of the students, I would suggest first that they visit a local high school or junior high and see if they are not as shocked as I often am at how students are dressing (or in some cases scarcely dressing).

Let the creativity of our young people manifest itself instead through music, science, writing, art, athletics, community service or any of countless other more constructive pursuits. And give our parents some support in not having to fight with their children about what they will wear to school or how much they can afford in the family budget.

School Safety and a Positive Environment

The final point to be made about schools is that they must be safe and supportive places to learn. This means children must not fear they will be the victims of bullying, hazing, or crime when they attend school. Allowing an unsafe physical or emotional environment in schools contributes to a host of problems including absenteeism, dropouts and lasting, lifelong emotional scarring of the victims and perpetrators.

In order to promote safer schools, all students, and their parents must be told explicitly that any conduct which jeopardizes the safety of the learning environment will not be tolerated. Early signs of problems must be identified promptly and interventions through skilled counselors, working closely with parents and faculty, must be directed to help remediate any problem behaviors.

Recognizing that it is not always possible to correct behaviors for all children, there must be practical, fair and constructive ways to remove from the regular school environment children whose behavior cannot be improved. For these children, specialized alternative educational opportunities should be provided so their needs are met without jeopardizing the learning environment for others.

Administration and Bureaucracy

We should vigorously cut the educational bureaucracy at every level - local, state and Federal and invest the money instead on teachers, principals and others who have direct contact with students.

As a member of the Congress, let me speak first about the Federal bureaucracy. Simply put, I do not think the Federal Department of Education has done a great deal of good in recent years. That may be changing with a new administration, but the record of the prior regime was not encouraging.

At state and local levels as well, close scrutiny should be given to the amount of administrative overhead in the budgets. In particular, redundancies and ineffective programs should be identified and eliminated. What is more, program evaluations should be conducted to ask teachers, principals, parents and others to identify what benefits or lack thereof are coming from the bureaucracy. Based on this evaluation, spending that is not producing results should be redirected and positions that are not contributing to actual improved outcomes should be eliminated.

School Boards

Since we are talking about education, here is a test that almost every one of us would likely fail – Name the members of your local school board and tell at least one fact about them relevant to their work on the board.

Fortunately, in spite of the fact that most voters could not answer this question with even one name, most school board members are nevertheless dedicated, caring people who overall do a good job for their districts. But this is more a matter of good fortune than an intentional result of how school boards are selected or function.

Considering the importance of local school boards, we need to do a much better job of informing the public about who board members are and the roles they play. We also must dramatically improve the information that is provided to the public about candidates for school boards during elections.

Providing more information in voters' pamphlets, providing school board candidates space on election websites, televising board meetings and other measures would all be improvements over current practices.

While doing a better job of informing voters about school boards and members, we also have an opportunity to give more support the board members themselves. One particularly promising effort to do so is the "Iowa lighthouse" project, which is working to identify and disseminate best practices to school boards across the nation. This project, which grew out of research conducted with school boards, has now expanded to a number of other states.

The Lighthouse project is not only encouraging because it is addressing what has perhaps been the single most overlooked element of our educational enterprise. It is also doing so by using sound research and assessing real world applications of that research.

Funding

One of the shameful aspects of our current educational effort nationwide is the profound and unjust inequities in the funding and resources available to children in certain districts versus others. If we honestly believe that every child in America should start with equal opportunities to make the most of their talents and motivation, it is simply unjust and wrong that some children attend dilapidated schools that are completely lacking in basic essentials.

For example, I have visited schools, especially in inner cities and rural areas, that have no laboratory space or equipment to teach science, lack adequate libraries, offer no musical equipment or space, and have no vocational training facilities whatsoever. By comparison, other students have virtually every opportunity and the very latest buildings and equipment at their disposal.

As I have emphasized throughout this chapter, I do not believe that throwing more money at new buildings or technology the solution, but we should make a national commitment to ensure that certain basics are available to every student in the country regardless of where they live or the wealth of their parents or specific district.

This will require a joint Federal, state, and local effort and will demand a substantial overhaul of current funding mechanisms. One such change is to de-link school funding from real estate taxes which tend to dramatically favor wealthy neighborhoods and districts over others.

Some have suggested that one source of funds for improving schools could be transportation dollars. The rationale for this is that many people who move outside of cities or live far from their place of employment do so in order to have their children attend better schools. If money were invested in improving the quality of schools and education throughout the nation, including in inner cities and rural areas, the transportation costs of those who relocate based on school quality could be substantially reduced.

Another intriguing suggestion put forth by a friend is to encourage parents who currently pay for their children to attend private school to instead invest the same amount in their local public schools. The money this would generate for public education would allow everyone's children to have better opportunities and strengthen our society as a whole. Given the state of some of our public schools today this proposal may not seem appealing to some parents, but if many of the other reforms described in this chapter were implemented, it might become much more compelling and viable for parents to invest in public, rather than private, education.

The Curriculum

While working to improve the quality of teachers, administrators, funding, and buildings, we should also change the curriculum by establishing voluntary national curricula combined with individualized instruction.

The U.S. Census Bureau reports that 40 million Americans, about 14 percent of the population, move each year[12]. This number includes nearly 9 million school age children. In some schools in my Congressional district, turnover of students from year to year exceeds forty percent.

This mobility presents substantial obstacles to our children and our educational system. With each new move, children not only have to adjust to the social and emotional challenges of new homes, schools, teachers, and friends, they also have to adapt to a different curriculum, different classes, and different

---

[12] *See* http://www.census.gov/prod/2004pubs/p20-549.pdf

textbooks. When a new student enters a school, the teachers, counselors and others have to assess the child's educational level and needs. This is unnecessary, expensive, inefficient and terribly hard for students and their families and for teachers and schools.

To avoid this expense and inefficiency, we should have a single, national curriculum with standard textbooks, educational software and technological aids for each of the major subjects we expect our children to master. There should also be a coordinated and confidential electronic record sharing system so schools, with parental permission and appropriate safeguards, can easily exchange academic records when students enter or leave a district.

With a consistent national curriculum, when students move from one district to another or one state to another, they can take up in their new school right where they left off in the prior one. They will be familiar with the books and other material, the courses will be taught in the same sequence, there will be no need for special testing each time a new student enters a school, and grade levels and courses will be comparable across schools.

A consistent national curriculum will also make it possible to train teachers consistently across the nation in course content and pedagogical approaches. Substitute teachers will especially benefit from this approach because there will be predictability and familiarity with what is going on in a classroom at a given level and point in time.

I recognize that this proposal may seem revolutionary in our country, which tends to leave curriculum and content up to local school districts or states. However, consistent national curricula are the norm rather than the exception in most of the foreign nations which are exceeding ours in test scores and rates of graduation. If other nations can do this and achieve success, surely we can too.

Not only can we do it, we should. It is in our national interest to know that all of our children are achieving in critical subject areas, and it is in our national interest to reduce the costs and inefficiencies in our educational system.

Individualized Instruction

While advocating a consistent national curriculum, two critical elements must also be present. First, we need to place much greater emphasis on individualized instruction. Second, it is essential that teacher creativity and spontaneity not be sacrificed.

These two principles may seem to be inconsistent with a standard national curriculum, but they are not. Individualized instruction is no less likely to occur with a national curriculum than it is with a locally selected course sequence. Indeed, individualized instruction is all too rare today under the standard regime of local control. This situation has been made worse by the requirements of "No Child Left Behind".

We need to place greater emphasis on individualized instruction and assistance because the normal curve of abilities is real and there are many different curves for many different abilities. To expect students who are largely grouped by age to all grasp information at similar rates is unrealistic. I know this not only professionally, as a clinical psychologist and teacher, but personally as the father of fraternal twin boys who differ greatly in abilities, interests, motivations and so forth.

Lumping all children together by age and teaching them as a group inevitably leaves the more capable or motivated students bored while those students who are struggling feel frustrated and lose confidence. This results in inefficient learning and dissatisfaction for most students. It also contributes to discipline problems as bored, frustrated or belittled students act out.

The key is first of all to change how we approach teaching and give teachers adequate time and class sizes to work individually with students. Along with this, we should make much more effective use of technology to allow students to study and advance at their own pace with targeted, individualized instructor help and focus to help each student succeed. This is especially important in areas such as mathematics and science.

The good news is that a number of proven programs exist which do exactly this. Under this approach, students work at individual computers completing lessons targeted specifically for their personal stage of knowledge and understanding. As concepts and skills are mastered, the students move to the next stage of learning.

Rather than giving all students the same lecture at the blackboard, teachers monitor the progress of each individual student from a central terminal and can identify when someone is having difficulty. The teacher then works one on one, using the technology as an aid, to help the individual student solve the particular challenge or learning goal he or she is working on at that moment.

To further enhance this approach, each student should have a personal laptop computer that is theirs to keep, to bring to the classroom and take home for homework and further study. Much progress has been made toward this possibility already, not only within our own nation but worldwide. Indeed, the One Laptop Per Child (OLPC) effort has produced a durable, inexpensive laptop that is equipped with educational software and wireless internet capability.

The idea of each student having his or her own laptop is much different than the more typical practice in which large investments are made to place desktop computers that are fixed in place in special computer labs within the school. Too often I have visited schools to see tremendously expensive computer labs filled with the very latest (though soon to be outdated or down) technology in front of which sit terribly bored or passive students.

I asked the creator of the OLPC, Dr. Nicholas Negroponte about this observation and his answer was telling – "Sure" he said, "The kids look disinterested because the computer isn't theirs. They don't have any real ownership with it. Their relationship to the device and to learning changes when they have a laptop of their own."

Dr. Negroponte also emphasized how personalized computers for every student is a tremendous boost to lower income students who are otherwise at a tremendous disadvantage compared to wealthier peers whose families can afford the very latest in technology.

Recently the OLCP effort has encountered some difficulties in its efforts to distribute computers to the poor worldwide, but I believe the concept and effort should be expanded within our own country with a goal of individual laptops for every child and individualized instruction within four years.

Having one's own laptop makes individualized instruction in the classroom much easier and allows every student the chance to take the device and the lessons home for further study. This possibility of enhanced home study raises another issue, which is one of the most important of all educational reforms.

Time on Task

The single most important variable across all studies of human learning is time on task. Even with the very best teachers, curricula, technology and lessons, it still takes time for us to learn things. All other things being equal, the person who spends more time studying something is more likely to master it.

Compared to other nations, on average students in U.S. schools spend much less time on education. Our school days tend to be shorter as are our school years. For example, the international average of instructional days in the school year is 193, compared to a U.S. average of 180. The U.S. average compares even less favorably to the highest nations, with Korea, Japan and China reporting 225, 223, and 221 instructional days per year respectively.

Translated into instructional hours per year, our nation fares better, with an international average of 1027 compared to the U.S. average of a better than average 1061. However, this relatively more positive figure should be considered in the context of research showing that distributed practice is generally superior to concentrated practice for learning. In other words, given a choice it is likely better to distribute learning time across more days rather than through more intensive hours in fewer days.

Beyond the study time spent in school, our nation also lags behind others in numbers of hours of extra school instruction. The average for Korean students is 2.2 hours and for Japanese students 1.8 hours per day beyond school. This compares to .9 hours on average for U.S. students.

These figures raise the obvious suggestion for how to improve the learning of U.S. students – more time on task. The school day should be longer, the school year should be longer, and there should be more time dedicated to learning away from school.

These changes would require several other modifications. Teachers would deserve substantial pay increases to compensate for greater time on the job. Teachers would also need more time in their day for lesson planning, grading papers and so forth.

With longer school days and years students would need some form of break for physical recreation during the school day. If properly managed, this might help reduce the epidemic of childhood obesity and associated health problems that are plaguing our youth.

In order to help make time away from school more effective, the previous discussion of personalized computers would be a great help. Online tutors, dedicated Webcasts coordinated with specific classes, and interactive methods to help parents help their children learn are all experimental possibilities that are producing encouraging results.

The key to these changes is to recognize that our traditional schedules for the school day and the school year have more to do with antiquated tradition, i.e. getting the kids free to work in the harvest on the farm each summer, than they do with current realities and demands.

No one is suggesting that children spend every waking hour studying, but there is clearly room for much more productive use of time. It is also clear that our children will increasingly be competing with people from other nations who are indeed spending their time more productively.

Testing

How do we know if our children are actually learning the things they are supposed to learn, mastering the skills they will need to succeed?

As someone who used to study and teach about educational and psychological testing before serving in Congress, I believe our approach to educational testing has simultaneously been too soft on children and too hard. Too soft because many people in our society have an attitude that what matters most is how children feel about themselves regardless of how they conduct themselves or what they know or can do. As a result we tolerate indolence, irresponsibility and ignorance and give young people the impression that education is or should be easy and they do not have to meet or be judged by any external standards.

On the other hand, we have been too hard because we have, from virtually the moment children begin school, repeatedly tested them on standardized, norm-based tests with the inevitable result that half our children and their parents are told from very early in their lives they are below average. This stems from the nature of norm-based standardized testing and from the definition of "average" itself. The result is incredibly dispiriting to children and their parents while at the same time doing almost nothing constructive to further the educational aspirations or motivation of the children or their parents.

What is needed is an approach that sets high standards for students then provides the tools and support needed to meet those standards. The solution lies in a process known as adaptive testing that utilizes computers to tailor each test to each individual student.

Rather than having every child take every test item, beginning with very easy and progressing to very difficult, adaptive testing begins with items of mid level difficulty for most students in a given age. If a child passes the first item given, the computer selects slightly more difficult items to administer. If a student fails an initial item, the computer goes down a few degrees in difficulty and gives a less challenging item. This approach takes much less time and is far less frustrating because more advanced students do not waste time with easier items while students who are less advanced do not get frustrated by repeated failures.

The result is more efficient and accurate results that allow the teaching of each student to be matched with that student's abilities. This form of teaching also allows an individual student's progress to be monitored throughout the school year. From an evaluation perspective, this approach allows for assessment of each student compared to their own earlier subject based test scores to see how they as individuals have progressed not simply how they stand relative to everyone else.

Special Education

It is not fully possible to understand the experiences of parents or children who have special needs unless one has been in that position personally. Depending on the specific needs and abilities of the child, the challenges of even the most basic activities of daily living can be extreme. The difficulties of education, on top of the other demands of life, can be insurmountable.

As a compassionate, caring society we have a moral obligation to help assist those who have special needs. In many instances schools, if given adequate funding and personnel, can provide the best opportunity to assist children with unique needs. This is particularly the case for children with learning disabilities or physical impairments that do not excessively impair their cognitive or behavioral performance.

We must recognize, however, that educating these children will take extra resources, including time, staff and materials. Those resources must be provided for as part of our educational funding. That investment and the ability to participate in regular schooling is worthwhile because it helps individuals maximize their potential and contribute constructively in life.

Unfortunately Federal mandates have required schools to provide education for students with special needs but the

Federal government has never provided the funding necessary to meet those needs. That must change.

We should also recognize the unfortunate reality that for some students the nature and extent of their cognitive or emotional challenges are such that participation in ordinary school settings is not in their best interest of in the interest of other students.

I am aware that this runs contrary to movements toward "mainstreaming", but I have visited many school and classes in which special needs students with profound behavioral or cognitive impairments were present in the classroom but were not necessarily benefiting from that placement. Forcing the educational system to meet the needs of students who are unmanageably disruptive, dangerous or profoundly cognitively impaired in regular classrooms does a disservice to all concerned, the students with special needs and the rest of their peers as well.

Recognizing this fact does not mean we can or should abandon our responsibility to help these young people and their families. Instead, for this group of students we must develop viable alternatives beyond regular school settings. This may mean a return to special schools or alternative "school within school" structures. It also means dedicated and specially trained staff must be available and financially compensated for giving this group focused attention and education.

Making these adaptations also means the educational goals should be tailored to the unique needs and talents of these students. It makes no sense and is unrealistic to demand, as the No Child Left Behind law does, that a school must try to make even profoundly disabled students achieve at average or better levels on academic tests or the entire school will be labeled as "failing."

Far more appropriate in many instances is to seek training in skills of daily living associated with simple trade, craft or service work. The goal should not be to ensure that every student should be at the same minimum level academically. Rather, it should be to help each individual to maximize their ability and opportunity to the greatest extent possible in the most caring and best suited settings.

Exceptional Talents and Motivation

Just as we must give students with unique cognitive or behavioral challenges the support they need to maximize their potential, we must do the same students with exceptional abilities. Not everyone in our society is fortunate enough to be born a genius, but we are all fortunate to benefit from the discoveries and contributions of those who are. Behind the achievements in technology, health, science and other fields that we often take for granted, are extraordinarily smart and motivated people who came up with and perfected products that have profoundly altered and improved the quality of our lives.

Because we all benefit from the contributions of exceptionally talented and highly motivated individuals, it is in everyone's interest to nurture that talent and motivation in our educational system. In fact, the "return on investment" from programs designed for this purpose may be among the highest in our educational enterprise.

To a significant degree, the adoption of a national curriculum combined with individualized instruction will go a long way toward supporting the most talented students. Able to work at their own pace and with appropriate guidance from qualified teachers, the very brightest young people can press ahead through the curriculum as rapidly as their talents, interests and drive will take them.

This opportunity can and should be supplemented by added opportunities for creative discovery and applied learning at higher levels. Wherever possible, such opportunities should be made available within the schools and we should implement specialized teacher training for such programs as part of the educational major.

We must also recognize that in many instances the most highly talented and motivated students will be, to put it bluntly, smarter than many of their teachers. This is not an easy thing to admit, and many teachers might find it offensive to state it so directly, but it happens to be a fact.

We should celebrate that fact and work with it rather than denying it and obstructing the progress of our students. Teachers should be trained in how to recognize and work with exceptionally bright students and in ways of helping maximize their abilities.

We also need to find opportunities beyond the school setting to help particularly talented students work with accomplished mentors in higher education or applied business or other settings. Facilitating applied and real world learning opportunities for students can be a tremendous incentive for further study and can give students a chance to advance their learning not only more rapidly but in ways that simply cannot be achieved within the ordinary resources of schools.

Career and Technical Education

Politicians, policy makers and our educational system place tremendous emphasis on and invest heavily in college and university education. As valuable as this education can be, our society as whole gives far too little attention or respect to career and technical, or, what used to be called "vocational" education.

As I meet with employers throughout the country, I hear again and again that there is a severe shortage of skilled workers. At a time of high unemployment, with many people needing and wanting work, employers consistently report that finding trained and reliable workers is one of their greatest challenges. Many of those workers need skills not taught in universities but best acquired through career and technical education and apprenticeship programs.

At the same time, an alarming number of students drop out of high school before graduation. These numbers are especially troubling among certain minority groups and in lower income urban or rural areas. For many of those who might otherwise fail to complete their academic schooling, the "hands on learning" opportunities of career and technical education are often a much better match with interests and abilities and offer constructive opportunities for both education and work.

Several measures will improve our support for career and technical education. First, we must get the word out that career and technical fields offer well-paying jobs with strong benefits and real opportunities for advancement. In fact, in many instances the starting wages of skilled machinists, electricians, advanced medical technicians and others exceeds the earnings of college graduates. This information needs to reach students, parents, teachers and school counselors. The latter, in particular, should approach students interested in career and technical education with equal respect and support as they would for college track students.

We must also ensure that adequate career and technical educational facilities are offered within our schools and that interested students have the chance to elect and pursue these opportunities. In recent years, Federal mandates and funding have driven attention away from career and technical opportunities. This trend needs to be reversed.

Along with information about job opportunities and wages, greater awareness is also needed regarding the level of skill and training that goes into many career and technical positions. A friend who is a journeyman electrical worker has a bumper sticker that reads "Apprenticeship – The Original Four Year Degree." Skilled career and technical workers earn high wages because their training and knowledge warrant it.

Further support for career and technical education must come from employers, labor unions and other groups with a vested interest in having skilled workers. Indeed, many unions and employer groups are already leading such efforts and their involvement deserves much greater recognition and support at all levels of government and the educational system.

Finally, we must make certain that financial aid and other forms of Federal and local support give adequate attention to career and technical education.

College

I once heard a joke that Bill Gates was planning to return to college and complete his Bachelors degree. He'd read that a college degree could increase earning by up to forty percent. At his income level, that's a lot of money.

The example of Mr. Gates notwithstanding, a college education has the potential to be of great value not only financially but in helping young people develop in a host of other ways. It is also true, however, that too many people are accruing too much debt and getting too little in return from their college experience.

Ask any member of Congress or other employer about the difficulty of finding college graduates who have strong writing and critical thinking skills and you are likely to hear a litany of frustrations and concerns. Considering how much students, their parents and our society, including the taxpayers, put into paying for college, this is unacceptable.

Colleges and Universities should certify in writing, signed by the faculty and the University Provost and President that every graduate possesses strong skills in writing, reasoning, and mathematics, plus a clear understanding of the basic documents and principals of our constitutional democratic republic. These skills and knowledge should be the *sine qua non* of graduation. Anyone who lacks them should not receive a degree.

This commitment should be absolutely clear before students enroll and pay their tuition. The college curriculum, courses, and teachers should then be geared toward developing, assessing, and strengthening the core skills and knowledge for all students.

Why emphasize the issue of performance and knowledge before talking about tuition costs, student loans, scholarships, and such matters? Because if the government is going to invest taxpayer dollars in grants, loans and other funding for higher education, the taxpayers have a right to expect that they are getting a quality result in return.

There are many possible ways in which the connection between financial support and demonstrated outcomes can be established. For example, student loans and scholarships could only be granted for students to attend institutions that meet specific performance criteria. And eligibility for continued scholarships and loans to students should be linked to the student's performance each quarter or semester.

As further incentives to academic institutions, other forms of Federal support, such as research grants, might also be linked to demonstrated overall or focused institutional success as reflected in the numbers of students meeting standards.

Funding Higher Education

With individual and institutional financial support directly linked to performance outcomes, it then makes sense to address how student aid should be provided, what form it should take and who should receive it.

Our educational aid system needs two fundamental changes. It should be simplified and it should reward financial responsibility and hard work.

Throughout this book I have described the difficult challenge of providing assistance to those deserving and in need without simultaneously punishing those who have acted responsibly and made wise decisions throughout their lives. There are few places where this is more evident than in financial aid for higher education.

Because much of our financial aid for higher education is related to need, families who have done the right thing and invested for their children's college education often feel deep frustration and resentment when they learn that because of their frugality, they are not eligible for many government scholarships and loans. We need to change this by doing more to reward, rather than punish, savings.

Simplification of financial aid is also essential because the current system is based on a confusing array of public and private scholarships, grants, loans, waivers, tax credits, tax deferred savings and many others. For most parents and students, tracking all this is difficult and, as a result, many legitimate opportunities are not used.

The first step toward simplification should be to disconnect educational support and incentives from the tax code. It is too complex, biased toward the wealthy and inefficient. Other proposals in this book for doing away with the tax code entirely would make this happen automatically, but if those proposals are not adopted, it still makes sense to stop linking college funding to tax complexities.

In an earlier chapter it was suggested that some level of matching money should be provided for low income workers who set aside money for savings. This should apply particularly to those families who save for their children's education.

We should also do more to encourage students themselves to work and save for their own education. We could create a special matching fund to augment earnings of students by investing in special savings accounts for students who maintain good grades and work to help pay for their educational costs.

Turn Off the Electronics

Beyond all the other changes recommended in this chapter, the single most economical and beneficial thing we can do to improve our children's education, and possibly their health, is turn off the television, video games and other electronic media and have children read, exercise and use their minds in other ways.

Television has always had enormous potential to transform education and our society for the good, but in actuality it has had a tremendously destructive impact on children and on our culture. The damage is caused by how much we watch, what we watch and how we watch.

How Much We Watch

A comprehensive study by the Kaiser Family Foundation[13] found that among U.S. children age 8 to 18, when time spent watching TV, videos and DVDs, listening to music, texting, surfing the web, social networking etc. is combined, average total media exposure is more than seven and a half hours per day. This compares to just 28 minutes per day consuming print media which, the authors of the study emphasize, is often done while the TV or other media is also turned on.

Such large amounts of time spent consuming electronic media results from a combination of factors. These include the increased mobility of media thanks to ipods, smart phones, mp3 players and other inventions, the fact that homes now have an average number of three TV sets and 71 percent of young people have their own TV, and the growing use of online media in general. What's more, fewer than half (46 percent) of 8 to 18 year olds reported that their families had any rules governing TV use.

The same survey also looked at self reported performance in school and found that in general young people who reported higher levels of media use reported lower grades than those with less use. What is more, a number of emotional and psychological variables, such as how the young people feel about themselves and life in general, showed a similar relationship.

Among the many adverse effects of such excessive time watching television is obesity. Although the Kaiser study did not find a relationship between amount of media time and self reported physical activity, numerous other studies[14] have shown strong relationships between amount of television watched and the likelihood of obesity. Particularly noteworthy, and troubling, is evidence that this relationship can begin as early as preschool years.

---

[13]*See* http://www.kff.org/entmedia/7251.cfm
[14] *See* http://www.mediafamily.org/facts/facts_tvandobchild.shtml

What We Watch

If a demented research psychologist put children for hours a day in front of a machine that projected violent and sexually provocative images, society would be outraged and insist the study be stopped immediately. Yet that is exactly what happens every day in homes across America and far from protesting it millions of people pay handsomely for the service.

Should we really be surprised at the results? Should we really be shocked at the levels of teen pregnancies, violence, suicide, eating disorders and drug use? And should we really be surprised if, having been fed a non-stop diet of television stimulation, children aren't as motivated or interested in their classes or homework?

What is needed is something that is never talked about – Discernment. All of us, especially as parents, need to ask ourselves, "Is this really good for me and my family to watch or do?"

Too often we simply "channel surf" and end up accepting whatever is least bad at the time. And far too often the choices on the TV, in spite of having hundreds of channels to choose from now, are worthless or destructive.

Discernment means we ask ourselves, "Is it really a good use of my time to watch two people beat each other senseless? Is it really good for me and my children to be bombarded by an endless stream of advertisements suggesting we cannot be happy unless we own more things or take new medications? Is it really good to fill our brains with stupid jingles? Is it really productive to watch 24 Hour News programming that is so focused on the latest tragedy or scandals, most of which we can do nothing about?"

Discernment means if the answers to these questions is "No!" (which it really should be most of the time), then we find something better to do with our time, lives and families.

How We Watch

As troublesome as the content on TV, the challenge for education is at least as much in how the process of watching television affects young minds.

Watching television is inherently a passive activity. What happens on the screen is completely independent of anything the viewer does. We have come to take that experience for granted, but it is by no means "normal" for human development and it may well have lasting and adverse neurological and cognitive impacts.

We know from countless research studies that the human brain develops as the result of interactions with the world. When research animals have been placed in experimental conditions that do not let them interact with the world but force them to merely observe passively, their brains do not develop normally. We learn to grasp, crawl, walk, throw, see, hear, speak and think because we act on the world and get feedback, sometimes good, sometimes painful, from that action. We learn, and our brains develop, through action and experience. We are not meant to be passive observers - we are meant to be active explorers. But television, by its nature, breeds passivity.

In saying all this, I know all too well that it won't be popular. Some years ago in fact we did a "focus group" in which we asked people how they felt about certain educational proposals. The idea of encouraging people to spend less time watching TV was one of those proposals and it drew the most strident and angry responses. It is so much easier to blame someone else, leave it to teachers, complain about "kids these days" or "society" or whatever else is convenient, than it is to do the simple, revolutionary act of turning off the box.

One person said, and this is an exact quote, "Who the hell is this guy to tell us to turn off the TV. In our house the TV's on all the time except at dinner, and even then we watch if there's something good on."

No one is suggesting that government should "FORCE" anyone to turn off the TV. The fact remains, however, that choices have consequences, time is limited and our children and society are being harmed. The fact too is that our children will have to compete with children from around the world who are studying and working much harder and who research shows are starting to outpace us in critical knowledge and skills.

It is hard to believe that at the end of their lives, most people today would list as one of their chief regrets that they did not spend enough time watching television. In fact, it might well be the reverse and that some of the things that people might regret not having done they might now find the time and energy to pursue.

The Meaning of Graduation

To conclude this chapter we should ask something that should actually at the very core of how we analyze any aspect of our education system. That is, "What is the purpose of our education system?"

The best answer I know is this, "To prepare young people so they will maximize their personal talents and interests, make good decisions about their lives, provide for their families, and have the knowledge, character and skills to accept and fulfill the responsibility of participation as citizens in a constitutional democratic republic."

Everything we do should in some way reflect this fundamental purpose. Graduation ceremonies should be the ritual through which we convey to our young people the sacred responsibility of participation as citizens in a constitutional democratic republic.

The Metric System and the Meaning of a Republic

One last note that I simply cannot resist before moving on – it is high time we adopt the metric system in our nation and begin training for it in our schools nationwide today. Whatever historical reasons we may have for not going metric, we can no longer afford the luxury of such cultural chauvinism and ignorance. In fact, if one wanted a simple but pretty good test of how well our schools are doing and how well informed our public is, we could simply ask why and how we should use metric rather than English measures.

We should also ask what it means to "Pledge allegiance to the Flag of the United States of America and to the Republic for which it stands?" Just what is a "Republic" that we are pledging allegiance to every day without really thinking or understanding? I have made hundreds of school visits during my time in Congress and when I ask this question more often than not only one or two students can give the correct answer and often their teachers don't know what a Republic is either.

When people can answer these questions, perhaps more importantly when people think critically enough to ask such questions, when they can understand and use metric measures in their daily lives, and when they have a sense of what the fundamental principal of our government really is, we will have made at least some significant progress. We will also have made an important stride toward better preparing our students and our society for this century and the global economy.

10.
IMMIGRATION

Amerika has long been enriched by immigrants. For the sake of our economy and our security we need to continue and strengthen that tradition. At the same time, however, sovereign nations have a right and responsibility to ensure their borders are secure and to admit only those legally allowed to enter or remain.

For far too long, our borders have been anything but secure with no reliable means of determining whether people have come in or are staying lawfully. There has also been insufficient national discussion about how overall immigration is affecting the size of our population and the implications on issues ranging from resource consumption to quality of life.

We need a comprehensive approach and significant reforms to deal with both lawful and unlawful immigration. I recognize some of what I will propose in this chapter will undoubtedly generate strong feelings. Nonetheless, I make these proposals because there are certain realities of immigration that will profoundly impact our nation and that must not be ignored.

Making Thoughtful Choices On Population Size

The foremost impact of immigration is extraordinary population growth. To those who find any proposal to limit immigration troublesome, it is fair to ask honestly how they believe we should deal with the following facts.

The Census Bureau estimates that at the current rate of population growth, the U.S. will reach 439 million people by the year 2050. That is an increase of 135 million people, 44 percent growth, in just 40 years. To put this number into context, it is nearly the equivalent of the entire current population of Mexico and Canada moving here.

This has profound impacts on virtually every aspect of our society, from the size of our cities to the demands for education, health care, water, energy, waste treatment and other infrastructure. To meet this demand, it has been estimated that 36,000 new schools would have to be constructed, highways would need to handle 106 million more vehicles, and 52 million housing units would need to be constructed. Such population growth also impacts quality of life, as it becomes difficult if not impossible to find places of solitude and wilderness.

Because the size of our population will influence so much of our nation's and our children's future, it is time for a serious discussion of how fast we believe our population should increase (if at all) and whether there should be a maximum desirable population level for the future.

Both lawful and unlawful immigration must be central to this discussion because immigration plus births to immigrants is the most prominent driving factor in growing the U.S. population. Indeed, some estimates suggest that immigration will account for 63 percent of population growth in the next 50 years.

In thinking about our own population growth, we must also recognize that immigration is significantly driven by overpopulation elsewhere in the world. If we want to deal with population growth in our own country we have to limit immigration. And if we hope to limit immigration we must work to limit population growth worldwide.

In talking about the rate and levels of population growth, the issue is not so much where people come from. Rather, it is about how many people we can and should have in this nation. If we do not have this honest and frank discussion, without either undercurrents of prejudice or reactionary charges of racism, the nation will change in ways that we have not imagined or consciously chosen and the effects of which we could have, and should have, foreseen and managed more purposefully.

My own belief is that we should seek to dramatically reduce the rate of population growth from all sources. In fact, national policy should seek to stabilize the nation's population at levels not significantly higher than current numbers. This goal should be one of the key principles around which all immigration policies are framed, but we must also keep in mind that immigration is not the sole cause of excessive U.S. population growth.

Ending Racism and Xenophobia

While confronting the impact of population growth, we must also recognize that the U.S. is the most diverse nation on earth. That is part of our greatest strength and something to be proud of. People of different faiths, ethnicity, skin color, culture and ideology are all given equal opportunity and protection under our Constitution and laws.

However one addresses the immigration issue, we must vigorously oppose any prejudice or racism. Unfortunately, too many of the arguments against immigration are either overtly or implicitly racist in nature. If we confront such rhetoric, it cannot withstand scrutiny.

When one considers the risks, effort and hardship that many immigrants endure to enter America, assertions that immigrants are lazy or unwilling to work hard are obviously foolish. Consider also that some of the most brilliant and successful entrepreneurs in America today and throughout our history came here from other nations. So too, many of the discoveries and inventions in technology, health care, software, aerospace, energy, engineering and other key fields were created by the genius and dedication of people who came from other lands and have enriched ours.

If these examples are not compelling, take just a few minutes to read aloud the names and look at the faces of those who have given their lives to this nation through military service. Let those who oppose immigration on racist or jingoist grounds contemplate this list and ponder the freedoms preserved for all Americans by those whose names or ethnicity would, in the minds of some, render them ineligible to be considered citizens.

If all we have to fall back on for pride is the color of our skin or heritage of our ancestry, things totally beyond our control or responsibility, then it does not say a great deal about us as individuals. If we feel superior to others simply because they were born in a different place than we were, how much say did we have in choosing our own birthplace or parentage?

I believe personally that we need to better manage immigration, both legal and illegal, but racist and prejudiced arguments cannot be justified or defended as the basis for this need. At the same time, it is also not justified to argue that anyone who supports constraints on immigration is therefore assumed to be motivated by prejudice or racism.

Stopping Illegal Immigration

Ending illegal immigration must come from a combination of measures including reducing the external conditions that drive people to emigrate from their own countries, reducing the internal U.S. demand and rewards for illegal immigration, improved enforcement of domestic labor and employment laws, and enhanced border security. We must also completely overhaul our immigration-related Federal agencies as they are among the most dysfunctional in the entire Federal government.

Reducing the Pressures That Cause Emigration

People come to the U.S., both legally and illegally, because life is better here than where they came from. If that were not true, it would not make sense for people to emigrate from their own lands.

Many Americans cannot fully imagine the poverty, warfare, natural disasters, human rights abuses, religious persecution, prejudice, overpopulation, sexual discrimination, famine and other circumstances that immigrants to our nation have fled. If we did understand such things, it might help temper some of the hostility, prejudice and demeaning attitudes that some express about immigrants. Indeed, if American citizens had faced the same circumstances, many of us would also have made a similar choice to emigrate for the sake of our families.

Understanding these conditions will help us see the humanity of immigrants and better manage immigration because we will have a better grasp of its causes. Not all of the circumstances that drive people to emigrate from their own lands are within our power to remedy, but to the extent that we can influence and reduce those pressures, the need and desire for people to enter our nation will be reduced.

I have already discussed the problem of population growth but this cannot be overstated. I believe we must lead the world in helping other nations manage and reduce population growth. Education, particularly for young women, birth control, improved health care, strong economic policies and all the other measures that have been proven to reduce population should be strongly encouraged. Simultaneously, in our foreign relations and aid strategies we should work to help improve economic conditions and reduce human rights abuses and other dangers that drive people to emigrate from their own lands.

Reducing Domestic Demand

While conditions in other nations drive people to emigrate from their own countries, there are also incentives within our nation that bring people to the U.S. Foremost among these attractions are the chance to obtain a better paying job, the prospect of citizenship, and access to social benefits like education and health care. To better manage immigration we must deal with each of these incentives.

Employment Verification

Stemming the tide of illegal immigration depends greatly on stopping the demand for undocumented workers. If it were not possible to work and make a living without being here legally, we would see a dramatic drop in illegal immigration.

To achieve that goal we must have a reliable means of verifying who has permission to work. We must then insist that all employers pay full wages and taxes, all workers rights are protected, and there must be significant penalties for violating these laws or intentionally hiring people who are not here legally.

A National Biometric Identification Card

For these measures to succeed, we need to establish a national, tamper proof, biometric ID card that is easily verified by employers and law enforcement. This must be coupled with an accurate and reliable database that protects confidential information but can readily be accessed to verify eligibility for work, driving, voting and other rights of responsible citizenship.

To assure that such a system is possible to create with current technology, I have consulted with several leading makers of secure ID systems and they all assure me that the technology exists today to create the ID cards and manage the data base securely and economically.

With this system in place, there must be strong penalties for employers who fail to conduct the necessary background checks or knowingly hire people who lack proper identification and permission to be in our country.

I am well aware that many people have serious reservations about establishing any form of national ID card, but, frankly, I do not know any other way to ensure that employers have an easy and valid way of determining whether or not someone is legally entitled to be and work here. Social Security cards, for example, could just as well come out of a cereal box. They are easily fabricated and carry no useful or reliable identification information.

The Congress tried to deal with this issue indirectly by passing the Federal REAL ID act, which essentially passed the responsibility and largely unfunded costs of verifying citizenship on to the states. What this accomplished, beyond generating a great deal of controversy, was to put substantial unfunded financial burdens on to the states without creating a single national standard ID or a corresponding central database for verification.

Instead of REAL ID, we need a single, nationwide standard biometric ID card coupled with a central database that links directly to a citizenship and immigration database. Lawful citizens would possess one type of card, lawful visitors, such as students or guest workers, get another. Those not here lawfully should not have such identifications and, hence, should not be able to work or stay.

With tamper-proof identification cards and a reliable database, employers would be able to readily check the status of job applicants. The standard would then be absolutely clear – no valid ID and work permission, no job and no voting.

Enforcing Employment and Tax Laws and Protecting Worker's Rights

While potential workers are drawn to the U.S. by the prospect of jobs, employers are also motivated to hire them by the prospect of having a cheaper workforce. The limbo status of undocumented workers makes them easy to exploit by paying substandard wages, no benefits, not withholding payroll or income taxes, and not paying unemployment or workers compensation insurance. Immigrants can also be placed in jobs with excessively long work hours or that are hazardous.

Creation of a foolproof identification and verification system should eliminate any excuse that an employer might have to hire someone without proper documentation. Additionally, any employer who does not pay taxes, unemployment insurance, workers compensation and other costs as required by law must face strong penalties, both civil and, where appropriate, criminal sentences.

At the same time, there must be more vigorous enforcement of labor laws. All workers must have certain rights protected. Among these rights are fair wages, safe working conditions, the right to participate in unions and collective bargaining, and the right to legal recourse if an employer has not complied with the law.

These measures, if taken together, would dramatically reduce the desire and incentives of certain unscrupulous employers to exploit undocumented workers. That, in turn, would protect all workers and would level the playing field for employers who follow the laws and treat their employees fairly.

Changing the Incentive of Citizenship

In addition to the prospect of employment, illegal immigration to the U.S. is also driven by desires to obtain citizenship after one arrives. This route to citizenship is profoundly unfair to those who have waited and gone through the legal process of obtaining citizenship.

In order to reduce this incentive for illegal immigration it must be absolutely clear that starting after a date certain anyone who is in this nation illegally and who lacks the requisite identification card described earlier will have no access to legal employment or citizenship. It must also be clear in the law that if individuals are identified as lacking requisite documentation and permissions to be here, they will be deported and will thereafter face permanent denial of U.S. citizenship. If someone wishes to one day become a U.S. citizen, they must arrive at that goal legally or suffer the loss of that opportunity forever.

Furthermore, this law itself must be permanent. After it is enacted, there should be no changes, no amnesty, no subsequent alternatives - period. From the moment of enactment on, no one should enter or stay illegally in the hopes of a future amnesty because that will not happen.

Ending "Birthright" Citizenship

If U.S. citizens take a moment to count their personal blessings, citizenship in this great country must surely be among the most precious and valued. That extraordinary value is why so many people work so hard, wait so long and go through all the steps and tests necessary to legally become naturalized citizens. It is why so many of our citizens, and a great many immigrants, are willing to die to protect this nation.

Considering how precious citizenship in our nation is and how many covet it, it is fair to ask if we should reward people who crossed our borders or stayed here illegally by granting automatic citizenship, and all its benefits, for any children they give birth to while on U.S. soil?

I believe that if we want to reduce illegal immigration and deal effectively with population growth, we must stop rewarding people for coming or staying here illegally. Ending birthright citizenship would take away one of the most valuable, and, to our nation, one of the most costly of those rewards.

This change would also help save on the health care and social expenses that accompany the care and education of children who are born here by illegal immigrants. In addition, ending birthright citizenship will help prevent the wrenching scenes of parents, who lack citizenship or documentation, being separated from children who were born here and hence have citizenship and the right to stay.

The principle of birthright citizenship derives, in our nation, from the 14th amendment to the Constitution, which begins "All persons born or naturalized in the U.S. and subject to the jurisdiction thereof, are citizens of the U.S. and of the State wherein they reside."

This amendment was originally necessary to correct the Dred Scott ruling, which had held that no black of African descent, even one who had been freed, could be a citizen of the U.S. That Supreme Court ruling, perhaps the most shameful in the history of the Court, was being used even after emancipation and the Civil War as a way to deprive blacks of their legitimate rights as citizens. The 14th amendment, therefore, sought to end such abuses. It was an absolutely necessary and justified amendment at the time.

Since its ratification, many have interpreted the 14th amendment to mean that anyone born on U.S. soil received automatic and immediate citizenship regardless of the status of their parents. As this is assumed to be a constitutionally protected right, it has also been assumed that to change it in any way would require a constitutional amendment.

Some scholars, however, have pointed out that the amendment speaks not only of being born or naturalized, but also contains the phrase "and subject to the jurisdiction thereof." Without going into extensive detail of the legal precedents, some have argued that both birth and being subject to jurisdiction must apply for citizenship to accrue. Therefore, it is argued, undocumented immigrants, who are not here lawfully do not meet the second part of the test and, hence, should not receive automatic citizenship at birth.

This interpretation is controversial but it can be tested if Congress enacts legislation clarifying that the 14th amendment does not grant such citizenship. Passage of such legislation would surely generate heated debate, but it would likely be easier than amending the Constitution. If passed, there would then undoubtedly be a challenge in the Supreme Court.

To my knowledge, no such challenge has ever actually been heard by the Court in relation to such Congressional action on this matter. Hence, the Court might uphold such Congressional action or it might overturn it and require that only a further amendment to the Constitution could have the desired impact of clarifying or ending birthright citizenship. If the court should in fact determine this, then I believe efforts should be made to amend the Constitution for this purpose.

Many who would oppose such changes would argue, legitimately, that the result might adversely affect numbers of people who were born in this country in rural or impoverished areas and lack birth certificates or other documentation. This is a very real concern and needs to be addressed. There are several ways to do this, either by using alternative documentation to demonstrate extended residence here or parentage by citizens. Other options would be to "grandfather" in those born before a certain date, then set a firm date after which only those with proper documentation that parents were here lawfully at the time of birth would have access to citizenship.

Again, in its time the 14th amendment was necessary and this is in no way an argument for its overall repeal. Rather, it is a sincere effort to reduce one of the most powerful incentives for people to enter and stay without documentation. To control the size of our population, to lower the social costs of births to undocumented persons, and to preserve the precious right of citizenship for those who follow our laws, we should make these changes.

Meeting Legitimate Agriculture Workforce Needs and Dealing With the Undocumented Already Here

As difficult and important as it is to implement measures to stop illegal immigration, a more vexing challenge still is how to deal some 12 to 20 million people (the actual number is probably even higher) living within the U.S. without legal documentation.

This issue is further complicated by the fact that our agricultural industry and certain other segments of our economy have come to depend on the labor provided by immigrant workers. Indeed, when I speak with orchardists, farmers, seafood processors, and others, I often hear that if all undocumented workers were all simultaneously to leave in mass, agriculture would virtually collapse and hundreds of millions of dollars of crops would be lost.

Recognizing these realities, let us first reject as impractical and counterproductive calls to make everyone who is here without documentation a felon. Instantly creating twenty million felons would overwhelm our law enforcement and judiciary system and would distract police, sheriffs and the courts from pursuing truly dangerous and destructive crimes.

So too, imposing harsh consequences on employers without first providing reliable background checks and identification is neither fair nor practical. Neither is it prudent to suddenly deprive honest farmers and others of a workforce without viable alternatives or time to adapt.

A more prudent course of action is to distinguish between three groups of undocumented residents. One group are those who came or stayed here without legal permission or documentation, but who have ever since violated no other laws and can demonstrate that they have worked and paid taxes for at least the past several years.

A second group includes those who came or stayed illegally, but who have either not been gainfully employed or cannot demonstrate that they have been paying taxes as part of their employment. A third group includes anyone here without legal documentation who has committed serious crimes.

Considering this last group first, there is near universal agreement that anyone here without documentation who has committed a serious crime must be deported as quickly as possible to their home country. For those whose home countries will not accept them, or for whom it is not possible to identify a home country, there should be special prisons established far from population centers and with very few amenities. Those who came here illegally and committed acts of crime and violence deserve only the most basic conditions of imprisonment and their further costs to our society should be kept to the barest minimum.

What to do about the two other groups of undocumented individuals is not so clear cut. Keeping in mind the earlier call for a national biometric identification card that is required for work, and recognizing the legitimate workforce needs that are currently filled by undocumented immigrants, what is the best course of action?

I believe those undocumented workers with no other criminal record who can demonstrate that they have been gainfully employed and, importantly, that they have paid full taxes should be given special permission to continue working.

As part of this permission, they should receive a unique identification card that entitles them to stay here as long as they are employed, to travel to and from this county within reasonable limits, and to apply for citizenship at the back of the current citizenship line without having to first leave the country. Immediate family members who are already here should also be allowed to stay and children who are attending school should be allowed to graduate and go on to continuing education.

Let me explain the reason for this proposal with a brief example from a local farmer in my district. This farmer is a respected community leader, known for growing quality produce and for treating his customers and employees well.

During a discussion about the issue of immigration and the challenges he faces in finding skilled, reliable workers, he confided that although he always performed the requisite check of documentation and paperwork before hiring anyone, and though he always paid full wages, plus taxes, unemployment and other fees, he could not fully vouch with confidence for the actual legal status of all his workers.

One family in particular had worked and lived on his farm for the past decade. The father of this family effectively managed many aspects of the farming operation, the mother worked in various positions in the processing operation, and the children went to local schools and were excellent students.

As the farmer put it, "These people are decent, hard working, good people who I would trust my life to and who I do trust the operation of much of my farm to. I pay them good wages and they earn every penny -- believe me. They are like family to me and to my family and I really could not afford to lose them. Whether or not they came here legally or not, I can't really say even though I've checked their paperwork every year. What I do know is that if I lost them I could not replace them. Under the current laws they have to live in fear of getting deported and I have to live in fear of losing them and possibly paying a fee to boot. There really has to be a better way."

Anticipating the argument that by employing this family of immigrants he was depriving non-immigrants of employment, the farmer spontaneously added,

"Anyone who says that I should just hire locals hasn't really tried to do that themselves. Every year me and the rest of the farmers around here try to get local folks or kids to work for us in the harvest or processing, and no one shows up. If someone does actually come and ask for work, we'll put them to work right away, but I can tell you the last few times we've tried that they've lasted less than a week. These are darn hard jobs and, to tell you the truth, many people today just don't want to work that hard. I'm sorry to have to say it, but it's true."

Having visited farms, fish processing plants, timber mills and other worksites throughout my district and elsewhere in the nation, I am certain that this story could be repeated by thousands of other farmers and employers. They are doing their best to follow the law, they desperately need the workers, they are paying full wages and taxes, and without the immigrant workers they'd be out of business and the rest of us would be out of food and other goods.

Given all that, it makes no sense to send away workers who have obeyed all other laws, paid their taxes, have learned and developed valuable skills, are contributing to our economy and society. If people in this group can demonstrate an employment history with valid records, and if an employer will personally attest that they have been gainfully employed and will demonstrate that taxes have been paid on their behalf, they should be allowed to stay and work here.

This leaves the third group of workers, those who lack documentation, have no other criminal record, but who have no record of documented employment and payment of taxes.

Personally, from a practical and emotional perspective, this is the most difficult of the three groups. I recognize the hardships many of these individuals and families would face if they were forced to leave and return to their countries of origin. I also know their absence could create disruptions for some industries and employers.

These hardships notwithstanding, we must not reward employers and workers who have not obeyed the law and paid taxes. There are also significant social costs, in the form of education, health care, and other public services that this group has benefited from without contributing equitably to themselves.

Recognizing these costs, and in the interest of not rewarding either the workers or their employers, I believe this group must be denied the required identification cards and, hence, permission to work. Lacking the identification and work permission, and with increased scrutiny by employers, most workers in this category would likely leave on their own.

To facilitate this, there should be some form of voluntary departure program in which special permission and protection from incarceration or prosecution is granted to those who self identify and return to their country of origin.

To further facilitate this voluntary departure, individuals in this group would, upon their return to their home country, be eligible to register at the back of the existing application queue, for eventual legal citizenship. This opportunity would not exist for those who chose to stay without documentation and were involuntarily deported.

In offering these proposals, I am fully aware that they may not be satisfactory to either extremes of the immigration continuum. The hardened "anti-immigration" forces might scream that allowing the taxpaying workers to continue working amounts to amnesty (which it does not), while the "immigrant rights" groups would likely protest the pressure on non- taxpaying undocumented immigrants to depart.

These concerns notwithstanding, our country must deal responsibly and humanely with the millions of people who are already here without documentation. What I have offered, in combination with other recommendations of this chapter, represent a practical approach that most Americans would likely support.

English Language Proficiency

English is the worldwide language of commerce, technology and is a unifying element for our nation. As part of a comprehensive approach to immigration issues, and in an effort to strengthen our economy and reduce costs, I believe we can and should do more to promote the knowledge and use of English for all those who live within our borders.

This will save governments, businesses, hospitals, schools and other institutions billions of dollars each year by reducing the need for translation services and reducing costly miscommunication. It will also help non-English speakers to be more successful in our country and will help reduce tensions from misunderstanding and frustrations related to communication gaps.

In Congress, I have introduced the *Access to Language Education Act*, which, if enacted, will utilize digital television signals to offer free, twenty-four hour a day television programming specifically designed to teach English to all levels of speakers regardless of country of origin.

Simultaneously, a second channel will provide instruction to native English speakers in other worldwide languages not widely taught in U.S. schools. Ultimately, for the health of our economy and our national security, it is in everyone's interest to speak English and for far more of our citizens to speak the languages of other nations. My legislation would go a long way toward achieving both goals.

With a standard, free, 24-7 nationwide television program dedicated to teaching English, specialized courses and adjunct material classes would undoubtedly become available through the private or social sector to help speakers of specific languages learn even more rapidly.

With this in place, there really would not be an excuse for people to not learn English. At that point, after three years of providing the television programming and giving sufficient time for classes and supporting material to emerge, I believe it would be fair for the Federal and state governments to announce multilingual translations of official documents or government funded translation services would be discontinued. People already here would have had ample time to learn basic English, and those planning to come to visit would have ample notice that they should endeavor to learn English beforehand.

Lest anyone consider this proposal somehow prejudiced or mean-spirited, I would ask how it is mean-spirited to invest in providing free instruction that will help people learn the most widely-used language not only in our own country but in the economically developed world?

No one is pulling the rug out from people or forcing them to do anything against their will. Instead, we are giving more than fair notice that conditions will be changing and then providing plenty of help and time to assist people in adapting to those changes. After that, it is a matter of personal choice and responsibility to do the wise thing or not, but society should not have to keep footing the costs for those who do not make that choice.

Speaking from personal experience, I have had the opportunity, and necessity, of learning a foreign language when

I lived overseas in Spain. While there, I did not assume that the Spanish people or government somehow owed it to me to speak English or translate their documents, signs, and so forth into my language. I was a guest in their country and it was my responsibility to do what it took to learn their language and culture as well and as quickly as I could.

Far from resenting this, I believe it was a tremendous opportunity and I am grateful to have had it. As a result, I speak Spanish fluently today. It is a beautiful language and I am eternally thankful to those who helped me learn it. I also believe we should return that favor to all those in our country who do not currently speak English but sincerely want to learn.

Reforming Legal Immigration

With so much current political attention given to the issue of unlawful immigration, far too little attention is given to how we manage lawful immigration. That is unfortunate because our legal immigration policies are not, for the most part, strategic or rational. Current policies do not intentionally allow in either those who could most productively contribute to our economy or those to whom we owe a moral responsibility because of our own nation's actions.

I believe we need to revise our legal immigration policies to be more strategic, to invite the best and brightest to stay or come to our nation, to honor our moral commitments to those who have risked their lives on our behalf, and to ensure a reliable source of workers for agriculture and other industries.

The challenge is to do all of this in a way that responsibly manages population size, avoids racism, and reduces any negative impact on U.S. workers or our economy. That may seem like a tall order, but the alternative of forcing the most talented people to leave, allowing illegal immigration to produce uncontrolled population growth and having insecure borders is not acceptable.

Reforming Family Reunification Policies

Current immigration law gives preferential treatment to the families of people who are already here. This is an understandable and generous gesture, but it goes too far and needs to be reformed.

When one makes the decision to leave their home country and emigrate to another, certain difficult and sometimes emotionally painful choices and consequences result. Among these consequences is the reality of living far from one's extended family. Having lived abroad for an extended time myself, I know how difficult this can be, especially if a loved one becomes ill or special events like births, weddings and so forth are celebrated.

As difficult as these things are for those living abroad, if we take seriously the issue of population growth, we cannot continue to give higher priority for citizenship to any people related to anyone already living here.

Admittedly, this is somewhat of an overstatement of how actual immigration policy regarding family members functions, but it is true that relatives by mere virtue of kinship are granted higher priority, regardless of their skills or talents.

My belief is that we should first set tight limits on the total number of immigrants who will be allowed to seek citizenship in a given year. Within those limits, we should then select the people who will bring the most needed skills that can contribute to our own economy. With limited number of citizenship and immigration opportunities available, of necessity preferential treatment of extended family members should effectively come to an end.

Encouraging The Best and Brightest from Abroad to Contribute to Our Economy

In many high technology industries the demand for talented workers exceeds the domestic supply. We simply do not produce enough top-flight researchers, engineers and other workers who are essential to the high technology enterprises. Because the industry is so extraordinarily competitive, with very rapid times for product development, a lack of skilled workers can create crippling delays and a competitive disadvantage. This puts pressure on U.S.-based companies to either seek skilled workers from elsewhere to come here or move their operations abroad to be closer to the needed workforce.

For the sake of our own economy the best thing to do is train more domestic workers. However, where those numbers fall short it is better to bring foreign workers here to grow businesses and pay taxes in our own country rather than moving operations abroad.

There are several key ways of making this happen. First, we should encourage foreign students who are trained in U.S. universities and have degrees in high demand fields to stay here after they complete their education. It doesn't make sense to invest heavily in training the very brightest people in the world only to then require them to leave our country rather than staying to grow our economy with their talents.

Some have suggested that in certain critical areas, such as advanced mathematics, computer science, medical research and other high technology efforts, we should attach a "green card" to every diploma. I believe we should do precisely that. Our visa and immigration laws should be changed so that visas allowing foreign students to study and train here are automatically converted and extended in ways that let individual with highly needed skills stay, work, pay taxes and, if they so desire, begin a path toward citizenship.

While encouraging the highest caliber international students and skilled professionals to study and work here, we should also increase the numbers of special H1-B visas but with several reforms to current practices.

These reforms include better enforcement of labor and wage requirements to ensure that domestic wages and labor standards are not being weakened by the use of foreign workers. We should also prevent "secondary" entities from monopolizing the H1-B visas and then brokering workers to other employers.

Finally, to be eligible to employ workers under H1-B visas each employer should be required to demonstrate a tangible commitment to educating the domestic workforce by supporting our educational system in a meaningful way. This goes well beyond the modest fees that are currently charged for H1-B applications. It might include providing mentoring for local schools, supplying them with advanced equipment, placing engineers and others in school classrooms to help with education.

Highest priority for access to a limited number of H1-Bs should then be allocated based on the commitment and success of an employer's efforts to train the U.S. workforce. Those who show a dedication to training our own students and workers would have access and be first in line for H1-B visas. Those who ride free and do not support domestic education would not have access to such visas and foreign workers.

Border Security

I purposefully reserved the discussion of border security till last because I believe the most effective solutions to immigration problems reside in addressing the demand and reward elements. The borders are simply too long and the visitors too many for security measures that do not address demand to succeed. In the long run it will be far more productive to address the external and internal drivers of immigration than it will be to patrol 1969 miles of border with Mexico, 5,525 miles of border with Canada, thousands of miles of coastline and track millions of foreign visitors annually.

That being said, we nevertheless need to do a much better job of securing the borders and coasts and tracking visitors. We also need to improve how legal visitors to our nation are welcomed and treated as they arrive and while here.

Far too many people come into our country across unguarded borders or through illegal smuggling at established points of entry. Of those who enter openly, and legally, too many overstay their visas without effective monitoring or consequences. To improve border security we must address both the legal points of entry to our nation and the unguarded borders and other routes of entrance.

The matter of unguarded borders is already being addressed to an extent by expanded fencing and increased border patrols. These measures are important and should be continued and expanded. But fencing and patrols must also be strengthened by greater cooperation from our neighbors.

As long as there is a lucrative industry of illegal human smuggling, coyotes, and other forms of human trafficking, creative people, driven by greed, will find new ways under, around, or over fences. Thus, one of our highest priorities for securing borders must be patrols and enforcement on both sides of the border with real and lasting incarceration and penalties by our neighbors for those engaged in illegal transit of people.

This same principal applies not only on the borders with our contiguous neighbors but also to nations with whom we trade, particularly those engaged in maritime trade through which individuals are smuggled into our country. For overall security against terrorism and to deal with immigration there must be continued gains in inspections and security at ports of destination. There must also be strict enforcement and penalties for those in foreign nations who traffic humans illegally into our own. Again, this has improved substantially in recent years, but there is much room for further gain. To achieve this gain, we should consider addressing enforcement of immigration by countries of origin as part of our trade or other international agreements.

Fencing, border patrols and cargo inspections are all needed, but we must also deal more effectively with managing the entry to our country through formal entry points at borders, airports, and maritime ports. Three main problems must be corrected.

First, if we truly want to monitor compliance with visas we must have biometric identification systems described earlier. Upon entry into the nation, visitors would receive an identification card with biometric information. Digitally encoded into the card would also be information about country of origin, date of arrival, authorized purpose of visit and duration of visit.

Anyone applying for work would have to display their identification card, which would then be checked against the national database. Those lacking a card or whose card did not grant permission to work would be denied employment. The same applies to education and other public services. These cards would also be cross checked by law enforcement.

Those lacking cards or whose visa duration had expired would be identified and referred to immigration authorities. Finally, persons who enter illegally or overstay visas would, upon deportation from this country, have biometric identification information recorded and would permanently be denied legal entry or access to citizenship.

Better monitoring and compliance with legally obtained visas and legal entrance must also be paired with significant improvements in how and why visas for visiting our country are granted or denied. Having dealt with this process for a number of years now, I believe it is profoundly dysfunctional, inconsistent, unrealistic and a detriment to both our economy and our security.

Granting Legal Visas and Treating Visitors With Courtesy and Hospitality

While arguing that we must do a much better job of managing unlawful entry into our country, I also believe we must substantially improve how we manage legal visits and visitors.

Under our present procedures, people who wish to visit our nation for tourism, business, education, family matters or other legitimate reasons often face unreasonably lengthy reviews and unrealistic demands in order to obtain required visas. As standard procedure, potential visitors must convince someone in our consulates or embassies that they have no intention of staying in our country permanently or longer than their visas allow.

This may sound reasonable, but as any scientist or defense attorney will attest, it can be virtually impossible to prove the negative, i.e. prove that you do not intend to do something before it has not been done.

The result is an extraordinarily time consuming, frustrating and often illogical process that ends up denying many perfectly legitimate people from coming to our country while letting others enter who should not be here. This process is also an increasing drain on our economy as business leaders, top scientists, scholars and artists find they do not want to deal with the headaches, personal insults, delays and uncertainties of merely obtaining a visa.

Just as tourism, scientific, business and cultural opportunities are increasingly being lost to other nations because of our visa review processes, some of the brightest students, who once saw the U.S. educational system as the best in the world, are now staying away. They are going elsewhere because the opportunities in other nations have improved, because it can take so long to get visas that they lose scholarships or other opportunities, and because, as one brilliant young mathematician from an Arab nation told me, they are afraid of being arrested, held without trial and possibly tortured.

The fact that these concerns exist, and are, to varying degrees based on reality, cannot be good for our nation. These business leaders, bright students, scientists, and cultural leaders may well have been able to help develop critical technology or cure diseases, or otherwise enrich our nation had they been encouraged to visit or study here.

What is more, and this fact cannot be overstated, one of the key reasons for the spread of democratic values around the world has been because so many international leaders, in politics, business, and other realms, have at one time or another studied in our country. These former students are now some of our closest and best friends. Losing such ties by making it hard for future students to study here is a hidden but tremendous loss, indeed danger, for our nation.

The sad irony is that in seeking to protect ourselves against terror, we are losing some of our best and most loyal friends and advocates. To remedy this, we simply must provide a way of expediting the visa review process and ending some of the illogical and insulting barriers that have been erected.

Once visas are issued and visitors come to our country, I believe we must also do a much better job of welcoming them here. Having traveled abroad and returned many times, and having also entered many other nations, I have had the privilege of encountering some truly outstanding border and immigration agents. They are professional, courteous, thorough and careful in their work, but they also treat visitors with humanity and courtesy. These agents deserve our gratitude and respect. They put forward a very positive face for our nation.

Unfortunately, there are some agents who do not show such qualities and who deserve to be replaced. Certain border agents display an attitude of hostility, disrespect, rudeness and intimidation. This is especially acute for foreign visitors, but it applies to U.S. citizens as well. I have experienced such conduct and attitude personally, I have witnessed it firsthand being applied to visitors, and I have heard truly outrageous stories of heavy handedness and frankly illegal and unconstitutional conduct on the part of some border agents.

As insulting as such conduct is to visitors and as damaging as it is to the image of our nation, it is also rather ridiculous when one thinks about it. True terrorists who wish to harm this nation are hardly likely to say to themselves, "I would travel to America and commit an act of terror, but those inspection people at the airport are so nasty I just won't risk it." Rudeness and discourtesy offend legitimate visitors but are unlikely to increase our real security to any degree at all.

Fortunately, things seem to be changing in this regard during the past couple of years, but I believe there needs to be a top to bottom review of the entire process from visa application, to how visitors are treated when they arrive in our country, and how we manage and track the visas after people enter the nation.

The fundamental message must be this - People are welcome to visit the U.S. They are welcome as tourists, as students, to conduct business, engage in scientific and cultural exchanges and to experience the very best we have to offer. We will have a reasonable, prompt, and fair process and adequate, trained staff to grant visas at our embassies and consulates. When people arrive at our nation through legal points of entry, we will have a pleasant, friendly attitude while still ensuring that documentation is in order and that contraband or dangerous materials are excluded.

If visitors follow the legal process and adhere to the terms of their visas, they will be treated with the utmost courtesy and hospitality at all stages of the process. At the same time, those who do not enter or stay legally or who violate the laws of our land should be aware that they will be recognized as doing so, will be deported, and will not be able to reenter in the future.

11.
FOREIGN POLICY

...nothing is more essential than that permanent, inveterate antipathies against particular nations, and passionate attachments for others, should be excluded; and that in place of them, just and amicable feelings towards all should be cultivated.

George Washington, from his farewell address

Multiple international polls have shown that the standing of the U.S. in world opinion was in precipitous decline for much of the past decade and, until recently, had reached its lowest point in many decades. Foreign policy mistakes, especially the invasion of Iraq, a perception of national and Presidential arrogance and ignorance, the pitiful response to Hurricane Katrina, obstructionist environmental positions, our national debt, the financial collapse, perceived and real inconsistencies in how we treat certain nations compared to others, and numerous other factors have substantially harmed our image. This is dangerous for our own nation and for the free world.

Fortunately, there are encouraging signs the international community is now looking at our country with new eyes and seeing us in a more favorable light. That gives us an opportunity to restore our standing, but only if we take the right actions.

This chapter describes the principles that should guide those actions. It does not attempt to spell out specific policies for specific regions. Rather, it looks at fundamentals that can help put our policies and our actions back on track around the world.

Our Core Values and Highest Ideals

The first and most important change needed in foreign relations is to once again live up to and support our highest ideals. For centuries now the principles on which our nation was founded have been a beacon for the world.

"We hold these truths to be self evident, that all men are created equal, that they are endowed by their Creator with certain unalienable rights, that among these are Life, Liberty and the pursuit of Happiness. – That to preserve these rights governments are instituted among Men deriving their just powers from the consent of the governed..."

On many occasions, we have sacrificed the blood and wealth of our nation to defend those principles not only for ourselves but for people around the world. For that, our nation deserves both credit and respect.

But when we are off course it is dangerous not only for us but for all who aspire to freedom, human rights, constitutional democracy and the rule of law. Without the U.S. at the forefront of these values, there is really no other superpower to fill that void. Certainly none of the other leading powers of the world right now is capable of filling that role and some of the most powerful nations embrace principles at odds with our core values. For our own sake and that of all who aspire to freedom, we must get back on stride and resume the role of leading by the power of our example more than the example of our power.

Understand Democracy Before "Exporting Democracy"

While emphasizing the importance of our core values, it is also important to note that the U.S. is not a democracy. It is a constitutional democratic republic and we forget that at our peril. When our foreign policy seeks to "export democracy" without really knowing what we are talking about, the results are too often the opposite of what may have been intended.

The Framers of our constitution were rightfully skeptical about democracy. They recognized that without checks and balances in and on government, and absent a constitution that protects fundamental rights, democracy can be just as oppressive or even more than monarchy.

Madison, for example, called democracy "the most vile form of government" and asserted that "democracies have.... ever been found incompatible with personal security or the rights of property and have in general been as short in their lives as they have been violent in their deaths."

Jefferson wrote that "A democracy is nothing more than mob rule, where fifty-one percent of the people may take away the rights of the other forty-nine."

When the primary authors of our Constitution and Declaration of Independence show such concern about democracy, one might wonder how it is that we place such a high priority on democracy abroad.

Politicians and pundits who laud democracy and call for it as a basis for our foreign policy are certainly well-intentioned but they are being careless about their words and ideas. Using "democracy" as shorthand for "constitutional democratic republic and protection of human rights" may make for easier speechmaking, but demanding elections in other countries without first establishing constitutional protections for civil rights and a political culture of public service rather than personal gain is unlikely to succeed.

This does not mean we should shy away from promoting democratic processes or elections. It does, however, mean we should not assume the mere act of voting, without other core ingredients, is likely to lead to a desirable result.

If we are to export our own ideas about government, our focus should first be on promoting basic human rights and constitutional government that protects those rights. We must also export the fundamental principle of serving in elective office as solely for the purpose of public service. Democratic elections should be an essential part of this overall goal, but elections alone are neither sufficient as a mechanism nor necessarily desirable in their consequences.

The State Department

Central to improving our international standing and relations must be rebuilding the Department of State. One of the greatest challenges facing the Department is inadequate staffing. In the middle of 2008, there were only 6,636 foreign-service officers and 4,919 support staff to cover the entire world. The number of State Department personnel in 2008 was only ten percent higher than twenty five years ago, even though the global population has grown by almost two billion people, nearly fifty percent since then, and there are now 24 more countries that did not exist at that time. In part because of the low staff numbers, the overseas vacancy rate stood at 21 percent in 2008.

To put minimal numbers of State Department personnel in context, contrast the total 11,555 with the nearly 3.2 million military personnel in the combined active-duty, Guard and Reserve, plus 673,000 civilian employees in the Defense Department. Those military personnel numbers were being increased by an additional 90,000 troops even as Congress failed to approve a requested 1,150 members of the Foreign Service corps.

Budgetary constraints also impede the ability of our diplomatic efforts. In 2008, only $7.5 billion went to the entire State Department diplomatic and consular programs. That included staffing and equipping the missions in Iraq and Afghanistan, plus some 265 other diplomatic locations in the world.

One consequence of this relatively low funding level is inadequate pay and benefits for staff. For example, during a recent trip abroad I learned that salaries and wages for locally hired staff at many of our embassies are not sufficient to meet even basic costs of housing, food, health care and so forth. This is not only an injustice to the local people we hire, it also poses a security risk as those unable to care for their families might be more easily targeted and tempted by offers to betray our interests.

Inadequate staff also costs economic opportunities and hurts relationships with those who might otherwise be friendly to our nation. When there are not adequate personnel to process requests for visas and other documents necessary to visit our nation, people become frustrated and, eventually, decide to take their tourism or investment dollars somewhere else.

I have met with some of the most prominent business, scientific and social leaders from around the world and time after time I hear troubling stories of excessive delays, discourtesies and mistakes in processing visa applications. Sometimes the problem is incompetent or rude personnel, other times the cause is simply excessive demand on too few staff. Both problems must be corrected.

There are many possible remedies to these staffing issues. One which I find particularly appealing, and which has in fact already existed to a limited degree, is the provision of scholarships for young people who are committed to and have the skills for a career in the Foreign Service.

I recently spoke to a graduate of this program who was serving overseas at an embassy and suggested that expansion of such programs would be a tremendous benefit. He also offered the intriguing idea that members of Congress might take on the role of nominating students to such programs much as is currently done for applicants to our military service academies. Both suggestions make great sense and would enhance both the standing and numbers of personnel in the State Department.

Citizen Diplomacy –
Educational, Scientific and Cultural Exchanges

One of the most effective of all aspects of U.S. foreign relations has been our once generous commitment to educational, scientific and cultural exchanges. Countless leaders throughout the world have warm affection for our country and an intimate knowledge of our culture, politics and economy because they studied and lived here at some point in their lives.

This level of personal knowledge and emotional connection is truly priceless. In many ways the friendships formed from these connections exceeds the value of all the other State Department, foreign aid, military assistance and other diplomatic efforts combined.

Sadly, in recent decades this commitment by our country has been in steady decline and reached its nadir in the post-September 11, 2001 era. Domestic security concerns following the attacks made it nearly impossible for people from certain nations to come to our country regardless of their purpose or background. At the same time, tales of incarceration without trial, fear of renditions to secret prisons, and discrimination against foreign visitors reduced the desire of many to visit the U.S.

These self-imposed wounds of our own policies have been exacerbated by a willingness of other nations to be more inviting and by growing educational and scientific investments abroad. The result is an unaccountable but undoubtedly profound loss of opportunity as friendships and contributions to our own nation have not been formed or created when they otherwise would have been. What is especially tragic from a security perspective is that in many cases the people who were most discriminated against when they sought to visit, work or study here were from regions in which our nation most needs to improve its standing and understanding.

It is in our urgent self-interest to reverse this trend and to do so quickly and publicly. To some degree this is happening already, as academic visas particularly are being processed more rapidly of late. That is a good start, but the change needs to be deeper and broader than that.

The State Department and Department of Homeland Security need to work together to conduct a bottom-to-top overhaul of how visiting scholars, scientists, business people, cultural artists and others are treated when they apply for visas. As discussed in the chapter on Immigration, there also needs to be a review and cultural change in our points of entry so that all visitors are made to feel truly welcome here.

Having led Congressional efforts to improve what we call "Science Diplomacy," I can say with confidence that taking these steps and publicizing the change around the world would have a profound and positive impact on our standing, our security and our economy. It would reestablish the extraordinary opportunities to build relationships, attract new talent, and educate both our own citizens and foreign guests about our mutual cultures and countries.

Supporting our friends and encouraging progress

Though I am mindful of and largely in agreement with Washington's sage advice about "passionate attachments" being as problematic as "inveterate antipathies," I am nevertheless aware that we too often pay disproportionate attention to areas of conflict, crisis or threat and give too little attention to long standing friends and areas of promise and progress.

Several years ago a delegation of members of the Japanese Diet came to meet with Members of Congress. One of the concerns they expressed had to do with the increasing disregard they felt from our country toward theirs and, at the same time, a growing infatuation they saw from us regarding their neighbor China.

They pointed out that Japan has a democratically elected parliamentary government with a strong human rights record. Their country has been a friend and ally of the U.S., is a strong trading partner, and has supported the U.S. in numerous political and foreign policy matters. From their perspective, these qualities were in contrast with how they saw China and, in their words, "We feel somewhat like the spouse who has been given up for the 'new girl' down the road."

The take home message for me was that even as we reach out to build new relationships, we must not forget those with whom we have worked closely for many years. This is not only a basic courtesy, it is also strategically prudent. If our nation comes to be perceived as a fickle partner, allies may not be with us when we are in greatest need and they too may seek other relationships at our expense.

So too, I believe we have a tendency to let our foreign affairs be bounced from crisis to crisis, threat to threat, ignoring in the process areas in which positive things are occurring and need to be nurtured. Multiple examples exist of nations and leaders who are making great strides, and in some instances running substantial personal and political risks to do so, yet they receive little attention and even less foreign aid. There are of course exceptions and examples of where we have invested heavily in countries that are making progress, but overall it is true that too much of our foreign spending goes to areas that are already in crisis, while too little goes to those who are managing to avoid conflict or breakdowns.

The solution to this is for the State Department to actively look for opportunities to give tangible support to those nations that are making gains. The power of this example would encourage other nations to follow suit and, just as importantly, would help strengthen friendships with the nations that are moving in the right direction. At the same time, support for progressive leaders helps show their constituencies that movement forward and constructive reforms will yield a better life than extremism or totalitarianism.

Minding the local hemispheres

Closely related to the principles of encouraging friends and rewarding progress is the need to pay more attention to what is happening in our own hemisphere. Because policy is so often crisis focused, our country has tended to neglect its neighbors to the North and South.

Considering politics as well as proximity, we have no closer friend than Canada, yet members of Congress on the whole pay less attention to Canadian politics and relations than to many other areas of the world. In the opposite direction of the compass, when attention has been given to Latin America, it has often been focused primarily on areas of crisis – "the drug war," adversarial leaders who have recently risen to prominence in several nations, or the periodic natural disasters get the attention and the funding. Meanwhile leaders and nations that have quietly and successfully built functioning constitutional democracies are given little attention. The ongoing failure of Congress to approve a free trade agreement with Colombia, which has made tremendous strides in recent years, is a case in point and is harming our relationship with that country and our standing in the region.

This regional neglect has been part of the reason extremists have been able to rise to power to begin with. It is also why other nations, most notably China and Russia, are giving much greater attention to the region and receiving a cordial welcome. As one diplomat from a country in South America said to me, "It's not that we naturally feel affection to the Chinese at all. But they have reached out, they're investing heavily, and, frankly, they're paying attention to us while the U.S. is not."

Does any more need to be said?

Keeping Foreign Policies Straight – U.S. Values and Interests

Notwithstanding the importance of maintaining strong relationships with friends, that does not mean we should unquestioningly or obediently support whatever a friendly nation chooses to do.

When Members of Congress and the Administration make decisions about foreign policy, their priority should be the highest principals and best interests of the U.S. Two questions should always be asked: Is this policy or action consistent with the highest values of our nation? Is this policy or action in the best near- and long-term interests of our nation?

Unfortunately, on a number of occasions we have strayed from these standards and usually to our own detriment. There are many reasons for this, perhaps most notably our dependence on foreign oil. In our quest to secure cheap oil we have backed dictatorships and sent trillions of dollars in consumer money and military aid and sales to regimes and regions whose values and actions are in direct conflict with our own. Meanwhile, we have led the world in polluting our planet.

Our foreign policy has also on occasion been directed away from core values and our own national interests by individuals and groups who have other nations as their highest priority. These groups have used campaign contributions, political pressure, and media to influence policies of Congress and the Administration.

President Washington, in the same farewell address quoted at the beginning of this chapter, cautioned against this danger:

"…history and experience prove that foreign influence is one of the most baneful foes of republican government…."

Washington saw in his own time, and would likely see again now, that such influences can produce: "…the illusion of an imaginary common interest in cases where no real common interest exists…infusing into one the enmities of the other" and leading to "participation in the quarrels and wars of the latter without adequate inducement or justification."

A recent example of how the priority of such groups can be the interests of nations other than the U.S. occurred when members of a particular organization visited my congressional office and began by saying, "Thank you for meeting with us Congressman. As you might imagine, our first priority is (fill in the blank with the name of a country other than our own), and we would like to ask that you (fill in the blank with a resolution or vote that in some way favors the other nation but may not actually be in our own national interest)."

In response to this, I replied, "I'm glad you are here, I'm interested in hearing from you, and I do share your concerns about this other nation. But I want to be clear from the start that my priority as a member of the U.S. House of Representatives is the values and interests of our own country, the United States of America, not any another nation."

The group seemed taken aback by this reply and there was a moment of awkward silence. Then one member spoke up and said of course that was their priority too, but of course our own nation's interest and that of the one they had mentioned were intrinsically linked.

Would that this were always so - unfortunately it is not.

Washington, again, warned of "…ambitious, corrupted or deluded citizens (who devote themselves to the favorite nation),…betray or sacrificed the interests of their own country…."

There is often real question about whether or not the positions being requested by such interest groups are consistent with our core national values or the interest of the U.S. There is also legitimate question about how the actions of other nations these groups support may adversely impact our domestic security and interests. What is more, in spite of the intentions of the groups involved in lobbying, in some instances what they are requesting may actually be contrary to the interests of the other nation they claim and intend to support.

It is a telling commentary on politics in our country that even raising this possibility can be seen as implying "disloyalty" to the other nation. But that is not where loyalty should be to begin with and unquestioning obedience to one group's wishes is certainly not the only way to show support for another nation even if one wants to. Ironically, in many instances a much more nuanced and open debate is being conducted in other countries, but raising questions or offering alternative perspectives is actively discouraged and punished politically here at home.

Much of the time when these sorts of conflicting interests arise they take one of two forms. Often the request from the interest group is to bring more foreign aid - military, civilian or both - to a particular nation. This is not necessarily contrary to our domestic interests. Well-targeted foreign aid is an essential part of our national interest and our moral responsibility to the world. In fact, in many ways strong arguments can be made that increasing foreign aid is in our near and long term interests as people and as a nation.

The key, however, lies in the reasons we are giving or withholding aid. Where does the aid go and how does it impact our own interests? What is the cost, what will the aid be used for and how will it be administered and monitored?

We must always keep in mind that if we give aid, especially military assistance, to a foreign government, what that government does with our assistance will inevitably and inescapably be tied directly to us. If we sell or give missiles, tanks or aircraft to another nation or group and they use those weapons to harm innocent civilians, suppress their citizens or launch attacks on another nation, the U.S. will be seen as substantially culpable for those actions.

Apart from foreign aid, members of Congress are also asked to vote on resolutions that praises or condemn another nation or group. To be sure, such measures are often absolutely justified, indeed demanded by circumstances and the actions of one group or nation. Truly egregious acts or regimes must be called to account publicly. Unfortunately, while many resolutions are well justified, there are also many occasions in which such requests are one-sided and inconsistent, sometimes even hypocritical when compared to our own policies and actions elsewhere in the world.

In response to resolutions and requests for foreign aid that may not be in the best interest of our own nation, Members of Congress must be willing to say no regardless of the political influence of the requesting group or lobbyist. Votes in elections and campaign contributions connected to legislation involving nations other than our own must always take second place to our domestic concerns and our core principles as a constitutional democratic republic and defender of human rights and rule of law.

This statement should be so obvious that it may seem surprising it must be made at all, but the reality is it must. Indeed, it might be a good idea for every member of Congress to post such a statement explicitly in large and bold print in their office.

"This office has a positive regard for international relations but the first and highest priority will be the preservation, prosperity and principles of our own constitutional

democratic republic and our core values of human rights, the rule of law, and respect for freedom and constitutional democracy at home and abroad."

In the example I gave earlier of the group saying their priority was another nation, I intentionally left out the name of the other country involved. The reason is that on different occasions I have heard essentially the same types of statements made by groups favoring or opposing several different countries other than our own.

It will come as no surprise that the most frequent and contentious foreign policy issues that come to Congressional attention involve Israel, the Palestinians, and various other nations in the Middle East.

Less frequent, but certainly not insignificant, are comparable requests and conflicts concerning Greece and Turkey, India and Pakistan, the two sides of our "One China" policy, and anti-Castro activists versus voices for more open relations with Cuba. Issues concerning other nations in our own hemisphere are also rising with greater frequency.

I mention all of these nations here to underscore the fact that, although certain regions and associated conflicts predominate in the political debate, the underlying issue of balancing our core values and domestic needs and interests with competing sides in foreign conflicts extends well beyond a single region. Explicitly naming some of the nations involved in these discussions is not to question the sincerity of those who are involved, nor does it suggest that the interests of the other nations are necessarily or always contrary to our own.

It is, however, important to be honest about the fact that such conflicts are shaping our policy to an excessive degree and interest groups, political donors, and voting blocs may, in some instances, advocate positions that are inconsistent with core values and long term interests of our own nation.

There is a strange game that occurs in Washington, D.C. as interest groups and individuals favoring one side or another proudly claim how effective they are to their own constituents, but then publicly deny that their influence sways U.S. policy.

At the same time, those on the other side of such issues, both in foreign nations and domestically, tend to exaggerate this influence and are too eager to suggest that it is the sole determinant of our foreign policy.

Those familiar with this general topic will likely recognize that merely stating things so bluntly is actually uncommon and politically risky for someone in elected office. That fact alone, however, should itself demonstrate the very point I am making. If we cannot even risk telling the truth about how policy is influenced in our own nation, is there any need for further evidence that the interests of other nations and the lobbying and campaign financing on behalf of those interests are distorting our policy and politics here at home?

As discussed elsewhere in this book, one of the most important remedies for this overall problem would be campaign finance reforms. Completely removing candidates and elected representatives from the money chase by banning direct solicitation or acceptance of contributions would substantially reduce the financial pressures and incentives that are attached to these issues.

No Apocalyptic Foreign Policy Vision

Conflicts of interest just described regarding U.S. foreign policy pose a threat to our security and stability, but that threat is paralleled by a potentially more dangerous tendency that has grown in recent years. Some within our own government and who have had a strong influence on government policy would like to direct our nation toward fulfilling a millennial vision of the future that they believe is guided by Biblical or other scripture.

To those who have not contemplated the connection between apocalyptic religious ideology and our foreign policy, let me emphasize two things. First, there is no question that the connection exists for some and has in fact influenced our policies and our politics. Second, people around the world have recognized this connection and are very concerned about it.

This is particularly evident in regards to U.S. policy in the Middle East, with some in our country arguing that it is the destiny of the U.S. to play a role in creating the conditions they believe will lead to Armageddon. That of course also means, according to their ideology, the destruction and eternal damnation of non-Christians worldwide and the second coming of Christ.

Based on that belief, certain policies regarding the Israeli/Palestinian conflict and broader Middle East policy are either approved or disapproved of and both votes and campaign contributions are tied to where candidates stand on those issues. Of course the matter is rarely stated so bluntly, but there is no question that some in the recent Bush administration held this belief as do some members of Congress and certainly many conservative supporters do as well. Merely watching television broadcasting and witnessing the apocalyptic preachers calling for the end of days on the one hand then championing one candidate or party over another, shows how the apocalyptic religious vision and political issues are directly connected.

When candidates for the Presidency or other high offices seek the endorsements and counsel of people who espouse such beliefs, there is reason for grave concern. So too, when elected officials at any level base or explain votes or other actions with reference to such beliefs, there is also reason to take note.

Beyond domestic politics and religion in the U.S., within the Middle East there are people on both sides of the Israeli/Palestinian conflict who believe they have a divine right to certain land and, therefore, virtually any behavior they engage in to acquire or defend that land is acceptable because it is in some way sanctioned by God. When U.S. policy is seen as favoring one side or another in this conflict of religious certainties and claims to land our own security and standing will necessarily be seen in that light.

How can we expect other nations of the world to respect or trust us if they have any reason whatsoever to believe that our ultimate goal as a nation is to bring about some form of apocalyptic religious vision that entails the horrific deaths and ultimate damnation of all but those of a certain belief? And how, if our own foreign policy is so twisted, can we condemn suicide bombers who kill innocent civilians while believing they will be rewarded by heavenly virgins for doing so?

Let me be absolutely direct about this kind of religious fanaticism as it applies to government policy - it is dangerous, delusional and has absolutely no place in guiding our foreign or domestic policy or politics. We must unequivocally disavow any intention whatsoever to allow any aspect of our foreign or domestic policy to be driven by any religious belief in an apocalyptic end of times.

If there is to be any religious basis for our foreign policy, let it be this – "Do unto others as you would have them do unto you" and "Love thy neighbor as thyself." And to that let us add "Do not do unto others what you would not want done to you, and Do not allow something done to others that you would not want done to yourself."

Military Aid and Arms Sales

The U.S. has for many years led the world in total arms sales to other nations. A recent study by William Hartung, of the New America Foundation, estimated that the some $32 billion worth of weapons were sold abroad in 2008. Hartung's report also noted that of the top 25 purchasers of U.S. made weapons, 13 could be considered undemocratic or to have been violators of human rights.

The ten largest recipients of arms in recent years have been (in order) Pakistan, Saudi Arabia, Israel, Iraq, Korea, the United Arab Emirates, Kuwait, Egypt, Colombia and Singapore. In some cases, most notably the oil rich nations above, weapons purchases have been funded with domestic resources of the purchasers, but in others the funding has come from the U.S. through ten or so different foreign military assistance programs. The total value of U.S. arms transfer agreements from 2000 to 2007 has been $123 billion – more than twice as much as the next largest arms seller, Russia.

For the period from 2002-2008 and including projected spending in 2009 these top five nations and their corresponding security assistance amounts were, in billions of dollars:

Afghanistan	$29.764
Iraq	27.492
Israel	21,610
Egypt	14,963
Pakistan	9.754

Looking at these figures, one must appreciate that there is often a legitimate need to provide military support to other nations, including through arms sales. But we must also be mindful that what is done with those weapons will reflect on our nation and we will be seen at least in part as culpable if innocent people suffer as a result or the weapons are used for domestic repression rather than defense. So too, we must be aware that, just as certain lobby groups may put foreign interests above domestic, the manufacturers of weapons for export may also put monetary gain over larger national interest and seek to influence policy accordingly.

I believe we should set a goal of gradually reducing our foreign arms sales of all types. While not being naive about the risks of the real world, excessive arms sales and the misuse of those weapons adds to that risk and embroils us in conflicts that we might well do better to avoid. Finally, we must also be cognizant that on more than one occasion weapons we have sold to others have ultimately been turned against our own troops, civilians and interests.

Peace and Service Memorial

Throughout our nation and our nation's capitol, monuments and memorials honor the sacrifice of those who have given their all for this country in times of war. This is right and fitting as we all owe an immeasurable gratitude to those who have sacrificed so others may live in freedom. Lacking, however, are fitting memorials to also honor those who have given their lives through service and peacemaking efforts.

Soldiers will be the first to tell you peace is better than war. That being the case, as we honor our fallen military dead and living we should also establish within Washington D.C. and at appropriate other locations across the nation memorials to peace and service.

As just one example of how appropriate this would be, consider that since President Kennedy initiated the Peace Corps in 1961, more than 180,000 volunteers have served. Of these, 274 have died while performing their Peace Corps missions.[15]

In addition to Peace Corps volunteers, hundreds of thousands of others have served in other service and relief groups, bringing aid and support to those in need. U.S. staff for the World Food Program, UNICEF, USAID, and many volunteer non-governmental organizations have served and among these a number have died while others have become ill or injured as the result of their service.

Honoring those who serve the cause of peace and service would provide powerful testimony and moving examples that people are willing to give their all for the sake of others. Just as military memorials can inspire our young people to enlist and serve this country in our armed forces, so too a memorial to peace and service can inspire our youth and citizens to volunteer for peace and service work around the world and at home.

In some ways this concept will become a reality when the permanent headquarters of the U.S. Institute of Peace (USIP) is completed in Washington D.C. This building, which is scheduled for completion in fall of 2010, will house, in addition to the USIP, a number of exhibits honoring peace-making and telling the stories of those who have sought to replace conflict with peace.

In addition to the USIP building and exhibits, I believe other memorials to both peace and service are warranted in the nation's capitol and in state capitols and other communities across the land. My hope would be that, just as veterans, their families, and others now make pilgrimages to the WWII memorial, Korean War Memorial, Vietnam Wall and to

---

[15] *See* For more information, see Fallen Peace Corps Volunteers Memorial Project at - FPCV.ORG

military cemeteries throughout the land and overseas, people might do the same to peace and service memorials to honor those sacrifices as well.

Congressional Travel

One final note to conclude this chapter -- Members of Congress ought to travel internationally more often, not less. There is simply no substitute for going places, seeing things with your own eyes, meeting people and having the give and take kinds of conversations that can only occur during direct, personal visits.

Are there some abuses of travel? Yes. Are there some Members of Congress who take advantage of the travel for personal pleasure without legitimate benefit to the country? Yes again and any excesses or abuses must be reduced and eliminated. But as easy and fun as it may be for the media to write or broadcast "exposes" about "congressional junkets," the fact is most congressional travel is legitimate and valuable, the schedules are often grueling, and the information and relationships that result can be invaluable.

Ours is the most influential nation in the world and, as such, it is a responsibility of U.S. Representatives to know something about that world so they can make informed decisions. Instead of criticizing their representative for taking periodic trips abroad or domestically, voters might do well to ask their member of Congress why he or she does not travel more internationally.

Only when members of Congress feel it is politically safe to journey abroad will they do so, and only when they do so will they really have an understanding of the international issues and opportunities before us today and in the future. Foreign or domestic policy made by people who have little knowledge of the rest of the world is not likely to be made as well as it could be and is highly likely to produce unknown and unintended consequences. Congressional travel cannot eliminate that possibility, but it can go a long way toward reducing it.

12.
NATIONAL SECURITY

*Our arms must be mighty, ready for instant action, so that no
potential aggressor may be tempted to risk his own
destruction....*

*This conjunction of an immense military establishment and a
large arms industry is new in the American experience. The
total influence – economic, political, even spiritual – is felt in
every city, every State house, every office of the Federal
government. We recognize the imperative need for this
development. Yet we must not fail to comprehend its grave
implications. Our toil, resources and livelihood are all
involved; so is the very structure of our society.*

President Dwight David Eisenhower
from his Farewell Address

I am writing this sentence while on a C-130 aircraft flying
into Kandahar airbase in Afghanistan to meet with our
troops just before Christmas 2008. Here in Afghanistan,
not far away in Iraq, and at countless bases around the world,
American soldiers, sailors, marines, coast guard and air force
personnel are away from their families, putting their lives on
the line for something greater than themselves.

Service to Country –
Our Military and Civilian Personnel

At home and abroad, at every rank and in every branch of
the services, some of the finest people I have every met wear
the uniforms of this nation. They are extraordinarily dedicated,
hard working, intelligent, motivated and diligent in their work.
The best are at once courageous and compassionate, willing
and able to fight if necessary, but equally willing and capable

of securing peace through the powerful example of their personal humanity and decency.

Our nation and the world are unimaginably fortunate that the most powerful military force in history is made up of people of this quality and character and with the fundamental human decency and motive of service. The United States of America would not exist and will not survive without the willingness of men and women to sacrifice their lives and everything they own for love of country.

It is tragic that this is the reality of the world, but reality it is and respecting that reality must be at the core of our understanding of national defense. Fundamental to our nation's security must be a readiness for Americans to dedicate, and if necessary give everything we have, including our lives, to defending our freedoms.

I begin this chapter with this core reality because our society as a whole seems to have lost sight of it. Of course we honor our troops at sporting events and on key days of remembrance like Veterans Day and Memorial Day, but the fact is only a small percentage of our population serves in uniform today and too many or our citizens seem willing to leave that responsibility to "someone else" or to have "other priorities" than serving the nation.

As our armed forces struggle to meet recruiting goals, and as ever higher and more costly financial and other incentives are employed to entice people into the military, we run the real risk of separating our military from the rest of our society. This is not healthy in a constitutional democratic republic and neither is it healthy for the military.

For the sake of our national security, we must reawaken the overall spirit of national service, renew the respect for military service among all Americans, and emphasize that the primary motivation for this service should be preserving our nation and its highest values.

If we choose to have an all volunteer force, then we must make enlistment in that volunteer force, either through active duty, The Guard or Reserve, something that all our young men and women consider when they reach the proper age. Only when the very best among our citizens are drawn to service will our military truly be all it can be. This means parents, educational institutions, counselors, teachers, clergy and other leaders and role models must give serious thought to encouraging those with the character and capacity to serve the country to enlist and do their part.

It must also be said that along with this commitment to defend and serve our nation there must be an equal commitment to do everything possible to prevent the need for people to lay down their lives for the nation and to seek means other than violent combat to prevent, manage and resolve conflict. We must choose wise leaders and representatives who do not take us into needless conflict and do not enter conflicts without adequate preparation or resources to prevail.

As mentioned in the prior chapter, we must also acknowledge the essential and courageous service of state department and other agency personnel serving overseas and at home. So too, relief and aid workers who put their lives on the line in conflict ridden, impoverished or disease ravaged areas also deserve our deep respect and gratitude.

Political Changes

As has been said so often in this book, both major political parties and our national policies need to change for our nation to truly be more secure. For their part, many Republicans have tended to emphasize the role of military force and neglected what is sometimes called "soft power," or better said, "smart engagement" – efforts to promote security through non-military means. Many Republicans have also wanted to pretend that we can increase military spending, conduct simultaneous major military campaigns, and grow our armed forces while also lowering taxes. That is simply not honest intellectually, mathematically or fiscally and it has contributed substantially to the growing deficit and debt and the financial chaos we are currently experiencing.

For their part, some Democrats, have suffered from the opposite tendency, a reluctance to acknowledge the essential reality that force is sometimes necessary in a dangerous world

228

and people must at times be willing and ready to lay down their lives and take the lives of others for the sake of our country and our values. Many Democrats have also failed to accept that providing for defense does have costs and those costs are substantial and must be fully paid for.

We will be most safe as a nation only when we wisely and responsibly address both the martial and peaceful sides of the defense and security challenges. The power of our example may be at least as important to our security as the example of our power, but both are necessary to defend and expand the cause of freedom.

Choices

As part of the visit to Afghanistan and Iraq, I also went to two places that highlight the difficult choices of our current defense policies. The first was a state-of-the-art U.S. Navy vessel the USS *San Antonio*. The ship was a marvel of the latest in naval technology and engineering. With sophisticated electronics, anti-missile defense systems, an impressive power plant controlled through fiber optics, a full medical and dental center, radar deflecting hull and upper deck - every element of modern naval combat for a ship of this class was included.

The ship's cargo, both human and material was just as impressive. It contained huge hovercraft landing craft that can carry hundreds of troops or their vehicles including M1 tanks. Also on board were amphibious armored personnel carriers, heavy trucks, up-armored Humvees, assault helicopters, Osprey vertical takeoff airplanes, plus weapons, ammunition, food, water and fuel for the vehicles all ready to go at short notice and high speed.

The sailors and marines on board are the best trained, best equipped fighting forces anywhere in the world. Each is not only armed with the most modern weaponry, but also the elements of modern integrated electronic war fighting – GPS navigation systems, sophisticated communication, night vision goggles and body armor.

As I toured the ship I was extraordinarily impressed by the capabilities of the people and the resources they have been given to do their jobs. I was proud of our sailors, Marines and soldiers, glad they had the very best tools to protect them and us, and glad that all of that personnel and hardware was on our side in a fight.

At the same time, as a member of the budget committee, and as our nation looks at a $1.6 trillion dollar annual deficit and $52 trillion present value of our future debt, and as word came from back home of a half million lost jobs in the preceding month, I was also painfully aware of the costs.

Rough estimates of ship and cargo indicate the following price tags: the ship itself $1.4 billion, landing hovercraft $24 million each, Osprey aircraft $96 million each, Expeditionary Fighting Vehicles $22 million, the list goes on. What's more, all of the vehicles just listed, from the ship itself to the landing craft and aircraft, all were associated with huge cost overruns and serious questions of performance.

Conservatively estimated, the total amount of floating physical assets in that one ship is somewhere over $3 billion. Again, I am glad we have such equipment on our side and it is vital that our troops have the very best equipment, but that equipment comes at both an economic cost and an opportunity cost. The latter was illustrated dramatically the very next day.

The day after seeing the *San Antonio*, we then went to tour the brand new campus of Carnegie Mellon University in Doha Qatar. That's right, Carnegie Mellon from Pittsburgh, also has a campus in Doha. The modern architecture, sophisticated classrooms, and the educational course offerings there would rival and likely be the envy of many colleges and universities in the U.S.

All of that construction was built from barren dirt to finished product in just a few years and was fully paid for by the government of the host nation. All of the faculty salaries and benefits, plus support staff, supplies, maintenance and so forth are also fully paid for by the host country. So too, tuition for the students from the region is free, again, paid for by the Qatari government.

As impressive as this building and its faculty are, this is just one of a half dozen American universities similarly invited and housed in equally impressive and sate of the art structures. Among the other U.S. institutions there are Texas A &M, Cornell medical, Virginia Commonwealth, Georgetown, and Northwestern all grouped together and coordinated in an "educational city" that will provide educational opportunities with faculty and physical resources rivaling anywhere in the world, including the U.S..

From the windows of these universities, visitors can observe two other remarkable developments. First, the nearby skyline of the main city of Doha itself is rising above the desert and sea with more new buildings and more daring architecture than anywhere in the U.S. In fact, in this one city alone there may well be more new and impressive skyscrapers under construction than in all major cities of the U.S. combined. The only rival to this boom is found elsewhere in the Gulf region or in cities of Asia.

The other visible development, which is nearing completion adjacent to the university complex, is a multi-billion dollar science research center rising up to parallel and complement the educational infrastructure. The goal is nothing less than attracting the most talented individuals in the world to the science center, then, in turn, utilizing that resource and the universities to train the next generation of scientists and engineers.

Virtually all this educational and scientific infrastructure plus the building boom of the city itself is funded from oil and gas revenues and designed to ensure that when the oil and gas eventually declines the Qataris will still lead and prosper from the next generation economy. Our dependence on foreign energy helps make that possible. So too does our national investment in defense capability, like the *San Antonio*, which in part is dedicated to defending the oil and gas supply to feed our dependence and that of other nations.

No nation on earth can rival our defense investment or capacity, but our nation is not now rivaling the development or educational and scientific investments taking place in numerous other nations. The question we must ask is which investment will pay the greatest dividends in the long run?

Defense Spending

To get a sense of what our nation spends on defense and related activities, consider the following. Defense spending for Fiscal Year (FY) 2009 was included in a continuing resolution which appropriated $487 billion specifically for defense purposes. In addition, the Military Construction and Veterans Affairs appropriations for 2009 amount to $72.9 billion. On top of this amount, $65.9 billion of "emergency" funding had already been approved in June of 2008 to cover operations in Iraq and Afghanistan through to early 2009.

To these figures, add in at least $10 billion for Department of Energy-housed funding for the nuclear arsenal. This brings the total appropriations for defense- and veteran-related funding to more than $635 billion for FY 2009. This figure is likely to rise still further before the fiscal year ends as some are calling for more "emergency" appropriations for Iraq and Afghanistan, with estimates of as much as $80 billion more to be requested.

It is helpful to put these figures into context from two different directions. On the one hand, those who argue for spending more on defense point to the need to fund ongoing military actions in Iraq and Afghanistan plus global efforts against terrorists. In addition, the increase in Chinese military activity, Russia's recent changes, plus other trouble spots in the world suggest to some we need still more military capacity and, hence, more spending.

Advocates of greater defense spending often contrast current expenditures as a percentage of gross domestic product (GDP) with prior years. Assuming an estimated GDP of around $15 trillion in FY 2009, and considering the $635 billion total defense appropriations figure cited above, this would put projected spending at around 4.23% of anticipated GDP for FY 2009.

Different groups have cited somewhat different percentages and it is likely that the GDP may actually be lower in 2010 due to the economic downturn, but as a working number somewhere around this value of just over 4% of GDP is still useful. For comparison purposes, during World War II defense spending averaged 37.4 percent of GDP. During the Korean conflict it was 14.2 percent, during Vietnam at the peak 9.5 percent, and during the Regan military buildup it was up to 6.2 percent of GDP. Given this comparison, and in the context of the current military actions and potential threats, many argue that we are in fact spending too little on defense today.

An alternative way of looking at U.S. defense spending points out that in inflation-adjusted terms, the U.S. is now spending six times as much on defense as it was in 1950. Indeed, in real dollars defense spending is now at the highest level since the Second World War. What is more, defense spending increased at an average rate of more than six percent annually in real dollars for nine out of the last ten years, which represents a sustained rate of growth not seen in more than fifty years.

Because overall GDP had grown so rapidly in recent years, the net defense spending as a percentage of GDP looks relatively small compared to prior conflict periods, but the absolute amount of dollars in inflation adjusted terms has increased substantially.

For example, major defense acquisition programs more than doubled in the last eight years, growing from $782 billion in budget authority in 2000 to $1.6 trillion in 2007. For each active-duty member of the armed services, annual costs in pay and benefits are estimated to be more than $100,000 each year. Those costs, it should be noted, have increased by more than 47 percent in the past eight years and more than 114 percent in the last three decades in real, inflation adjusted, dollars.

U.S. defense spending can also be considered in comparison to spending by other nations. This analysis indicates that the U.S. alone spends very close to half of the total global military spending in a given year. In other words, our nation spends about as much on defense as the entire rest of the world combined.

It is also worth noting that, according to the Government Accountability Office, there are real problems in knowing where substantial amounts of the defense money is actually going and how it is being spent. When GAO prepares its annual financial report, it is unable to provide confident audit statements about the Department of Defense because of what it describes as "serious financial management problems at the Department of Defense."

Specifically, GAO was not able to confidently report on expenditures of DOD, noting that, "the Federal government was unable to support significant portions of the total net cost of operations, most notably related to DOD."

GAO also reported that "With respect to disbursements, DOD and certain other Federal agencies reported continued control deficiencies in reconciling disbursement activity...." resulting in " ...unreconciled differences between Federal agencies' and Treasury's records of disbursement and unsupported Federal agency adjustments, totaling billions of dollars."

Not Asking "How Much?"
But Rather "On What?" and "For What?"

As interesting as it is to consider levels of defense spending from different perspectives, my own belief is that, as in other areas of government, we should not evaluate the quality or success of an endeavor based solely on how much money we can throw at it.

Rather, we need to ask the more important questions of how well we are achieving the goal of providing for our national security and how we can better achieve that goal. We also need to keep in mind the opportunity cost of all spending and consider the contrast I described earlier between the state of the art of our own military hardware compared with the state of the university and science centers of other nations.

Throughout this book I have argued that the current and future financial conditions of this nation will require a combination of growing the economy while cutting expenditures and increasing revenues. I also maintain that spending cuts must be sought in all aspects of the budget, with no category exempt from scrutiny or reduction. That principle must apply to Defense spending as well and I am convinced we can reduce spending on defense without endangering our security.

The Military Industrial Complex

One of the first places we can look to find ways of providing more effective security for less money is to ask how the most costly defense and weapons expenditures are chosen and funded. To better understand the importance of this, it is helpful to consider the admonition of someone who knew well what was at stake.

In his 1961 farewell address to the nation, a portion of which provides the quotation that begins this chapter, President and former General Dwight D. Eisenhower advised that:

> In councils of government, we must guard against the acquisition of unwarranted influence, whether sought or unsought, by the military industrial complex. The potential rise of misplaced power exists and will persist....Only an alert and knowledgeable citizenry can compel the proper meshing of the huge industrial and military machinery of defense with our peaceful methods and goals, so that security and liberty may prosper together.

Eisenhower was right when he said this more than forty years ago, and he would be shocked at how the military industrial complex functions today. The sophisticated integration of political lobbying, campaign contributions and spending earmarks, plus the complexity and opaqueness of the military procurement system have all made defense spending more costly than it needs to be and less effective than it should be.

At the same time, an increasing pattern of former military personnel leaving the uniformed ranks to join high-priced and higher-paying lobbying firms is drawing from the ranks of our services and creating dangerous conflicts of interest within the military and in the lobbying world itself.

At least six key measures would substantially reduce both total defense costs and the adverse impacts of the military industrial complex that Eisenhower warned of. They are:

- Increase clarity, transparency, fairness and oversight of defense procurement and acquisition;
- Reform campaign finance to prohibit contributions to candidates;
- Require full transparency and justification of earmarks;
- Lobbying reform that closes the revolving door from the Pentagon to lobbying firms;
- Improved contract management and oversight with real financial penalties for cost overruns; and
- Changes to arms sales of U.S.-made weapons to foreign nations.

Because reforms to campaigns, earmarks and lobbying are addressed elsewhere in this book, let us focus here on defense specific issues of acquisitions and arms sales.

Clarity, Transparency, Competition and Oversight of Acquisitions

My guess would be that if you asked every Member of Congress how defense procurement works, fewer than a couple dozen or so could come close to offering an educated answer. That might not be so surprising, as most members tend to know what goes on in their own committee and those not on the Armed Services Committees would have relatively little reason to acquaint themselves with this rather arcane matter.

At the same time, however, considering that hundreds of billions of dollars per year are spent on defense, and, given that the security of our nation depends in large part on our defense capabilities, the taxpayers have a right to ask how well this system is working.

The answer, unfortunately, is that in many cases it is not working very well. This is demonstrated by numerous examples of cost overruns, faulty equipment, delivery delays and other snafus. It is also evident in the fact that the Government Accountability Office has reported that the Department of Defense financial records are not in condition to allow them to be audited.

Clearly, this is a system in need of review and reform. The good news here is that one of the undertakings of the House Armed Services Committee in 2009 was the creation of a Panel on Defense Acquisition Reform. The mission of this panel was to conduct a comprehensive review of the structure and performance of current defense acquisition procedures and identify areas of needed reforms. The panel completed its work in early 2010. Congress and the administration would do well to carefully consider its recommendations and make whatever changes are needed to prevent the kinds of costly errors and over expenditures that have plagued defense spending in recent years.

Further good news on this front comes from Defense Secretary Gate's recent position statements and budget proposals for future defense programs and spending. Once again, however, it will be up to Congress to demonstrate the political will and courage to make these changes for the good of the country, even if it means one or another weapons system needs to be cancelled in the process.

Veterans and Disability Benefits

As mentioned elsewhere, before serving in Congress I worked as a psychologist, including a period working in a VA hospital. Based on that work I am absolutely committed to ensuring that our wounded warriors and their families receive the best possible medical care and educational benefits they have earned through their service.

I am also aware, however, that escalating costs and finite financial resources are realities that must be dealt with responsibly. This is not easily achieved because our nation owes a real debt to those who have served in uniform. What's more, veteran's organizations comprise powerful voting blocks and mount effective lobbying campaigns calling for increases in benefits.

Here then is the challenge, stated in its most blunt terms: On the one hand many veterans and non-veterans alike believe those who have served in the armed forces are entitled to substantial health, education, retirement and other benefits. On the other hand, if all veterans received all the benefits that some advocates seek on their behalf, the costs would be crippling to the nation.

"Well you'll just have to solve that Mr. Congressman," said one constituent when I raised this at a town hall. "I served my country and I demand my rights and my benefits and I don't care where you have to get the money from."

Another veteran responded to that statement in a much different way.

"I'm not asking for anything," he said. "I was proud to serve my country. I believe it was my duty. And the only pay or benefit I ask is to live in freedom. The guys we really owe the most are the ones who can't claim disability or other benefits because they gave their all and gave their lives for us. People have been sacrificing for this country since the Revolutionary War. Most of them didn't do it for money or disability compensation, they did it for love of country – nothing more."

These two statements reflect strikingly different attitudes about the purpose and rewards of military service. They also have profoundly different implications for the nation's defense, financial future and, importantly, for the health of the individual veterans as well.

Let me say a few things that are rarely said but need to be acknowledged. Without any doubt, there are many veterans who have been severely injured in the line of duty and are deserving of every medical expenditure and disability payment that comes their way. Those who have lost limbs or been paralyzed, suffered severe burns, been blinded, or sustained serious brain injuries are all among this group.

Even for this group, however, from a clinical perspective it is important to emphasize that restoring the maximum ability possible should be the primary goal, not focusing primarily on compensation for disability.

It is a difficult thing to say, but in some circles and for some individuals a culture of disability and entitlement has replaced a standard of the individual can do spirit and service to country. This is not healthy for the individuals or their families, for the services, or for the nation.

Disability payments may be well-intended compensation for service to country, and, again, in many cases they are both needed and deserved. But for some veterans, such payments and an infrastructure of interest groups dedicated to helping obtain them can have the iatrogenic consequence of prolonging disability and inhibiting progress rather than enhancing treatment and recovery.

In both my clinical and Congressional experience I have seen individuals who spend virtually their entire lives in pursuit of disability payments. The sad effect of this can sometimes be that people become so committed to and dependent on disability payments that their opportunities and motivation to improve their condition, be it physical or psychological, is impaired.

Even stating this is sure to elicit angry denunciations of insensitivity or disrespect, but it should be just as questionable to encourage people who might otherwise reach higher levels of emotional or physical function to instead accentuate deficits for the sake of financial compensation.

To be honest, I do not have an easy solution to this except to state the matter as plainly as I can and encourage all those who are involved in it to consider as objectively as they can if there is not some truth to what I have just said. The toll on the emotional and physical recovery of veterans created by "rewarding disability" is my greatest concern, but there are also real and substantial financial costs to the nation that must be addressed.

Nuclear Weapons

As part of our strategy for national defense, we need to seriously evaluate the role of nuclear weapons. Among the questions we should ask are what the total costs are for building, maintaining, protecting and ultimately decommissioning such weapons and dealing with their waste.

Of particular concern in this regard is a shortage of scientists and engineers who are knowledgeable in weapons production and maintenance. Maintenance is a growing question mark as our existing nuclear arsenal and that of other nations ages with uncertain impacts. If we are going to maintain a nuclear inventory as part of our defense weaponry, it is absolutely essential that we invest now in the education and training of a new cadre of scientists and engineers who will have the knowhow to build and maintain the arsenal we already have and build new devices to replace those that must be taken out of ready service.

The other key question that must be asked is more fundamental still, and that is the question of whether or not nuclear weapons should be part of our arsenal at all. In my judgment, the answer to this is not as clear as some might think.

Having been involved personally in citizen efforts to reduce nuclear threats during the Cold War, I appreciate the horrific potential of nuclear weapons, particularly if used against civilian targets. I am also aware, both from classified briefings and publically available information, of the dangers posed by so called "loose nukes," i.e. actual weapons or weapons grade material falling into the wrong hands. A further concern is that our own nuclear capabilities make it more difficult to argue against proliferation by other nations, such as Iran, North Korea or others.

Taking this later point first, I do not agree with the argument that says we must disarm if we want to oppose nuclear capabilities of other nations. The fact is, nations differ in their motives, their histories, their values, their leadership and their respect for such things as rule of law. Keeping weapons of mass destruction from certain nations makes perfect sense in its own right, whether or not we possess such weapons ourselves. What is more, if such nations do eventually develop their own nuclear capacity, it would put our own nation at risk if we lacked any credible threat of comparable response.

I truly wish it were not necessary to make this argument and that reality were different. Wishing, however, does not change that reality. Neither does it change a second reality which is this.

War, death, and mass destruction are horrible events under all circumstances. Read the accounts of historical battles, from the Trojan war, Agincourt, Napoleon's retreat from Moscow, Antietam, D-Day, Guadalcanal, Pork Chop Hill, Dak To, Faluja, and others, listen to those who participated in the fighting, and it is clear that war is grisly whatever the weaponry of the era.

Nuclear weapons, along with chemical and biological weapons of mass destruction, have the potential to vastly increase the numbers of deaths and are especially indiscriminate in their targeting and victims, but disarming our own nation does not in itself protect us from such horrors. If we lack nuclear weapons but are subject to massive attack from more conventional forces, what alternatives would we have for defending our nation at home or our forces abroad?

Unfortunately, the alternative might well be still more massive expenditures on conventional weapons and much larger military forces, including a draft.

Certainly, I have argued elsewhere in this book that we must do much more to prevent armed conflict to begin with, to promote diplomacy and peacemaking, and to conduct our actions in ways which are more likely to gain allies than adversaries. All of that notwithstanding, we may still face attack from a variety of sources and we must be prepared to dissuade and defend against such attacks.

It may be that we will one day choose to not include nuclear weapons as part of that strategy, and it is certainly true that we can and should reduce the numbers of devices currently ready and deployed around the world. But at the present time,

I do not believe it would be sound policy to completely disarm our nuclear arsenal.

Sexual Orientation and Military Service

With difficult and costly military engagements in Iraq and Afghanistan, with an operations tempo that is rapidly exhausting troops and equipment and with certain specialized skills in high demand, our nation cannot afford to exclude qualified, motivated and patriotic Americans from military service for reasons that have absolutely nothing to do with their ability to serve and perform their missions.

I have met with brilliant computer experts, foreign language interpreters who speak fluent Arabic, Farsi and Pashto, skilled fighter pilots, doctors and nurses, all of whom have served their country well or would like to serve, but who have been discharged or denied because of their sexual orientation. This makes no sense. We need people with those skills and as loyal Americans they should have every bit as much right to serve their country and defend our security as anyone else.

The old prejudices that prevent this from happening need to be vigorously challenged just as prejudices against people of color were challenged in an earlier era. Arguments that homosexuals would act out sexually with other soldiers are based on stereotypes not fact. The numbers of women reporting sexual assault in the military and the numbers of pregnant soldiers suggest that if the mere possibility of sexual activity is grounds for discharge then we must exclude heterosexuals as well. That's going to leave a very small force of abstemious eunuchs left to defend the country.

Simply put, there is no valid reason, other than prejudice and stereotype, that sexual orientation per se should disqualify someone from service. The penalties for sexual conduct, such as harassment, fraternization and other offenses, is another matter and should apply equally to all troops, hetero and homosexual alike, but discrimination based on orientation should stop.

Non-traditional Threats and Terrorism

Since September 11, 2001, our understanding of national defense has changed in many ways. We have learned that threats are not limited to combat between large military forces deployed overseas. Rather, they can come at anytime, anywhere, with civilians as primary targets and the attackers not part of any national military force.

The challenge this poses to national defense are many, but one of the most significant realizations is that our vast expenditures on traditional defense may not be able to protect us as we would wish. The same is true of much of the expenditure on "homeland security," which, in spite of the hundreds of billions spent, still leaves gaping vulnerabilities for terrorists to exploit.

One of the implications of this is that individual citizens must do much more to prevent and prepare for possible attacks. On the prevention side, ongoing vigilance and reporting is essential. On the preparation side, every American ought to have a personal disaster preparedness plan and supplies to be ready for natural disasters or terror attack.

Unfortunately, most Americans have little idea what they would do if a dirty bomb or biological weapons attack struck their community. In fact, some surveys suggest people might do precisely the wrong thing and expose themselves and their families to greater risk. Equally problematic is the fact that only a very small percentage of people have sufficient supplies to allow them to survive disruptions in basic services like water, electricity, gas and so forth.

What is troubling about this is that we ought to know better and take action, but most people don't. Certainly scenes of the devastation from earthquakes, hurricanes, floods etc., and the realization that help in such large scale disasters may be weeks away, ought to convince everyone to have at least a week's supply of water, medicines, food, and emergency supplies stored in a safe and accessible place. Yet few people do.

We need to launch a national education and preparedness plan and establish an annual "Disaster Preparedness Week" that encourages people to prepare for terrorist event or natural disaster and check their preparedness on an annual basis. This should be coordinated with all media outlets plus the businesses which sell the necessary supplies. Our goal should be nothing less than to ensure that every single American knows exactly what to do in different scenarios and that every American has sufficient supplies to survive at least a full week, and preferably several weeks, without any external support and without the basic infrastructure and service needs being met.

Continuity of Government

As troubling as it may be that few Americans have taken adequate disaster preparations for their families and homes, it is even more disconcerting that the Federal government itself is woefully unprepared to deal with catastrophic events. The shocking fact is that all three major branches of the Federal government, the Legislative, Executive, and Judicial branches, have either no continuity plan whatsoever or have plans that are deeply flawed constitutionally or practically.

I have been working to address this issue since the night of September 11th, but thus far there has been no real progress. Consider, for example, what happens if a nuclear weapon detonates near the Capitol, wiping out the Congress, the Supreme Court, the President and Vice President. During the Cold War we might have had some warning of an incoming missile or bomber, and we hoped the deterrence effect of nuclear retaliation could have prevented an attack to begin with. Those conditions no longer apply in an era of loose nukes and non-state suicidal terrorism.

If Congress were wiped out, the Senate could largely be restored to functioning relatively quickly through gubernatorial appointments. The House of Representatives, however, requires direct election to replace members. If large numbers of House members were killed or incapacitated several months would pass before the House could be fully reconstituted. Since legislation, including declarations of war, establishment of a draft, defense appropriations and countless other likely responses requires passage by both the House and Senate, this would leave the legislative branch either paralyzed or forced to act in an extra-constitutional capacity of questionable legal validity.

Bear in mind too that the Speaker of the House is next in line to the Presidency if both the President and Vice President perish. A terrorist attack could easily alter the elected political makeup of the House, perhaps installing a new Speaker who may well be from the prior minority party and perhaps from the party opposite the President. If this were to be accomplished with fewer members than the constitutionally required majority for a quorum, a constitutional crisis would likely result.

The most appropriate arbiter of such a crisis would normally be the Supreme Court, but, in the case of a nuclear attack, the Court might also be eliminated. Just as there is currently no valid plan for continuity of Congress, there is also no plan for continuity of the Supreme Court.

It is also worth considering that next behind the Speaker of the House is the President pro tempore of the Senate who, by tradition, is typically the most senior senator in the majority party. Without referring to specific members of the Senate, suffice it to say that the most senior member of that body has not always been someone well equipped to serve as President in time of crisis.

During Congressional testimony an expert on terrorism and national security asserted that this situation of inadequate and flawed continuity provisions virtually invites a terrorist attack on the capitol, knowing that such an attack would profoundly disrupt central elements of our constitutional republic.

To address these concerns a collaborative effort by the American Enterprise Institute and the Brookings Institution has brought together a non non-partisan blue ribbon commission of legal scholars, security experts, and former members of Congress. This Continuity of Government Commission has reviewed the dangers faced by current lack of continuity plans and has put forward a series of recommendations for how to prepare for such events. Several members of Congress, including myself, have also offered proposed remedies.

Sadly, the response from Congressional leadership and members has been dismal. I have heard otherwise respected colleagues say such things as "Why should I care, I'll be dead anyway," "Don't ask me to think about my own death, it's too disturbing," "There is no way terrorists could kill us, we don't have to worry about that," and "I'm sure someone would survive and they would do the right thing. We don't have time to worry about that now," and, perhaps most disturbing of all, "I'm not sure that polls very well."

The American people, and for that matter the rest of the world, deserve better than this. The current situation practically invites terrorists, foreign or domestic, to profoundly disrupt our government and change the political balance of power. Alternatives exist that would maintain political balance and allow the House, Senate, Executive Branch and Supreme Court to be fully and constitutionally functioning within twenty four hours of an attack. We should implement those measures before they are needed. Since we cannot know when that moment might come, it is essential that we act now.

13.

CONGRESSIONAL REFORMS

Article I of the Constitution defines the responsibilities of the Legislative branch of government - the Congress. The Framers purposefully did not start by describing the Presidency or the Courts, they began with the Congress.

Most Americans recognize this, but we too often look to the President as if the Executive Branch made the laws. In reality, and in the Constitution, the Executive Branch is supposed to be just that, the branch which executes the laws made by Congress. If we truly want to get our nation back on track, we should call on Congress to do its job. The trouble is, certain rules, structures and procedures within Congress make it terribly difficult to get things done in responsible, timely ways.

How Congress Raises and Spends Money

Suppose your spouse, colleague or employees kept coming up with ways to spend money without in some way linking the new expenditures to realistic sources of income. At the same time, imagine that others in your family and business keep finding ways to reduce your income without significantly altering spending. Now suppose that decisions about exactly how money would be spent for the coming year have to be made by a certain date but year after year that critical date is missed.

If this happened, it would not take long for you, your family or your business to be in debt or bankrupt. Unfortunately, this is essentially how Congress and the Administration have been operating for some time, and it is one of the key reasons the national debt continues to increase.

To get a sense of why our fiscal situation is in the state it is, it helps to understand a bit about how Congress functions or, perhaps better said, "dysfunctions" today. Looking closely at many of the processes in Congress one may begin to wonder if the whole system was not designed by an "inefficiency" expert or, worse, a committee of inefficiency committees.

Within the Congress, different committees are responsible for what is known as "authorizing" and "appropriating" the expenditure of money. To put these titles in terms everyone can understand if a teenager asks his parents for permission to go to the movies and the parents say yes, the teenager has the "authorization". But only when the parents accompany that authorization with, say twenty bucks or so, does the teenager actually receive the necessary "appropriation."

Authorizing committees in Congress have the prerogative to come up with new programs and, hence, in most cases, new ways to spend money. Authorizing committees do not typically have to decide where the money is coming from. Decisions about actually spending money on discretionary programs are made by the Appropriations committee and its various subcommittees. These committees do not necessarily have to spend any money on what the authorizing committees have authorized, nor, in most cases, can they determine where the money they will appropriate to spend actually comes from.

The committees tasked with raising money through taxes, i.e. the powerful Ways and Means committee in the House and the Finance committee in the Senate, do not get a direct say over how much money actually gets spent, at least not on most discretionary programs. On the other side of the equation, if the Ways and Means committee decides to lower taxes, and hence revenues, they usually bear little or no direct responsibility for determining which current spending commitments or programs actually have to get cut as a result.

What all this means in practice is that one set of committees and people in Congress can create new programs with no responsibility for how to pay for them. A second set of committees can actually spend money, but this group lacks the requirement or the authority to determine where the money comes from. Meanwhile, the committee that actually does raise the money can't control where or how much of it is spent

248

on the discretionary side, nor are they responsible for what happens if they decide to raise less money.

As if this structure were itself not inherently doomed to failure, keep in mind that many government programs, once established, run on "autopilot" with spending on them considered to be "mandatory" under the terms of the law that created the programs to begin with. "Entitlement" programs are examples of this and, as discussed earlier in this book, the spending "autopilot" that guides these programs seems only set on climb. Rarely if ever is it set to descend and when that does happen Congress usually intervenes to manually override the descent.

Even discretionary programs have the potential to run on indefinitely once created. To return to the teenager analogy, when the teenager returns home, a responsible parent is likely going to try to be sure the teen actually went to the movie as promised. They might ask "How was the movie?" In Congress-speak, this would be called "oversight." "Authorizing" committees have the responsibility for oversight. It is also within their authority to eliminate programs, which does actually happen on rare occasions but not nearly often enough.

The Administration's Role

Congressional processes certainly deserve a great deal of blame for our current fiscal situation, but when it comes to Federal tax and spending policies, administration officials and the office of the President can be every bit as profligate, biased, and political -- and this applies to Presidents from both parties.

The Broader Context

To appreciate the context in which spending decisions occur, consider that as this paragraph was first being written in early 2008, Congress had just voted to essentially give away $168 billion dollars in "stimulus" money through tax rebates with no idea whatsoever of how it would be paid for and, unfortunately, through a procedure that allowed no consideration or votes on any alternative ways of spending the money. Voting against that bill, and essentially telling millions of people they would not get a "free check", was not easy.

Updating what you just read, the paragraph you are reading now had to be added in late September of 2008 as Congress contemplated a proposed $700 billion bailout (now known as the TARP) of financial companies. In the Bush Administration's initial request, there was no proposal suggesting how we would pay for this expense. To the credit of Congress, the final bill included key provisions, some of which I helped insert into the legislation, that ensure the taxpayers will be protected and the financial industry will ultimately foot the costs of the program.

The continuing financial chaos of our government is further indicated by the need for yet another additional paragraph, this one added in February of 2009 as the Congress passed a nearly $800 billion economic recovery and reinvestment package. Most economists believe this spending was necessary to prevent a slide into depression, but the significant increase in the deficit is nevertheless a problem.

Though Congress did its best in the face of the unprecedented situation of September 2008 and again in early 2009, looking at the overall process one must ask if it is any wonder that we are in such a financial mess in both the private and public sectors? More importantly, does it seem very likely that the system which got us here is likely to solve that mess?

The fact is, the way Congress and the Administration make decisions about how to raise and spend money just doesn't make sense, doesn't work anymore and ought to change. Common sense and simple math says that if budgets are to balance spending should not exceed revenues and the processes by which spending and revenue decisions are made ought to be connected. Achieving that goal in the current crisis may not be possible immediately, but it should be our objective to get there as soon as responsibly possible. Let's consider what needs to change structurally in Congress to bring that about.

Key Problems In Congressional Appropriations

Within the House and Senate the Chairs of the appropriations committees are sometimes referred to as "Cardinals" because the power they wield is comparable to the power of cardinals within the Catholic Church. My own experience in Congress has come in the House of Representatives, so that is the side of the Legislative branch I will focus on here.

Of the four hundred thirty five voting members of the House, only 60 serve on appropriations committees and only 13 are subcommittee chairs or "Cardinals." The total annual discretionary expenditures, including supplemental appropriations, for fiscal year 2009 was nearly $1.5 trillion

One of the legitimate questions raised by this is how such a relatively small number of people can possibly make informed decisions about spending such incredible amounts of money on literally thousands of different programs throughout the government.

A second concern has to do with the inequalities that result from a handful of powerful members controlling so much money. Stories of appropriations chairs "earmarking" vast sums to their districts, at the expense of others, may be the exception but they are nevertheless too common. This abuse of power has undoubtedly contributed to much of the cynicism and disregard that people increasingly hold toward the institution.

One of the chief outcomes of this disdain has been a call for earmark elimination. The real problem, however, is not so much earmarks per se' as it is the system that entrusts so few individuals with so much control over so much of other people's money. Changing that inherent structure, and implementing political reforms addressed in the next chapter, will go a long way, and likely much farther toward restoring balance, than most of the proposed earmark reforms.

A third problem with the current structure is what happens when authorizing committees, for example those dealing with education, veterans affairs, or transportation, create programs or establish legislation with no direct connection to how much money will be made available from the appropriations committee to support the programs or enact the laws.

Examples of this disconnect are evident throughout government. The "No Child Left Behind Act" is a case in point. States were mandated to comply with a host of Federal requirements in order to receive Federal education funding, but the money that was supposed to be made available to help meet those mandates was never fully appropriated.

Ending the Authorizing/Appropriations Disconnect

To address all of these problems, the committee structure of Congress and House rules should be fundamentally changed. The authorizing/appropriating distinction should end and responsibility for appropriating money should be more broadly and evenly distributed throughout the Congress.

Committees that have direct authorization jurisdiction over program areas and agencies should also have direct appropriations capabilities, and there should be no specific separate "appropriations" committee that determines funding for all the other committees and members of Congress. Broad spending and revenue levels for different government functions should be set by the Budget committees, with the specific details of how money should be spent and raised left to the specific committees of jurisdiction.

In practice, this reform would mean that a committee dealing with education policy would have authorizing, appropriating and oversight responsibilities. It would be their role and responsibility to review what is working, what is not and evaluate proposals for how to improve our educational system.

If that committee believed a certain new program was needed, they could put forward measures to establish such a program and, importantly, they would have the authority, within the parameters set by the Budget, to also propose specific spending amounts to support such programs. So too, if the committee felt that money was not being well spent on a particular education program, that committee would have the responsibility and authority to recommend to the full House that funding be cut or eliminated for such programs.

One might think that this proposal would be appealing to most members of Congress because under the current structure those who are not on appropriations are largely excluded from the appropriations process and relegated to the role of supplicants, humbly asking the "Cardinals" to grant them this or that earmark. However, the entrenched power of appropriators was well illustrated by the response of one member of Congress who, hearing of these proposed reforms said, "You'd better not let the Appropriations committee hear about this or you can kiss your earmarks goodbye."

Changing the system as suggested would obviate this concern and distribute the responsibility and power much more evenly across the Congressional membership. Members would have more time to focus carefully and specifically on the area of primary interest to their committee jurisdiction and no programs could be authorized without corresponding decisions to appropriate the needed funds.

Ending the Appropriations/Revenue Disconnect

Merely merging authorizing and appropriating functions and distributing appropriating authority more broadly would have a number of benefits, but in and of itself would not likely be sufficient to rein in spending and reduce the deficit. If we are truly to reduce the deficit, members of Congress and the Administration must constantly ask, on every item of spending for every program, "Is this really necessary and do the benefits merit the costs?"

These questions, if simply rhetorical, can often be answered with more rhetoric. To make the questions and answers go beyond rhetoric to reality, any proposed spending, both on new programs or existing ones, must be directly connected to a specific revenue amount and source.

This principle is fundamental to how families and businesses conduct their financial affairs, but it is so alien to Congress that most members of Congress who hear of it ask,

"Well how would you ever do that?" The first answer to that question is itself a question, "If you don't directly link spending and revenue decisions, how do you ever expect to balance your budget?"

The substantive answer is this – for any proposed spending, specific revenue amounts should be identified and accounted for in revenue legislation for the corresponding year. At the end of the revenue and spending decision process, the total amount in the spending column would have to equal that in the revenue column. This principle should also apply to amendments offered during floor debate on either spending or revenue legislation.

Let's illustrate this with an example. If a committee dealing with education wanted to create a national program for providing scholarships to science teachers, the proposed program would have to be associated with a specific amount of money to be spent. The committee that determined the new program was necessary would also be able to appropriate money to fund it, but only if the amount of that money were also included in the revenue legislation for the year.

In practice, this means when the measure creating the program was voted on by the members of Congress, they would know they were voting not only on establishing the program in theory, but also on spending the money and on either raising that money through revenue or through transferring money from other existing programs that would see their total funding reduced. The amount and source of that money would then have to be specified as part of the legislation setting revenue and amounts for the year.

If fifty million dollars were proposed for a program, money for that could come by reducing spending on other programs, dedicating a specific portion of sales tax revenues, drawing funding from other revenue sources, or some combination thereof. This funding source would then also be reflected in annual tax legislation or through changes in spending on other programs.

This change would force elected representatives to make explicit choices between spending on different programs and between spending and revenue decisions. No longer could one committee simply create a new program or appropriate spending without that proposal also being tied to a designated source of funding.

Ending the Revenue/Spending Disconnect

Linking spending decisions to revenue sources deals with one direction of the financial ledger, but we must also address the other direction and link revenue decisions to spending. Just as it is far too easy now to propose continued or increased spending on new programs without having to worry about paying for them, it is also far too easy to promise to cut taxes without being explicit about what programs and individuals would lose out as a result.

To remedy this, anyone wishing to enact revenue cuts would have to be explicit about which programs would see reduced spending as the result of those cuts. In practice this would mean that if a legislator or the administration sought to reduce tax rates or eliminate all estate taxes, they would have to specify precisely what specific program cuts they would propose as a result of the lost revenue or, alternatively, what other taxes might be increased to keep the net revenue constant or in balance with spending.

Earmarks

Much has been made of the supposed "evils" of earmarks in appropriations bills. The first thing that must be recognized about Congressional earmarks is that the framers of the Constitution purposefully put "the power of the purse" in the hands of the Congress, not the administrative branch. That being said, it is true that there have been far too many instances in which powerful members of the House or Senate inserted special targeted spending to benefit their districts, financial backers or special interest groups.

The same is true of tax bills in which some members have added tax breaks that benefited only a few individuals or special interests. Although these "tax earmarks" have received far less attention than spending earmarks, they are every bit as costly to the treasury and equally prone to abuse.

Estimates by Citizens against Government Waste and Taxpayers for Common Sense indicate that the total amount of money earmarked in fiscal year 2008 was somewhere between $17 to $18 billion. This is a lot of money to be sure, but put it against the total discretionary spending of over a trillion dollars, or annual deficits exceeding a trillion dollars, and it is clear that one will not "solve the deficit" by eliminating earmarks. What is more, under current procedures eliminating all earmarks would, in most instances, have no net effect on total spending because earmarks merely designate spending within established appropriation amounts, they do not add to the total.

It should also be emphasized that, Congress is not the only entity that "earmarks" spending and tax breaks. In fact, overall, the President designates far more spending in his annual Budget than any member of Congress. Taking power away from Congress and giving more to political appointees is certainly no guarantee of impartiality. It is all too easy for politically motivated agency heads, who never have to face the voters themselves, to tip the scales toward members of Congress who are friendly or facing difficult reelection battles.

At least in the case of Congressional earmarks, there is an opportunity to see who spent what money where and then demand that they explain why. This is much more difficult in the case of administration and bureaucratic earmarking.

Transparency and Limits

The most important remedy to the abuse of earmarks is transparency. If there is concern about unjustified or excessive earmarking, the best solution is to make each member of Congress publicly identify any requested funds that are actually included in spending bills. The opportunity for the public and media to see who is spending how much, where and why they are spending it will quickly reveal those who are guilty of abuses.

There also need to be limits on how much any one individual member of Congress is allowed to direct to his or her district or to specific programs. It is understood that chairs of committees will likely have greater discretion and receive somewhat greater benefits through designated projects, but when a powerful chairman can direct vastly disproportionate amounts it distorts the process and deprives other members and districts of needed resources.

Ideally, information about earmarks should come before, not after legislation is passed into law. For that to happen changes are needed in House and Senate rules that govern debate on appropriations and revenue bills.

Floor Debates on Spending and Taxes

In recent years, it is not at all uncommon for legislation that calls for spending hundreds of billions of taxpayer dollars to be available for just a few hours before votes are taken. Examples include the so called "omnibus" appropriations bills passed at the end of each year, the Medicare prescription drug bill, the energy and climate bill of 2009, recent stimulus packages and many others.

Passing such important and expensive legislation with too little time to read the actual language and no opportunities for amendments does not make sense and is an insult to the institution and to the voters. Indeed, it is remarkable such a blatantly irresponsible practice has become standard operating procedure regardless of which party is in the majority and with very few members raising any objections.

In contrast to current practices, I have introduced legislation to require that all legislation should be available to Members of Congress and to the public online, for at least 72 hours before being submitted to a vote. In addition to a 72 hour rule for time to read the base legislation, House rules should also require that proposed amendments be available for at least 24 hours and these too should be published on the Internet for public access. To maintain some flexibility and immediacy to the process, exceptions to this latter rule on amendments could be made if approved by, for example, a fifty-five percent majority of those voting.

The first benefit of this rule would be that Members of Congress and their staffs would actually have an opportunity to study legislation before voting on it. They would also have a chance to offer meaningful amendments and to adequately review proposed amendments offered by other members.

Not only would members of Congress be able to study and understand the impacts of proposed legislation and amendments, the public and the media would have the same opportunity. This would have an extraordinarily salutary impact on the spending and revenue process and would go a long way toward restoring responsibility and balance to Federal spending and revenue decisions.

No longer could powerful chairmen slip last-minute items into bills with the hope they would not be discovered till well after a bill was passed. Truly unjustified projects would be recognized for what they are before votes were taken, not afterwards, and investigative journalists would have time to check out just who would benefit from such projects built at taxpayer expense.

On a positive note, my calls and those of others demanding time to read legislation have borne some fruit very recently. Indeed, the health care reform legislation that became law in March of 2010 had been debated extensively in the House and Senate, with the core text of the legislation being available for months. When final modifications were brought to a vote, the legislative language had been available and posted on the internet for more than 72 hours, and even the nine page managers amendment was available for more than 24 hours before the vote.

Observing this process from the inside, I am certain this time was absolutely essential to allow members on all sides and the public sufficient opportunity to evaluate the strengths and weaknesses of the legislation. Let us hope that similar transparency is followed on future legislation regardless of which party is in the majority, but we should go beyond hope an insist that Congress firmly establish this principle in the rules package at the beginning of each session.

Allowing Amendments to Revenue Bills

Allowing sufficient time for debate must be accompanied by opportunities to amend the legislation. Unfortunately, procedures governing revenue bills typically allow no amendments. This leaves the rank and file House member who is not on the Ways and Means committee with little say in revenue bills other than a simple up or down vote on the entire package or, often, a single alternative offered by the minority party.

I should emphasize that to a large degree amending complex tax legislation would be obviated if the simpler tax code I have advocated earlier in this book were enacted. Under that system, debate might focus on levels of taxation within a given revenue category, but all the targeted "tax expenditures," "tax earmarks," special interest provisions, complex formulas, and so forth of the current approach would be eliminated.

Still, even under a sales tax system, and especially considering the current tax system and code, Members of Congress should have opportunities to offer and vote on amendments of revenue bills just as they do on spending packages. And, just as proposed for spending packages, any proposed revenue cuts or increases would have to be linked to specific program changes and all revenue bills should be available to be read online for at least 72 hours, with amendments available for at least 24 hours.

The Fiscal Year and Biannual Budgets

In theory, and in law, all of the thirteen major appropriations spending bills are supposed to be passed by both the House and Senate and signed into law by the time the fiscal year begins on October 1. In practice, this rarely happens. Indeed, since 1974, when the fiscal year was reset from July 1 to October 1, there have only been three occasions on which all of the spending bills were actually enacted on time.

In the past 12 years, the record has been especially disappointing, with an average of only 1.5 appropriations bills passed into law on time each year. When bills are eventually passed after the deadline, they are increasingly joined together into so called "omnibus" packages combining multiple bills running hundreds or even thousands of pages in length, with hundreds of billions of dollars in spending and typically very little time allowed for members to actually read the bills before voting on them.

This now predictable unpredictability creates enormous problems for the government agencies that must function from year to year without knowing what their actual budgets will be. Agency directors cannot make decisions about hiring staff, repairing equipment or issuing grants without knowing what the funding for the year will actually be. In some recent years that information has not been available until the fiscal year was already more than one quarter complete.

To reduce such problems Congress should establish biannual budgets including both revenue and spending levels. Under this system, each revenue and spending bill would span funding or taxation for two years, thus allowing agencies, businesses, and individuals to plan ahead with more accuracy and confidence. An added and important advantage of this timeframe is that it would allow the respective committees of jurisdiction more time to conduct genuine oversight and performance reviews in the "off years" between appropriations.

A constructive variation on this would be to divide biannual appropriations in such a way that half of the appropriations for spending are considered each year, with the remaining half of the biannual appropriations the subsequent year. This way, if each appropriation and corresponding revenue package spanned two years, that would give more time for consideration of each of the spending bills for a given year. I have discussed this proposal with a number of agency directors who have indicated that it would indeed be a tremendous help to plan reliably for two year periods.

The Congressional Schedule

Biannual appropriations have the potential to make it easier for Congress to hit the scheduled timelines for spending bills, but appropriations delays are symptomatic of much deeper and more sweeping shortcomings in Congressional procedures and schedules.

For at least the past decade, the day to day and week to week Congressional schedule has lacked coordination, planning, or predictability. This has been true regardless of which party was in the majority and it is one of the causes of Congress failing repeatedly to complete its business on time.

It is common in Congress for different committees to schedule hearings or markups (votes) for the same time and day. Since many members of Congress serve on multiple committees and subcommittees, these scheduling conflicts are part of the reason hearings in the House so often have rooms packed with observers, experts and staff, but only a handful of members are actually in attendance.

The challenge of simultaneous committee meetings is particularly acute when votes are scheduled in more than one committee at once. This leaves members literally running from building to building to vote in two different places, or, alternatively, choosing between which issues and votes are more important.

Meanwhile, constituents wishing to meet with members personally rather than with staff must also jockey for a place on the schedule and a physical space in offices. To further complicate matters, debate on the floor of the House is also going on with the possibility of votes being called there at any time. Understanding that most members are involved with committee activities or constituent meetings while the House is also in session, helps explain why so often the House looks virtually empty even as important matters are being debated.

When votes are called on the House floor, all other business, including committee hearings, constituent meetings, yes even fundraising receptions, necessarily stop or continue without the members of Congress. Hearing witnesses, who may be cabinet officials, generals, world leaders in their fields, and average citizens with something important to say, are all put on hold while members of Congress race off to vote. It is not at all uncommon for such interruptions to last an hour or more.

There is a better way.

The Weekly Work Schedule

To put order and efficiency, and perhaps even sanity, into schedules, Congress should initiate five day workweeks separated every three or four weeks by full week-long district work periods.

During workdays in the Capitol, the schedule should limit conflict between committees and between committee work and floor action.

This could largely be achieved by scheduling most or all committee hearings for the mornings. Floor votes could then begin after 1 pm without fear of votes interrupting committee hearings or markups.

Separating committee time from floor action would obviate the interruption of committee hearings by votes, thereby making committee time much more productive and saving witnesses and others from the discourtesy and inconvenience of interruptions. This would also allow members who wish to participate in or observe floor debate time more to do so without sacrificing their committee duties and vice versa.

To reduce schedule conflicts between committees, set days each week should be designated for hearings by certain committees and subcommittees, with other days reserved for other committees. This would not eliminate all overlap, but with a bit of study and strategic planning, it could substantially reduce the conflict and make it much easier for members to plan and schedule their time in order to attend a higher percentage of hearings.

Congressional Hearing Reforms

Scheduling changes could help reduce conflicts and make hearings more productive, but other changes should also be made. The most significant of these would be for members of Congress to talk less and listen more. After all, the name of the event is a "hearing" not a "talking."

In some instances, hearings have begun with as much as an hour and a half of member "opening comments" before ever hearing a word from the witnesses. Meanwhile, the panel of witnesses and everyone else waits patiently at their table listening to member after member posing for the cameras and the Congressional record reading aloud what their staff has written for them as if anyone outside the hearing room actually cared about what they said.

This really should change. Hearings are expensive to arrange, time is precious and finite, and if members do not really want to hear what the witnesses, rather than other members, have to say, why call the hearing to begin with? Standard practice in all committees should be for the Chair and Ranking Member to each offer brief introductory remarks and any other member who wants to chime in at the outset should do so for the record in writing but not take time to read what they could just as easily introduce in print.

District Work or Congressional Travel Periods

In contrast to the current practice, in which members race home every weekend but have little midweek time in their districts, Congress should institute five day work weeks in the Capitol with periodic and predictable week long district work or travel periods.

Some may argue that five day work weeks in D.C. would reduce the time members have with their constituents. In fact, however, if full district work weeks were scheduled frequently, Members of Congress would have more usable time in their districts.

Ideally, district work weeks should be staggered to take place in different weeks of different months. For example, in one month the break might occur during the first week of the month, the next month the break might be the second week and so on. By staggering weeks on different months, it would be easier to meet at some point in the year with constituent groups that regularly hold meetings, for example, on the first Thursday or second Wednesday of every month.

Weekends Between Congressional Workweeks

A less obvious but important benefit from the proposed schedule changes would be the prospect of increased civility among members of Congress. Much has been said and written about the decline of comity in the Congress in recent years. In part, that decline is due to the schedule.

With members racing back and forth from their districts every week there is very little time to get to know each other as people or to interact with families. By comparison, if Congress met Monday through Friday for consecutive weeks, it is more likely that members would stay in Washington on weekends and would have free time on weekends to interact with one another and with each others' families.

Such interactions were once the norm, but now are rare. Having time to get together away from the partisan political world could go a long way toward restoring civility and cooperation. If you have dinner with another person and their family or take a day to go fishing or play golf together on a weekend, it is not so easy the next day to block your friend's right to be heard on the House floor or cut them to ribbons in your remarks during a committee debate.

Families

While the Congressional schedule should be set to provide for the most effective and efficient functioning of the institution itself, the unfortunate reality of Congress is that no schedule will truly be "family friendly." Nevertheless, if there is predictability about when the workdays begin or end, members who base their families in the D.C. area can work with their spouses and with schools or care providers to plan each day.

A second step that should be implemented is the provision of modest dedicated travel budgets to allow the immediate families of members to travel to or from their home district for a limited number of visits. Any family travel beyond this would be at the member's personal expense.

Finally, for all members of Congress, especially those who choose to bring their families to the D.C. area, the basic tax deduction for living expenses should be expanded to more realistically reflect actual expenses and to take into account the added costs of moving and maintaining a family while serving. This deduction, of course, would be unnecessary if a sales tax system were implemented, but barring that, it has merit under the current code

While on this subject, contrary to internet rumors, Members of Congress, unlike many state legislators, receive no "per-diem" expenses for housing meals or anything else while serving in Washington DC. Their total tax deduction for living expenses is $3000, in contrast to most other workers who deduct the full costs of living while working away from home.

It is also worth noting that, again contrary to Internet rumor, Members of Congress do not retire on full salary, nor do they receive free health care, and they do in fact all pay into Social Security and Medicare just like every other working American. This is by no means to complain about these facts, it is merely to state that they are facts..

Senate Rules

Because my experience in Congress is confined to the House of Representatives, I am mindful that it is somewhat presumptuous to offer suggested reforms to procedures in what we House members refer to as "the other body." Nevertheless, certain procedures in the Senate make it very hard to get real work done and excessively empower a very few extremist members to the detriment of the institution and the Nation's business.

The most needed and undoubtedly controversial reforms to get the Senate moving would be modification of the Filibuster and rules for obtaining cloture. It is also worth considering whether or not the Senate should consider a "germaneness" rule to ensure that bills are less often amalgams of unrelated measures glued together for political effect. This suggestion is certainly not original with me, but I have long believed it is necessary and recent events have only confirmed that belief.

As most people know, Senate rules allow an individual Senator or group of Senators to speak as long as they wish about anything they wish unless or until three-fifths of the Senators vote to close debate through a process known as "cloture." This is in contrast to House rules which provide strict time limits for total debate and individual speeches.

Because it can be difficult to muster the requisite Senate votes for cloture, small groups, or even a single member, can effectively block action on legislation or other business. To be sure, there have been many occasions in which the use or threat of a filibuster has, depending on one's political orientation, prevented undesirable actions or appointments, or provided sufficient political leverage to produce desired compromises.

Increasingly, however, in recent years a very small number of Senators at the extremes of the political continuum are employing actual or threatened filibusters, and associated "holds" on numerous matters before the Congress.

To get a sense of this increase, during the 1960s no Senate term had more than seven filibusters. By comparison, in the 110th Congress, from January 4th 2007 through November 20th 2008, 138 cloture motions had been filed to break actual or, more typically, threatened filibusters. The 111th Congress may well be on pace to break that record. As a result of such frequent filibustering, much needed work is not being completed simply because it does not satisfy the demands of a very few individuals.

At least two reforms to filibusters should be considered. First, there should be a limit to the number of times or issues on which any individual Senator exercises the filibuster. While it may be arguable that the Senate's deference to individual voices has merit and must be preserved, allowing single individuals to repeatedly block action on virtually everything the Senate hopes to achieve is counterproductive and unfair to everyone else. Limiting the numbers of times an individual utilizes the filibuster would cause those individuals to be more discerning and selective about what they chose to block.

The second reform to consider is reducing the number required for cloture from 60 to 55. I should hasten to emphasize that this proposal is not new and it was included in this chapter before the outcome of the 2008 elections. Hence, it is not a response to a favorable or unfavorable result in any specific election or for any specific party. Rather, it is a recommendation that would allow the Senate to move forward on key legislation. Sometimes, one party or another might not want that, but allowing a handful of Senators from either side to repeatedly and excessively obstruct legislation or confirmations blocks meaningful progress for the good of the country.

14.
POLITICAL REFORMS

Changes in how things work within Congress and the policy recommendations offered in this book will be more easily achieved if there are corresponding changes in how people get to Congress to begin with.

Campaign Finance Reform

If only one policy recommendation from this entire book could be put into place, the most beneficial overall effect would come from this – **completely prohibit candidates from accepting or raising campaign contributions or spending any personal money on their own elections**.

The way politics is currently practiced in the U.S., anyone seriously hoping to win an election to Federal office needs to raise and spend substantial amounts of money. Having been through seven races for Congress now, I have had to do this many times.

I am profoundly grateful to all of the donors who have invested their confidence and contributions to help me in my own campaigns. As grateful as I am for those contributions, and as necessary as they were, I also recognize that the need for and influence of money to finance campaigns distorts and damages our political process. The perpetual demand to raise money for campaigns takes far too much time from members of Congress or other elected officials and candidates. What is more, it inevitably raises the specter and reality of money unduly influencing votes or giving unfair advantages to one candidate over another.

To appreciate the time taken from members by fundraising, consider that competitive House races can easily cost several million dollars every two years. Quick math reveals that in order to raise two million dollars in two years, candidates must bring in an average of more than nineteen thousand dollars each and every week for the entire two year period.

Raising that money requires members of Congress and candidates to spend hour after hour after hour, day after day calling people on the phone to essentially beg for contributions. Then there is all the time spent attending fundraisers and other receptions with the goal of raising money or making connections that will lead to money.

All this effort spent on fundraising is time not spent studying policy, reading legislation, working with colleagues or meeting constituents. It is not uncommon on Capitol Hill for "call time," i.e. time spent making fundraising appeals, to be referred to as "doing the Lord's work." If one forsakes this work for the sake of policy concerns or other activities actually related to the job of making responsible legislation, it is akin to dereliction of duty. This pressure is especially acute for new members from swing districts who are under the watchful eyes of party leaders and for whom a low fundraising total in a given quarter can signal vulnerability and hence, even more attacks and more pressure to raise more money.

Fundraising pressures are exacerbated by the tacit, in some instances explicit, link between campaign contributions and votes or co-sponsorships. For new candidates, questionnaires are often sent by interest groups as litmus tests one must pass in order to receive financial contributions. This can easily cause candidates to make commitments to how they will vote before they are even in office. For incumbents, votes and co-sponsorships are "scored" by interest groups and everyone knows that a vote one way or another can easily cost tens or even hundreds of thousands of dollars in contributions.

Such outside pressures to take certain positions are added to by the internal pressure within political parties to raise money for the party or for other members. Raising money is not only about winning one's own election. It is also about gaining status and position within one's party.

Members of Congress seek assignments to certain committees at least in part because it is easier to raise campaign money if one is on those committees. Because the money that will be raised through service on the committees is likely to come from individuals, PACs, or others with interests before the committee, it is all too easy for policy and legislative decisions to be influenced by concerns about campaign contributions. This can lead to an effective "capture" of the committee, with those who have issues before the committee influencing the make-up of the committee membership and the direction of the committee decisions.

To take one example, consider that service on the Financial Services committee is considered to be an "exclusive" committee assignment. This means members who serve on this committee theoretically do not have other committee assignments. One of the unspoken reasons for this "exclusivity" is that this committee is a good place to raise campaign contributions. The trouble is, those contributions will more often than not come from the entities over which the committee is supposed to have oversight and regulatory responsibilities. If one seriously engages in such oversight and regulations, how likely is one to receive contributions?

Fundraising pressures can also influence and distort foreign policy as interest groups supportive of one foreign nation or another make campaign contributions to candidates who essentially pledge or vote in a certain way relative to those other nations.

This influence is especially powerful, and distorting, in regard to policies regarding the Middle East. It is no secret in Congress that voting, "the wrong way" on measures backed by certain pro-Israel groups can easily cost a member a hundred thousand dollars or more in lost contributions that may well wind up in the coffers of a primary or general election opponent who promises to "vote the right way" on these issues. More is said about this elsewhere in this book in the chapter on Foreign Relations, but the key point here is that U.S. Foreign policy should not be driven by considerations over campaign contributions, and the election of people to public office should be based on U.S. interests, not the interests of any foreign nation.

How The Money Is Spent

As pernicious and damaging as all of the issues just described are, the process is made worse by the realization that all the money being raised is ultimately going to pay for meaningless or downright mean television adds, robo-calls and slick mailers that don't really say anything of substance.

Freedom of speech is cherished, but speech is not really free if candidates have to sell their souls to pay for it, and our constitutional protections do little good for the republic if what is said is blatant pandering or nasty smears.

Banning Individual Fundraising by Candidates

Recognizing all of these problems, is it possible to give elected officials time to study issues instead of raising money? Is there a way to prevent the outcomes of elections and representative government itself from being excessively influenced, if not outright controlled, by those with the greatest amounts of wealth and most extreme positions?

The answer is yes.

Again, the best way I know of to achieve these goals would be to make it illegal for candidates to raise or accept money for their campaigns or to spend any personal funds on campaign activity.

In place of the existing money game, candidates and parties who demonstrate a base level of support would receive limited and equal amounts of public funding with limited time periods during which this money can be spent. This level required for eligibility could be shown by gathering sufficient numbers of signatures on petitions of support for a candidate. Levels of public funding should be set at reasonable levels that would allow a candidate to convey their messages to voters without overwhelming the airwaves, newspapers or mailboxes.

Of course no one would be required to accept public financing, but there would be no alternative direct source of money for candidates. No other funds could be spent or raised by candidates, period.

If public funding is provided, strict constraints should also be placed on when it can be used. The increasing trend toward endless campaigns is driving costs higher and higher and exhausting the tolerance and interest of the electorate. Limiting the time period for use of public funds could reduce this trend.

As someone who has spent fifteen years under the present system, and in the process burned far too many precious hours of life on fundraising calls and events, the thought of such a fundamental change is really remarkable. It is truly difficult, but also exhilarating, to imagine running for and serving in Congress without the pressure or even the ability to raise money.

How much time would come back to our lives that could better be spent on substantive policy work? What would it be like to not have somewhere in the back of one's mind the financial impact of votes, co-sponsorships and so forth? Imagine never having to worry that an "expose" in a paper or hit piece from an opponent is somehow going to smear you because of the conduct of or association with one of thousands of campaign contributors. And what would it be like if Congressional races and candidates were evaluated not on the basis of "cash on hand" on quarterly FEC reports, but on actual personal qualifications, true grass roots support, and real stands on real issues?

The answer to these rhetorical questions is simple – it would be profoundly better – better for the people involved in politics, better for the political process itself, and better for the nation.

"Independent" Expenditures

The problem of individual candidates being forced to constantly raise money and consider financial consequences of votes is paralleled and complicated by the growing influence of extreme "independent" groups on both sides of the political spectrum. This problem was exacerbated exponentially by a January 2010 Supreme Court decision allowing direct and virtually unlimited campaign spending by Corporations, Unions and other groups that had previously been constrained under campaign spending laws.

One manifestation of independent expenditures that existed prior to the new court rulings the so called 527s, so named because of a provision of the tax code which governs their tax status. In 2008, combined spending by these groups exceeded $487 million.

Many of these groups are essentially surrogate attack organs of the two major political parties. The well known "Swift Boat" adds of the Kerry v Bush presidential contest is one such example. Certain labor union affiliated ads are examples from the other side of the political spectrum.

In addition to the independent groups that act as party surrogates, there are also groups that focus many of their attacks on candidates or elected representatives who are not "liberal or conservative enough" within their own parties. This self policing and political culling by extremists tends to drive a wedge of division still more deeply into the body politic and makes it even harder for reasonable, thoughtful people to work together for the common good from the center. Because such groups have access to so much money, their influence further complicates and compounds the financial and political pressures on candidates.

What to do about these groups and expenditures is by no means an easy question. Having supported various attempts at campaign finance reform during my time in Congress, I know the difficulty in crafting solutions that do not violate the first amendment, make the problem even worse, or do both at the same time. Some of most well intentioned reforms passed into law thus far have actually made things worse and put more money into independent groups at the extreme ends of the political spectrum with even less transparency or accountability than direct contributions to candidates.

In fact, the earlier suggestion that we outlaw individual fundraising by candidates, if not accompanied by reforms of independent expenditures, could itself be counterproductive. Candidates would quite understandably complain that if they could not raise money themselves they would be left virtually defenseless against attacks from so called independent groups that under current rules can spend virtually limitless amounts.

What is needed then are substantial reforms on independent expenditures. The most important of these are:

- Firm limits on the amounts that can be contributed to such groups both in terms of total contributions from an individual, per period, to all groups and total contributions to any one group, per person, per period;
- Complete transparency with real-time, up-to-date listing of all donors to any such group, the amounts they have contributed, and their employment or other current and former affiliations;
- Complete transparency with real time listing of all expenditures by any groups including how much was spent, for what purpose, through what media channels and at what prices;
- Clearly legible or audible identification of the group or individual associated with any political or issue advertising and, as just described, readily available Internet posting of all donors and group expenditures;
- The immediate availability of additional public matching funds to any candidate who is the target of campaign advertising by independent groups or whose opponent is directly referenced favorably by independent groups; and
- Personal appearances and statements of responsibility by corporate or union heads in every advertisement if corporate or union money is used.

The Need for An Amendment

In light of not only the most recent but also prior Supreme Court decisions, it is evident that a constitutional amendment will be required to achieve the recommended limits on independent expenditures and candidate fundraising and spending. Such an endeavor, particularly when matters of speech are concerned, is never to be taken lightly.

Nevertheless, for the good of the Republic I believe this is in fact necessary and that it must be done in a way that does not constrain the content of political discourse but rather allows for open and honest limits on the sources and quantities of money spent on political campaigns.

Ultimate Responsibility for Reform

The reforms proposed above, have the potential to substantially alter the influence of money in politics. Ultimately, however, we will only be able to reduce the influence of money on politics when "we the people" fully accept and exercise our rights and responsibilities as citizens.

This means citizens must think carefully and critically and seek out and analyze information about candidates and positions well beyond thirty second television ads and slick mailers. The Internet and other technologies make this information more accessible than ever before, but only if people avail themselves of this resource and use it wisely. Citizenship is not a free ride, it is a responsibility and meeting that responsibility is at least a part time job.

Finally, just as citizenship is a responsibility so is seeking or serving in elective office. Holding office is not meant to be a risk-free occupation. In spite of, indeed, in some cases because of the power of money, candidates and elected officials must have the courage to take difficult, principled positions even though it may mean the loss of political contributions and even when the result means one will be targeted by extreme interest groups.

Ending Congressional Gerrymandering

Most states now set Congressional and legislative borders based on partisan legislative manipulations, with district boundaries drawn in order to give one party or candidate the greatest political advantage. The results produce disproportionate partisan political outcomes and congressional districts formed into weirdly contorted jigsaw puzzle pieces rather than reasoned contiguous communities. This is unfair to citizens, distorts the task of the representative, and skews the balance of legislative power in ways that do not truly represent the views of voters.

This practice should end. Congressional and legislative districts should not be based on political power lines or incumbent protection (or endangerment) but on logical, rational boundaries reflecting geographic coherence and fair representation.

Some states, including my own state of Washington, already achieve this relatively well by using independent or bipartisan commissions to establish new congressional boundaries in response to census data. To appreciate the difference in results between independent commissions versus legislated boundaries, look at maps of the Congressional Districts in states where legislatures have had control versus independent commissions. In general, if you find states with districts that look literally "all over the map", you are looking at a legislated, very likely gerrymandered outcome.

Because the legislatures that currently control the drawing of Congressional district boundaries do so for their own partisan advantage, it is not likely that many will voluntary relinquish that privilege. This is especially true if one majority has effectively used legislative boundary control to stack their majority and limit minority access.

As a result, to make real changes will almost certainly require Federal government direction and strong legal standards for independent commissions and their results. Legislation has been introduced to do precisely this and it should be passed into law before the next census and redistricting.

Ending the Electoral College

The Electoral College as a vehicle for choosing Presidents is an anachronism that should be abolished and replaced by direct vote. Established in an age when communications were poor, literacy was low, and the "big state/small state" divide threatened ratification, the Electoral College may have made sense at one time, but it no longer serves the nation well.

This odd manner of electing a president has failed four times to represent the will of the majority of Americans, most recently in the 2000 presidential election. In that election, a few hundred disputed votes in one state determined an election in which over 100 million people voted, and the candidate who received the most votes was not the individual who eventually took office.

In addition to allowing candidates to gain office who actually received fewer overall votes, the Electoral College disenfranchises millions of voters who cast ballots for candidates who do not get a majority in the voter's particular state. This violates the "One person one vote" principle that is so central to core democratic philosophy, but it happens every four years as we select what is arguably the single most important elected office in the land.

Considering this, it is really rather astonishing that voters have put up with the Electoral College as long as they have. Indeed, if the status quo today were direct election, it is hard to imagine any scenario in which the Electoral College system could be seriously considered as an improvement or replacement. The more likely response would be outrage and uprising as voters demanded that every vote count. They would be right to do so.

The American people are perfectly capable of making educated decisions in electing our President, and they deserve the right to do so. Every vote should carry the same weight, no matter where in the nation it was cast, and Presidential candidates should not wage a handful of separate campaigns in a few swing electoral states, but one campaign, in all states, for all the people.

To change this of course requires an amendment to the Constitution. That is not easy, but it is the right thing to do and the sooner it happens, the better for our nation.

There is also, it should be noted, an alternative to a constitutional amendment which is passage of state laws and in interstate compact requiring that states will allocate one hundred percent of their electoral vote to whoever prevails in the popular vote. To date, only four states have agreed to the compact but others are considering it. Some scholars have also suggested that if it were actually to take effect this approach might raise concerns under the Compact Clause of the Constitution. My own belief is that I appreciate and am willing to support this effort as a second best alternative, but the real and preferred solution remains to amend the Constitution and end the Electoral College entirely.

Instant Runoff Voting

Abolishing the Electoral College and moving to a popular vote for President, would be a substantial improvement over the status quo, but there are still other problems that should be addressed. Preeminent among these is the possibility that even under direct elections candidates who were not supported by a majority of voters, nevertheless can and do take office as President, Governor, Members of Congress and other offices.

Setting aside the controversy over vote counting in Florida and elsewhere, and setting aside the Electoral College issues that were just discussed, it is indisputable that the eventual winner of the Presidential race did not have the majority of all votes cast in 2000. George W. Bush received only 47.87 percent of the popular vote compared to Al Gore's 48.38 percent.

A somewhat similar result, without the ballot irregularities or Supreme Court intervention, occurred in the election that put Bill Clinton into office as President in 1992. In that race Clinton received only 43 percent of the popular vote, while Ross Perot, running as an independent garnered 18.9 percent and George H.W. Bush 37.7 percent.

Some estimate that throughout our history this sort of outcome has occurred in about one out of ten Presidential races. If we believe it is better for a person to have the support of the majority in order to be elected, should we really accept a ten percent failure rate from a process that determines one of the most important positions not only in our nation but the world?

Having reviewed a number of options that have been suggested to solve this problem, I believe "instant runoff" voting (IRV) would be an improvement over our standard practice. IRV is the least likely to be "gamed" and the most likely to produce an outcome in which the person with the broadest overall support will eventually prevail.

Under instant-runoff voting, voters do not simply cast one vote for one candidate. Rather, each voter has the option on the ballot of ranking all of the candidates who are running for a given position. When votes are counted, if no individual candidate gains a majority of first preference votes on the first count, the candidate receiving the least first preference votes is then eliminated automatically from the next count. (It's kind of like being "voted off the island" because of lack of support). The preference votes of supporters whose first choice have thus been eliminated are then given to other candidates based on what those voters had identified as their second choice. This continues until one candidate has received a majority of the total votes among those candidates who have not been eliminated.

If this sounds complicated, it really isn't. The first and most important thing to understand is that if any candidate has the first preference support of the majority of votes, that person will be elected on the first counting of ballots and the election is over. If, however, there are multiple candidates, the mere fact that one candidate may have received slightly more votes than any other, but far less than a real majority, does not mean that person will be elected. Others, who might have much broader overall support would be able to demonstrate that broader support on the second or later round of counting among the remaining candidates.

For most Americans this approach is certainly not familiar, and many people have a natural tendency to reject anything with which they are unfamiliar. This is understandable, but before rejecting this out of hand, people might want to ask themselves this question – "Do you think it is generally good for a democratic republic to have an election process that relatively often puts people in office who are not supported by a majority of voters?"

If you believe, as I think most people do, that the answer to this question should be "NO", then we should at least consider how often that happens in our present system and how we can avoid it in the future.

It may also help to know that IRV has actually been applied with substantial success in a number of localities within the U.S. and in other nations, including Australia, Ireland, and New Zealand.

Term Limits Are Not The Answer

Having proposed some changes to improve the political process, it is also worthwhile to take a moment to argue against one common proposed political reform – term limits.

On the face of it, when people are angry about government it can seem like an appealing idea to simply "throw all the bums out" after a fixed number of years. As attractive and simple as this idea may appear, it would in practice have a ruinous impact on government of the people, by the people and for the people. What is more, there is in fact more turnover in Congress than most people realize.

Comparing the membership of the 110th Congress with the 111th reveals that 65 of the 435 voting members of the House of Representatives who served in the 110th are no longer there in the 111th Congress. That is a turnover rate of more than one in every seven members in a single Congressional cycle.

In large part this came about because the framers of the Constitution purposefully included the best form of term limits that you can have in a constitutional democratic republic - elections. By having every single member of the House of Representatives and one-third of the Senate face the voters every two years, the Constitution ensures that the voters themselves have the right and the responsibility to decide whether or not someone has been in office too long or deserve to continue.

It is absolutely true that there are some members of Congress, and some staff as well, who have indeed been there too long. Either they have lost touch with their constituents, are no longer competent mentally, or they have forgotten the real purpose of serving the people. But these qualities are not limited to the longest serving members. In my experience one is just as likely to find incompetence, questionable motives, flawed character and downright stupidity among some relatively junior and younger members as among the more senior. The statement applies even more strongly to many of those who call so vehemently for 'throwing the bums out." but are themselves no more meritorious than those they would replace.

Whatever benefit there might be to automatically term limiting the incompetent, out of touch, or power mad at the end of just a few terms, you would also lose the many hard working, principled representatives who serve their constituents and country well and who have acquired essential knowledge to do their jobs even better from year to year.

Still more problematic and dangerous to a democratic republic is the fact that, if elected representatives are automatically removed by term limits, the actual process of making laws and managing the government will be given over to unelected staff and the influence of paid lobbyists. However upset the public may be with the elected members of Congress, without some institutional and issue knowledge on the part of elected officials who have been at the job for more than just a few years, the power of information will be held even more by staff than it is today.

For a government to derive its just powers from the consent of the governed, those who are governed must have the chance to elect, or, if they chose, to un-elect that government. Term limits take away the right of the public to truly choose who they think is best to represent them and, at the same time, they actually give greater power to people who were never elected to begin with.

Lobbyists

The Center for Responsive Politics estimates that in 2009 approximately $3.49 billion was spent on lobbying Congress and Federal Agencies, and a total of nearly 4,000 individuals were involved in lobbying. Without a doubt, some lobbyists provide a valuable service to their clients and help our system function more efficiently and effectively. In my experience, however, this is not the norm. Based on personal observation, and corroborated by a number of colleagues, a great many lobbyists are vastly overpaid, under-qualified, provide little added value, and in many instances distort the legitimate process of government.

That statement's going to cost more than a few campaign contributions I'm sure, but it also happens to be true. Let me give a few examples.

At the beginning of every session of Congress, members' offices are inundated with letters written by lobbyists on behalf of clients requesting a meeting with the member of Congress. The apparent belief of those who have employed the lobbyists to request the meeting is that somehow the letter from the lobbyist carries special weight and will help get special or higher access than they otherwise would. In most cases, it does nothing of the sort.

Why does a major university, county, city, port, large employer, school district or other substantial entity in a Congressional district need to pay someone to write a letter and schedule an appointment? The fact is, all of the aforementioned already have an advocate in Washington DC -- their member of Congress.

Any Representative worth his or her salt will gladly meet with local governments, schools, business, labor and for that matter most other legitimate groups if they simply schedule a meeting. And most members of Congress will do whatever they can to help constituents out if their needs and requests are legitimate and realistic. In my office, the signature of the lobbyist does absolutely nothing, zero, to increase the likelihood that I will personally meet with someone or take up their cause. I recognize that this is not always the case in every office, but it should be.

Now let me give the other side of the lobbying story, which is actually more pernicious and troublesome. While lobbyists who are unnecessary and ineffective are common, it also happens that some lobbyists do manage to get "special access" to influential people in Congress and the Administration and this can substantially distort the legitimate process of legislation. On more than one occasion in my own experience lobbyists have contacted Congressional offices urging yes or no votes or co-sponsorship of legislation before most members of Congress themselves have had an opportunity to view the legislation.

Lobbyists also work to influence the administration. Under the Bush administration the energy policy was notoriously drafted with a large amount of input by paid lobbyists for the energy companies. As the 111th Congress and Obama Administration sought to address climate and energy policy in 2009, the Center for Public Integrity reported that more than 770 companies and interest groups employed more than 2, 340 lobbyists to influence Federal policy.

The situation then, is that, on the one hand, a great many lobbyists are incompetent, ineffective, unnecessary and overpriced. On the other hand, a select group of lobbyists is far too effective with certain legislators and administration officials, thus distorting the legitimate process of representative government.

Lobbying Reform

The most important reform to lobbying abuses is campaign reform that bans contributions. With that reform, "buying access" through campaign contributions would not be possible. The second reform is for many of those who currently believe they are lost without lobbyists to realize they are not – they simply need to work more closely with their member of Congress and his or her staff.

Related to this recommendation, a third reform would be to require that every city, county, school or other public entity and every business, association or other private entity make widely available and public the amounts of money they are paying to lobbyists and the specific purpose for that spending, i.e. what exactly is the lobbyist requesting from Congress and what specific services is the lobbyist supposedly providing.

On this same topic there should be a complete prohibition on "pay for performance" compensation that links lobbyist compensation to legislative outcome. This sort of compensation can all too easily lead to lobbyist "getting a cut" for an appropriation or other legislative goal at the ultimate expense of the taxpayer.

Another needed reform is to end the revolving door from Congressional office to lobby firm by putting in place strict limits on when or if former staff members can lobby the Congress. Members of Congress and top staff are already under such restrictions. Frankly, I am not certain this restriction on former members and top staff is all that beneficial, but if these restrictions apply to members and top staff, they should apply to all Congressional and Administrative staff as well. Why should second tier and often not as competent staff be exempt while more knowledgeable and skilled staffers are not? Lobbying limits should also apply to former military officers for the same reasons.

Finally, those who still wish to employ lobbyists, and I actually do believe there are legitimate reasons to do so, would be wise to conduct thorough and careful performance appraisals of what the people they employ to lobby are actually doing for their money and how those particular people are in fact perceived by those who they purport to be influencing. In many instances, the results would be surprising and a fair bit of money could be saved that is now largely wasted.

An Independent Speaker and Fair Rules for the House of Representatives

The Constitution of the United States says simply, "The House shall chuse its own speaker." No direction is provided for how this shall be done, nor is there a requirement that the Speaker be a member of Congress. This raises the possibility that a neutral, impartial individual could be elected Speaker to ensure that the house runs efficiently and fairly as "The People's House," rather than as the "Majority Party's House."

The traditional practice of selecting the Speaker is for the majority and minority parties to each nominate a candidate from among their own ranks, then, with very few exceptions, members of each party dutifully vote for their party's chosen candidate with the majority party candidate prevailing. In recent years, the Speakers, Democratic and Republican alike, have tended to use the position of Speaker for partisan advantage.

For the good of the institution of the Congress and the Country, it is worth considering an alternative.

If an election year for Congress results in a close margin between the two parties in the House, a portion of both parties could work together and propose to vote for an independent, neutral speaker.

The goal would be to choose an individual of impeccable integrity, someone not currently in the House, who could be respected and trusted by all sides to conduct the business of the house in a fair and efficient manner.

The key benefits of this approach would be to restore impartiality to the Speaker position and, at the same time, strengthen the center. As increasingly partisan divides and pressures from interest groups have made it harder and harder for centrists from either party to survive and have an impact, giving centrists on either side an option to help elect a more moderate and impartial Speaker would empower those voices relative to the extremes.

In addition to electing an independent Speaker, it would also be necessary to implement a more equitable package of House Rules. Including such measures as sufficient time to read legislation, opportunities for both parties to offer constructive amendments, improved schedules etc. could all be included in such a package. Procedurally, this would take place by having the newly elected independent Speaker call up an alternative rules package to that which would have been offered by the majority speaker had he or she been elected. Voting for this rules package would again entail the minority party plus the group from the majority who had chosen that speaker also voting the alternative rules package.

I recognize that this action of electing an independent speaker not from the House is unprecedented in the history of Congress. I also know that the mere mention of this concept and how it could come about is likely to be perceived as a threat by those on either side who see themselves or their close allies as likely "heirs to the throne" of Speaker.

Those considerations notwithstanding, there is in fact an extraordinarily powerful precedent, perhaps the most powerful precedent of all, which argues for precisely this kind of speaker.

When the Constitutional Convention convened in 1787, the natural choice for presiding officer was George Washington. There were no established political parties at the time and, indeed, Washington and many of the other founders often warned of the dangers of such partisanship. The words "political party" occur nowhere in the constitution for good reason.

Consistent with that principle, history records that Washington himself spoke very little at the convention. His role was, instead, primarily to ensure that the process moved forward in a constructive fashion and, by his own presence, stature and personal example, encourage members to keep the greater good first and foremost in their deliberations and debate.

Had Washington not chosen this strategy, but instead presented himself as overtly biased toward certain interests or coalitions over others, had he in some way denied one group or another an opportunity to be heard, history could easily have turned out much differently and there might well not have been a constitution or, for that matter, even a country as we know it today.

In modern times of course, partisanship is a way of life and one could easily anticipate that the majority party would feel betrayed and seek vengeance in some way if an independent speaker were chosen. This strategy, however, is by no means inevitable.

To begin with and most importantly, it is likely the public at large, "we the people', would in fact welcome an independent, non-partisan speaker and rules for the House. Hard core partisans notwithstanding, most Americans believe in fair play and care more about their institutions and elected representatives serving the greater good rather than their partisan agendas. I believe they would welcome a Speaker who put functioning of the House and service to the country above partisan advantage, campaign fundraising, and all of the other concerns that contaminate the process today.

At the very least, it would behoove both the majority and minority party leadership and members to give the speaker and rules package a chance to work rather than making a political spectacle of the very sort that people are so sick of. Let the debate be about substance and let the individual representatives and parties prevail in the court of debate and public opinion, with fair rules and an independent arbiter working for the good of the process.

CONCLUSION

Any book about public policy and the political process is by nature aiming at a moving target. Facts change, people change, elections happen, new laws are proposed or enacted, and as soon as something is written it can be overtaken by events.

This has been especially true as I have worked on this book for the past four-plus years. On multiple occasions, I have been ready to release the final draft, but economic changes, elections, or other concerns have required modifications and updates. This process could go on forever.

At some point, one has to make a decision that there are core ideas and proposals that transcend the transitory changes in specific facts. So too, so much of what has passed for reforms in the past has been more like a rearrangement of deck chairs on the Titanic. While dickering over whether the chairs should be red or blue, the ship of state is sailing full steam ahead toward catastrophe. Waiting for that impact is not an option.

Someone has to not only shout "Disaster ahead," but change how the ship itself is steered.

I know that some of what is proposed in this book will be easily dismissed by cynics as improbable or hopelessly idealistic or perhaps as simply bad ideas. That eagerness to dismiss any serious call for change is itself part of the problem.

Cynics aside, this nation, from the revolution that allowed its formation to the Constitution and Bill of Rights that codify its governance, is by its nature and origin both idealistic and pragmatic. That is why our country is, in spite of its flaws, a great nation and at its best still an inspiration for the world.

We will only maintain and further that greatness if we are not afraid to face the challenges and embrace solutions based on true character - honesty, integrity, responsibility, community, courage and humility. That is what I have tried to do with this book.

LaVergne, TN USA
02 November 2010

203261LV00001B/3/P